W.B. YEATS AND

W.B. Yeats and the Muses explores how nine fascinating women inspired much of W.B. Yeats's poetry. These women are particularly important because Yeats perceived them in terms of beliefs about poetic inspiration akin to the Greek notion that a great poet is inspired and possessed by the feminine voices of the Muses. Influenced by the Pre-Raphaelite idea of woman as 'romantic and mysterious, still the priestess of her shrine', Yeats found his Muses in living women. His extraordinarily long and fruitful poetic career was fuelled by passionate relationships with women to and about whom he wrote some of his most compelling poetry. The book summarizes the different Muse traditions that were congenial to Yeats and shows how his perception of these women as Muses underlies his poetry. Newly available letters and manuscripts are used to explore the creative process and interpret the poems.

Because Yeats believed that lyric poetry 'is no rootless flower, but the speech of a man,' exploring the relationship between poem and Muse brings new coherence to the poetry, illuminates the process of its creation, and unlocks the 'second beauty' to which Yeats referred when he claimed that 'works of lyric genius, when the circumstances of their origin is known, gain a second a beauty, passing as it were out of literature and becoming life.'

As life emerges from the literature, the Muses are shown to be vibrant, multi-faceted personalities who shatter the idea of the Muse as a passive stereotype and take their proper place as begetters of timeless poetry.

W.B. YEATS AND THE MUSES

JOSEPH M. HASSETT

*For Lucy,
with thanks again
for your help at
the 'Muse of Yeats 2016'
best wishes x
Aisling.*

OXFORD
UNIVERSITY PRESS

OXFORD
UNIVERSITY PRESS

Great Clarendon Street, Oxford, OX2 6DP,
United Kingdom

Oxford University Press is a department of the University of Oxford.
It furthers the University's objective of excellence in research, scholarship,
and education by publishing worldwide. Oxford is a registered trade mark of
Oxford University Press in the UK and in certain other countries

© Joseph M. Hassett 2010

The moral rights of the author have been asserted

First published 2010
First published in paperback 2015

All rights reserved. No part of this publication may be reproduced, stored in
a retrieval system, or transmitted, in any form or by any means, without the
prior permission in writing of Oxford University Press, or as expressly permitted
by law, by licence or under terms agreed with the appropriate reprographics
rights organization. Enquiries concerning reproduction outside the scope of the
above should be sent to the Rights Department, Oxford University Press, at the
address above

You must not circulate this book in any other form
and you must impose this same condition on any acquirer

Published in the United States of America by Oxford University Press
198 Madison Avenue, New York, NY 10016, United States of America

British Library Cataloguing in Publication Data

Data available

Library of Congress Cataloging in Publication Data

Data available

ISBN 978–0–19–958290–7 (Hbk.)
ISBN 978–0–19–874602–7 (Pbk.)

Links to third party websites are provided by Oxford in good faith and
for information only. Oxford disclaims any resposibility for the materials
contained in any third party website referenced in this work.

Contents

List of Plates	vi
Acknowledgments	vii
Abbreviations	x
Manuscript Material Abbreviations	xiii
Introduction	1
1. White Woman That Passion Has Worn: Olivia Shakespear	11
2. Where the Blessed Dance: Florence Farr	37
3. The Apple on the Bough Most Out of Reach: Maud Gonne	65
4. The Living Beauty: Iseult Gonne	103
5. Out of a Medium's Mouth: George Hyde-Lees	131
6. In Search of the Muse: Memories of Love and Lyrics for Imaginary People	157
7. A Foolish, Passionate Man: Margot Ruddock and Ethel Mannin	169
8. Fury: Dorothy Wellesley	185
9. Golden Codger and Siren: Yeats and Edith Shackleton Heald	199
Finale	209
Endnotes	213
Bibliography	235
Index	245

List of Plates

1. Olivia Shakespear, from *Literary Yearbook*, 1897. 10
2. Florence Farr in *A Sicilian Idyll*. 36
3. Maud Gonne, *c.*1890–92. 64
4. Iseult Gonne, *c.*1918. 102
5. George and W.B. Yeats, 1920. 130
6. Margot Ruddock, from *Ah, Sweet Dancer*. 168
7. Ethel Mannin. 180
8. Dorothy Wellesley and Yeats, at Penns in the Rocks, *c.*1936. 184
9. Edith Shackleton Heald and Yeats at Chantry House in 1937 or 1938. 198

Acknowledgments

This book would be impossible but for the fact that its author stands on the shoulders of giants: Roy Foster, author of the incomparable *W.B. Yeats: A Life*; John Kelly, general editor of the magnificently edited and annotated ongoing edition of Yeats's letters; Warwick Gould and Deirdre Toomey, editor and long-time research editor of *Yeats Annual;* Ann Saddlemyer, author of the informative *Becoming George;* and Stephen Parrish, Ann Saddlemyer, Phillip L. Marcus and Jon Stallworthy, general editors of *The Cornell Yeats*.

To explore any area of Yeats's life or work in detail is necessarily to marvel at Foster's ability simultaneously to master significant detail and articulate it in the context of broader themes. The annotations in Kelly's edition of the letters never fail to enlighten, fascinate, and amuse. The extraordinary devotion and scholarship of Warwick Gould and Deirdre Toomey make the *Yeats Annual* an essential source of context and depth. The *Cornell Yeats* provides scholars with the great gift of easy access to Yeats's manuscripts.

I have been particularly fortunate to have had the enormous benefit and pleasure of conversing with Roy Foster, John Kelly, Warwick Gould, Deirdre Toomey and Ann Saddlemyer about all things Yeatsian – and beyond. I have benefited from the generosity and kindness of the late Michael and Anne Yeats over many years, and the courtesy of Gráinne and Caitríona Yeats.

I am grateful to Bernard O'Donoghue for his insight and suggestions; Hermione Lee whose pointed questions always signaled the need for a deeper analysis; Patrick Crotty who invited me to lecture at the Yeats International Summer School while the ideas in the book were taking shape; the students at the school for their comments and suggestions; Andrew McNeillie who, as commissioning editor, supported the idea of this book from its inception; Jacqueline Baker and Ariane Petit, who saw it to completion; scholars and writers who shared their ideas and friendship, including James Pethica, Christine Kelly, A. David Moody, Tony Gibbs, and Colin Smythe. I am eternally indebted to the late Gus Martin for showing me how satisfying Yeats scholarship can be, and to the late Derry Jeffares for his very helpful assistance at the beginning of the road.

Special thanks are due to the President and Fellows of St. John's College, Oxford for their hospitality and support. Custodians and librarians have been uniformly helpful, in particular, Dr. Issac Gewirtz, Berg Collection, New York Public Library; Katherine Reagan, Cornell University Library; Teresa Burk, Robert W. Woodruff Library, Emory University; Erin Chase, The Huntington Library; Dena Williams, Lilly Library, University of Indiana; Richard Temple, Shannen Chu, and Tansy Barton, Senate House Library, University of London; Laura Ruttum, New York Public Library; Colette O'Daly and Maíre ni Chonallaín, National Library of Ireland; Dr. B.C. Barker-Benfield, the Bodleian Library, University of Oxford; Verity Andrews, University of Reading Library Special Collections; Kristin J. Nyitray, Stony Brook University Libraries; Marc Carlson, Milissa Burkart, and Brenda Brown, McFarlin Library, University of Tulsa; and Eva Guggemos, Beinecke Rare Book and Manuscripts Library, Yale University. I am grateful to Dr. Eva Hesse and The Lady Elizabeth Clyde for their courtesy and assistance.

Certain poetry, prose, and unpublished writings by W.B. Yeats appear by permission of United Agents on behalf of Catríona Yeats, and Scribner, a division of Simon & Schuster, Inc. The poem 'Portrait d'une Femme' by Ezra Pound from PERSONAE, copyright © 1926 by Ezra Pound, is reprinted by permission of New Directions Publishing Corp. 'Letter to Eva Hesse, November 5, 1954' by Ezra Pound, from PREVIOUSLY UNPUBLISHED MATERIAL, copyright © 2010 Mary de Rachewiltz and Omar S. Pound is reprinted by permission of New Directions Publishing Corp. Bernard Shaw's letter of 29 March 1894 to Elizabeth Robbins is quoted with the permission of the Society of Authors on behalf of the Bernard Shaw Estate. 'The Shadow of Noon' by Iseult Gonne is quoted by kind permission of Christina Bridgewater. I am also grateful to the following holders who have granted access to previously unpublished material: John Quinn Papers, Manuscript and Archives Division, The New York Public Library, Astor, Lenox and Tilden Foundations; the National Library of Ireland owner of the unpublished draft of *Per Amica Silentia Lunae* and Yeats's P.I.A.L. Notebook; and McFarlin Library, University of Tulsa (Marc Carlson, Special Collections Librarian).

I am grateful for the help of a great many individuals who assisted me in obtaining permissions, including Jane Cram, Ruth Tellis, Declan Spring, Lisa Dowdeswell, and, especially, Emily Kitchin of AP Watt Ltd and Yessenia Santos of Simon & Schuster, Inc. for their gracious and diligent assistance. I am deeply indebted to Leslie Gibbs for her careful attention to the typescript.

Every effort has been made to establish contact with the holders of original copyrights; in cases where this has not been possible, I hope this general acknowledgment will be taken as sufficient.

Abbreviations

Au	*Autobiographies* (London: Macmillan, 1955).
AVA	*A Vision: An Explanation of Life Founded upon the Writings of Giraldus and upon certain Doctrines attributed to Kusta Ben Luka* (London: privately printed for subscribers only by T. Werner Laurie, Ltd., 1925).
AVB	*A Vision* (London: Macmillan, 1962).
CL 1, 2, 3, 4	*The Collected Letters of W.B. Yeats: Volume I, 1865–1895*, ed. John Kelly and Eric Domville; *Volume II, 1896–1900*, ed. Warwick Gould, John Kelly, Deirdre Toomey; *Volume III, 1901–1904*, and *Volume IV, 1905–1907*, eds. John Kelly and Ronald Schuchard (Oxford: Clarendon Press, 1986, 1997, 1994, 2005).
CL InteLex	*The Collected Letters of W.B. Yeats*, gen. ed. John Kelly, Oxford University Press (InteLex Electronic Edition) 2002. Letters cited by Accession number.
E&I	*Essays and Introductions* (London and New York: Macmillan, 1961).
G-YL	*The Gonne-Yeats Letters 1893–1938: Always Your Friend*, ed. Anna MacBride White and A. Norman Jeffares (London: Hutchinson, 1992).
L	*The Letters of W.B. Yeats*, ed. Allan Wade (London: Rupert Hart-Davis, 1954; New York: Macmillan, 1955).
LDW	*Letters on Poetry from W.B. Yeats to Dorothy Wellesley*, intro. Kathleen Raine (London and New York: Oxford University Press, 1964).
Life 1	*W.B. Yeats: A Life, I: The Apprentice Mage*, by R. F. Foster (Oxford and New York: Oxford University Press, 1997).
Life 2	*W.B. Yeats: A Life II: The Arch-Poet*, by R. F. Foster (Oxford and New York: Oxford University Press, 2003).
Mem	*Memoirs: Autobiography – First Draft: Journal*, transcribed and edited by Denis Donoghue (London: Macmillan, 1972; New York: Macmillan, 1973).
Myth	*Mythologies* (London and New York: Macmillan, 1959).

Abbreviations xi

M 2005	*Mythologies*, ed. by Warwick Gould and Deirdre Toomey (Houndmills, Basingstoke: Palgrave Macmillan, 2005).
MYV 1, 2	*The Making of Yeats's "A Vision": A study of the Automatic Script By George Mills Harper* (London: Macmillan; Carbondale and Edwardsville, Ill.: Southern Illinois University Press, 1987). 2 vols.
NC	*A New Commentary on the Poems of W.B. Yeats by A. Norman Jeffares* (London: Macmillan; Stanford: Stanford University Press, 1984).
SB	*The Speckled Bird by William Butler Yeats: an Autobiographical Novel with Variant Versions: New Edition, incorporating recently discovered manuscripts*, edited and annotated by William H. O'Donnell (Basingstoke: Palgrave Macmillan, 2003).
TSMC	*W.B. Yeats and T. Sturge Moore: Their Correspondence, 1901–1937* ed. Ursula Bridge (London: Routledge and Kegan Paul; New York: Oxford University Press, 1953).
UP 1, 2	*Uncollected Prose*, ed. John P. Frayne, (New York: Columbia University Press, 1970–76).
VP	*The Variorum Edition of the Poems of W.B. Yeats*, ed. Peter Allt and Russell K. Alspach (New York: The Macmillan Company, 1957). Cited from the corrected third printing of 1966.
VPl	*The Variorum Edition of the Plays of W.B. Yeats*, ed. Russell K. Alspach, assisted by Catherine C. Alspach (New York: Macmillan, 1969).
VSR	*The Secret Rose, Stories by W.B. Yeats: A Variorum Edition*, eds. Warwick Gould, Phillip L. Marcus, and Michael J. Sidnell (London: Macmillan 1992). Second edition, rev. & enl.
WWB 1, 2, 3	*The Works of William Blake Poetic, Symbolic, and Critical*, edited with lithographs of the illustrated "Prophetic Books", and a memoir and interpretation by Edwin John Ellis and William Butler Yeats, 3 vols. (London: Bernard Quaritch, 1893).
YA	*Yeats Annual* (London: Macmillan, 1982–) cited by no.
YAACTS	*Yeats: An Annual of Critical and Textual Studies*, ed. Richard J. Finneran (publishers vary, 1983–1999) cited by no.
YL	*A Descriptive Catalogue of W.B. Yeats's Library, Edward O'Shea* (New York and London: Garland Publishing, 1985).

YVP 1, 2, 3, 4   *Yeats's Vision Papers* (London: Macmillan, 1992; Palgrave 2001), George Mills Harper (general editor) assisted by Mary Jane Harper, *Vol. 1: The Automatic Script: 5 November 1917–18 June 1918,* eds. Steve L. Adams, Barbara J. Frieling and Sandra L. Sprayberry; *Vol. 2: The Automatic Scripts: 25 June 1918–29 March 1920* eds. Steve L. Adams, Barbara J. Frieling and Sandra Sprayberry; *Volume 3: Sleep and Dream Notebooks, Vision Notebooks 1 and 2, Card File,* eds. Robert Anthony Martinich and Margaret Mills Harper; *Vol. 4: 'The Discoveries of Michael Robartes' Version B ['The Great Wheel' and 'The Twenty-Eight Embodiments'],* eds. George Mills Harper and Margaret Mills Harper assisted by Richard W. Stoops, Jr.

Manuscript Material Abbreviations

PF MM — David R. Clark, ed., *W.B. Yeats 'Parnell's Funeral and Other Poems' from 'A Full Moon in March', Manuscript Materials* (Ithaca: Cornell University Press, 2003).

WFMP MM — David R. Clark, ed., *W.B. Yeats Words for Music Perhaps and other Poems Manuscript Materials* (Ithaca: Cornell University Press, 1999).

Tower MM — Richard J. Finneran, ed., with Jared Curtis and Ann Saddlemyer, *W.B. Yeats The Tower Manuscript Materials* (Ithaca: Cornell University Press, 2007).

ISW MM — David Holdeman, ed., *W.B. Yeats 'In the Seven Woods' and 'The Green Helmet and Other Poems' Manuscript Materials* (Ithaca: Cornell University Press, 2002).

WR MM — Carolyn Holdsworth, ed., *W.B. Yeats The Wind Among the Reeds Manuscript Materials* (Ithaca: Cornell University Press, 1993).

NP MM — J.C.C. Mays and Stephen Parrish, eds., *W.B. Yeats New Poems Manuscript Materials* (Ithaca: Cornell University Press, 2000).

Resp. MM — William H. O'Donnell, ed., *W.B. Yeats Responsibilities Manuscript Materials* (Ithaca: Cornell University Press, 2003).

MRD MM — Thomas Parkinson, ed., with Anne Brannen, *W.B. Yeats Michael Robartes and the Dancer Manuscript Materials* (Ithaca: Cornell University Press, 1994).

WSC MM — Stephen Parrish, ed., *W.B. Yeats The Wild Swans at Coole Manuscript Materials* (Ithaca: Cornell University Press, 1994).

LP MM — James Pethica, ed., *W.B. Yeats Last Poems Manuscript Materials* (Ithaca: Cornell University Press, 1997).

OJE MM — Steven Winnett, ed., *W.B. Yeats 'The Only Jealousy of Emer' and 'Fighting the Waves' Manuscript Materials* (Ithaca: Cornell University Press, 2004).

Introduction

Yeats's relationships with nine exceptional women profoundly influenced his poetry. These relationships were especially fruitful because Yeats experienced them in terms of his belief in Muses as sources of inspiration. Throughout his remarkably long and prolific career, Yeats was convinced that his poetry arose from an influx of knowledge or power from beyond his mind. As he often did when hedging his convictions against a skeptical audience, he put his belief in the form of a question: '[w]hen a man writes any work of genius, or invents some creative action,' he asked, 'is it not because some knowledge or power has come into his mind from beyond his mind?' (*Au* 272) The question reflects his predisposition to be attracted to the Greek notion that poetry was inspired by the Muses, daughters of powerful Zeus and Mnemosyne, goddess of memory.[1] The Greek idea of the Muse is captured in Plato's dictum that 'all good poets, epic as well as lyric, compose their beautiful poems not by art [*techne*] but because they are inspired and possessed' by the Muse, who speaks through the poet.[2] This direct role of the Muse is apparent, for example, in Homer's appeal that his Muse 'Tell me' of the exploits of Odysseus,[3] and in Hesiod's assertion that 'the reedy-voiced daughters of great Zeus... breathed into me a divine voice.'[4]

Endlessly fascinated by women, Yeats was particularly drawn to the idea that the Muse could reside in a living woman who, like Petrarch's Laura, would inspire by 'drawing out sweet words' from her admiring suitor.[5] His mentor here was Dante Rossetti, a powerful 'subconscious influence' on his early work, who fueled the Yeatsian tendency to see '[w]oman herself' as 'romantic and mysterious, still the priestess of her shrine....' (*Au* 302)

Yeats's concept of the Muse was informed both by the Gnostic belief in a divine feminine Wisdom principle symbolized by the moon, and by the courtly love tradition in which erotic attraction to an idealized woman inspires the poet to create beautiful lyrics. The Wisdom figure as Muse, which Yeats knew from Flaubert and his friend G.R.S. Mead's work on Simon Magus, can be understood in terms of Robert Graves' theory that all true love poets are conscious or unconscious worshipers of the ancient White Goddess figured in the moon, and that poetic inspiration is 'the poet's inner communion' with her human representative.[6] For Graves, the Muse poet – in contrast to an Apollonian poet of intellect and order – 'is in love with the White Goddess, with Truth,' and inspiration flows from his duty to 'tell the truth about himself and her in his own passionate and peculiar words.' (*Id.* 435, 439) The Muse poet knows that he is fated to sacrifice himself for his Muse, but must keep pursuing her: 'A poet cannot continue to be a poet if he feels that he has made a permanent conquest of the Muse, that she is always his for the asking.' (*Id.* 435) The subject of the courtly love poem is even more remote. She is unattainable by definition, an idea epitomized for Yeats by Dante's pursuit of the unreachable Beatrice.

Early in his career, Yeats made a choice that propelled him to see his poetic enterprise in terms of his relationship to a Muse. Believing that 'if a man is to write lyric poetry he must be shaped by nature and art to some one out of half a dozen traditional poses, and be lover or saint, sage or sensualist, or mere mocker of all life' (*Au* 87), he made a fundamental choice of the role of lover, and thus sought the basic emotion out of which many of his most enduring poems would be built in his experiences as a lover. His sense that intense experience of women would open the door to inspiration is implicit in his comment that his conversations with his fellow members of the Rhymers Club, who 'kept the Muses' sterner laws' (*VP* 273), focused on life 'at its most intense moment,' one 'in which one discovers something supernatural, a stirring as it were of the roots of the hair.' (*Au* 320) Like Wordsworth, Yeats would construct his poetry from 'emotion recollected in tranquility,'[7] but he would look to his experiences as a lover, rather than to nature, as the primary source of emotion from which to fashion his poetry.

Following Yeats's dictum that 'lyric poetry is no rootless flower but the speech of a man,'[8] this book seeks to enhance understanding and enjoyment of the poetry by examining the role of the Muses in its creation.

OLIVIA SHAKESPEAR

Chapter 1 shows that some of the best poems in Yeats's first great collection, *The Wind Among the Reeds* (1899), were written to Olivia Shakespear, his first lover, and reflect his association of Shakespear with the White Goddess. For example, 'He remembers Forgotten Beauty'

Introduction 3

(*VP* 155), read in light of Yeats's discussion of the moon as symbol in his essays on Shelley and Spenser, suggests that when the poet hears 'White Beauty sighing, too' in the sighs of his lover, he is hearing the loveliness of the White Goddess '[t]hat has long faded from the world.'

However, Shakespear did not conform to the rubric of the Muse as a stern mistress who cannot be possessed. Yeats too readily won her, and thus lost her as Muse. Rather than exhibiting the unattainability that caused Petrarch to speak of Laura as his 'beloved enemy', Shakespear was, as Yeats said in *Memoirs*, 'too near my soul, too salutary and wholesome to my inmost being.' (*Mem* 88) Although he forsook Shakespear to pursue other Muses, she returned to his poetry as the subject of his great celebration of love as friendship, 'After Long Silence' (*VP* 523).

FLORENCE FARR

From the outset of Yeats's relationship with Florence Farr Emery, there was a powerful impetus to see her as a priestess of the White Goddess. On the night of 5 May 1890, Yeats was in the audience at the clubhouse in Bedford Park to hear Farr, playing a priestess, summon the Egyptian Moon Goddess Selene. The occult studies she would soon undertake with Yeats led her to identify the Wisdom Goddess as the essential source of artistic inspiration.

Yeats and Farr became lovers, and she inspired his work in fundamentally important ways, but she could not maintain a status as Muse because she refused to assume the role of dominant dispenser of wisdom. Rather, as Yeats told her in a moving letter, she enabled him to be his 'own self, and to be this not because one has created some absurd delusion that all is wisdom ... but because one has found an equal....' (*CL* 4, 327–8) Nonetheless, Farr reclaimed her status as Muse after her death. Chapter 2 shows how the poem she wrote and sent to Yeats from her death-bed gave birth to 'All Souls' Night' (*VP* 470), that magnificent poem about the ability of the dead to inspire the living poet.

MAUD GONNE

Yeats's poems about Maud Gonne were consciously written in the courtly love tradition, 'the old high way of love', as he called it in 'Adam's Curse' (*VP* 204). Reading these poems as part of the courtly love tradition explains how Yeats found the endurance required for a nearly fruitless, twenty-eight-year pursuit of Gonne. Her unattainability was a *sine qua non* of the courtly tradition, in which to win the beloved is to lose her. Gonne understood this perfectly. In rejecting one of Yeats's proposals, she focussed sharply on her role as Muse: 'you make beautiful poetry out of what you call your unhappiness and you are happy in that,' she said. 'Marriage would be such a dull affair. Poets should never marry', a declaration that placed her squarely in the tradition of Dante's Beatrice.[9]

Yeats's deeply moving poem 'Words' (*VP* 255) meditates on his understanding that the turmoil engendered by his Muse powered his poetic engine, and that, were it not for the turmoil, there might have been no poetry: 'I might have thrown poor words away/And been content to live.' (*VP* 255–6) Chapter 3 explores Yeats's memorable poems to Gonne in terms of the differing ways she functioned as Muse over the course of their long relationship.

ISEULT GONNE

Yeats's conversations with Maud Gonne's daughter, Iseult, during the summer of 1916 inform the intriguing essay on poetic creativity that he wrote while wrestling with the idea that Iseult might succeed her mother as Muse. In the essay, called *Per Amica Silentia Lunae*, he says that he seeks inspiration by 'invit[ing] a marmorean Muse' (*Myth* 325), thus invoking the image in the accompanying poem, 'Ego Dominus Tuus', of Dante setting his chisel to the hardest stone and hungering for 'the apple on the bough/Most out of reach.' Yeats asks whether advancing age requires that he abandon his quest for an unattainable Muse: 'A poet, when he is growing old, will ask himself if he cannot keep his mask and his vision without new bitterness, new disappointment.' (*Id.* 342) He concludes that there is no alternative to the 'bitter crust' of unrequited pursuit of the Muse – a conclusion fraught with peril because it suggested that, in order to retain his access to poetic inspiration, he needed to relive his unsatisfied quest for Maud Gonne in uncanny pursuit of her daughter. Chapter 4 examines the way in which Iseult Gonne propelled Yeats's career forward when it threatened to stall upon his abandonment of her mother as Muse.

Yeats proposed marriage to Iseult in August 1917. She declined, but seemed unwilling to let him go completely. The prospect of a second generation of pursuing the unattainable was unnerving. Almost immediately, Yeats decided to marry George Hyde-Lees, a young woman to whom Olivia Shakespear had introduced him a few years earlier.

GEORGE HYDE-LEES

Seeking refuge in marriage to George Hyde-Lees posed a potentially lethal threat to Yeats's poetic enterprise. Because the essence of the courtly love poem was its praise of an unattainable woman, marriage and sexual satisfaction threatened to cut off the source of inspiration.

Yeats found his way out of the inspirational impasse, but this time it took what he described in a letter to Lady Augusta Gregory as 'something very like a miraculous intervention.' Just days after his marriage, Yeats found himself 'in great gloom.'[10] To improve her husband's mood, Mrs. Yeats feigned receipt of a consolatory message through automatic handwriting. Suddenly, she maintained, a superior force took over, guiding her hand to write words from beyond her mind. Fascinated, Yeats pressed her into five years of intensive communication with the unknown spirits.

Just as the Pythias answered questions with ambiguous oracles, Yeats proceeded by suggestive questions, and George's responses left great latitude for him to believe that he was discovering his own creations. These exchanges clarified the analogy between *daimon* – the anti-self who opened the door to creativity – and sweetheart that had puzzled him in *Per Amica Silentia Lunae*. George's communicators taught him that the 'moment of sexual union' is the locus of the 'supreme activity of the *daimons*.'

They also answered the question whether sexual success would still the voice of the Muse. *Au contraire*, they said, 'What is important is that the desire of the medium and her desire for your desire be satisfied' because 'there cannot be intellectual *desire*... without *sexual* & *emotional* satisfaction' and 'without intellectual desire there is no force – *or* truth especially *truth* because truth is intensity.' (*YVP ii*, 487) In other words, whereas sexual fulfillment was inconsistent with the courtly lover's access to inspiration, it was the *sine qua non* of revelation from George's instructors.

Chapter 5 explores Yeats's *A Vision* in terms of muse theory, and examines the way in which the great poems of Yeats's maturity reflect the influence of George Yeats as oracle and Muse.

MARGOT RUDDOCK AND ETHEL MANNIN

The corollary to Yeats's recognition that an erotic relationship with his wife was essential to her functioning as a medium was that, as one aspect of their relationship faded, the other languished as well. Chapter 6 traces the extraordinary transition in which Yeats, fearing he must 'bid the Muse go pack,' rekindled his inspiration through a meditation on past Muses that gave birth to the idea of timeless singing masters of the poetic soul that drives the magnificent 'Sailing to Byzantium.' As the inspirational fumes of memory began to fail, Yeats, feeling that 'he had lost all inspiration,' underwent the Steinach rejuvenation operation in 1934, hoping it would cure sexual impotence and reopen the path to inspiration. He believed the operation a success, and so it was. His June 1935 letter to Dorothy Wellesley celebrated 'the strange second puberty the operation has given me, the ferment that has come upon my imagination.'[11] 'If I write more poetry,' he confided, 'it will be unlike anything I have done.' He was convinced that the operation, revived both 'my creative power' and 'also sexual desire....'[12]

Chapter 7 examines the poetry engendered by two beautiful women Yeats met in the wake of the Steinach operation who were both Sirens – who sing erotic but ultimately destructive songs – and Muses. The unpublished 'Margot' suggests that Margot Ruddock was initially a Siren, but when Yeats viewed her through the lens of dance as a symbol of creativity in 'A Crazed Girl' (*VP* 578), she became a Muse. The austerely beautiful draft 'Portrayed Before His Eyes,' which may owe its genesis to both Ruddock and Ethel Mannin, clearly shows the influence of an inspiring Muse.

The poem presents its subject as initially something of a marmorean muse – she is 'Implacably lipped' – but ultimately 'she moved' and found her way to 'Love's levelling bed.' Her role as Muse is signified by her association with Artemis, the Hellenic equivalent of Diana, who displaced Selene as the goddess of the moon. Yeats likely had Mannin in mind as moon goddess. He addressed her as 'Mother Goddess' and told her 'You are doubly a woman, first because of yourself & secondly because of the Muses whereas I am but once a woman.'[13]

DOROTHY WELLESLEY

Yeats's experimentation with the ideas developed in *Per Amica* and *A Vision* took a startling turn in June 1935 when he met Dorothy Wellesley. His letters to Wellesley reflect beliefs that her role as Muse would be coloured by her lesbianism, and that her Muse was located at the intersection of what he perceived as the masculine and feminine aspects of her personality. 'What makes your work so good,' he wrote

Introduction 7

her, 'is its masculine element amid so much feminine charm – your lines have the magnificent swing of your boyish body. I wish I could be a girl of nineteen for certain hours that I might feel it even more acutely.'[14] He had already suggested to Wellesley that his own creativity arose out of 'the woman in me.'[15]

'To Dorothy Wellesley' (*VP* 579), the centerpiece of Chapter 8, suggests that Wellesley's Muses are Furies, primitive earth goddesses who, as Erich Neumann has shown, represent angry emotional forces that are opposite to those of the Muses but, because of the tendency of opposites to merge into each other, can be forerunners of inspiration.[16] Yeats's own Muse was now a Fury as well. The beast of hatred had replaced concentration on Gonne as the besom that could clear his soul and open the way to inspiration.

EDITH SHACKLETON HEALD

Yeats extended his last, yearning grasp for the Muse toward Edith Shackleton Heald, whose Siren's evocation of the twin impulses of *Eros* and *Thanatos* propelled him to pursue sexual desire for the sake of desire, even as he learned to relinquish longing for life or death. Chapter 9 follows these remarkable developments to their culmination in Yeats's recognition that 'lust and rage,' as he put it in 'The Spur' (*VP* 591), were unreliable sources of inspiration. Their sterility is apparent in 'The Circus Animals' Desertion' (*VP* 629), which describes Yeats's vain search for a theme. His next poem, 'Politics,' the one he intended to complete his last volume,[17] eschews the Furies and returns to the Muses. The poet focuses on 'That girl standing there,' and his longing – that of a true Muse poet – 'that I were young again/And held her in my arms!' (*VP* 631)

The wheel had come full circle with Yeats's decision to end his body of work with quite a different song from 'Words,' where his Muse's unattainability was essential to generating his poetry. The poet of 'Politics' it a devotee of a Muse who, speaking in 'The Three Bushes' (*VP* 569), insists on being captured:

> Said lady once to lover,
> 'None can rely upon
> A love that lacks its proper food;
> And if your love were gone

How could you sing those songs of love?
I should be blamed, young man.'

A CHORUS OF MUSES

Tracing the relationship of Yeats to his Muses will show how his idea of the Muse underwent sea changes according to his own life changes, as different women fulfilled different needs at different times, propelling him through a poetic career of exceptional longevity. Examination of the differing ways in which different Muses inspired particular poems will unlock that 'second beauty' to which Yeats referred when he said, in a preface to a book of verses by one of his Muses, that '[w]orks of lyric genius, when the circumstances of their origin is known, gain a second beauty, passing as it were out of literature and becoming life.'[18] Reading Yeats's *Collected Poems* against the background of their author's relationships with his Muses gives his poetry a new coherence, and reveals ways in which his sometimes opaque prose informs the poetry.

The demonstrable relationships between Muses and poems supports Yeats's assertion that his poetry was no rootless flower. His love poems were rooted in real and identifiable relationships, a fact that distinguishes them from traditional courtly lyrics which, as Julia Kristeva observed, had 'no object,' the purported object being simply 'an imaginary addressee, the pretext for the incantation' in the poem.[19] Although Jahan Ramazani has enthusiastically applied Kristeva's theory to Yeats, arguing that 'the real women [are] occluded... to the aesthetic and psychic structures' of the poems, he ultimately asserts only that the poetry 'is inexplicable in terms of *superficial* biography.'[20] Readers of Yeats's poetry, however, are blessed with a cornucopia of biographical sources that permit an in-depth exploration of the relationship between Muse and poem.

These materials – including notebooks, letters, journals, autobiographies, an unpublished memoir, drafts of the poems, and a detailed record of a probing analysis of his love life undertaken jointly with his wife – confirm Yeats's own understanding of a symbiotic relationship between his life and work.[21] Writing from the center of that symbiosis, Yeats insisted that '[a] poet writes always of his personal life,' thus encouraging explication of the poems in terms of their inspiring Muses and validating reference to the speaker in the poem as 'Yeats.' At the same time, he also recognized that the poem is more than autobiography because the poet 'never speaks directly as to someone at the breakfast table, there is always a phantasmagoria,' a persona who is 'intended, complete.'[22] The poet is thus constructed out of the man, and, as Yeats said in *The Trembling of the Veil*, the masterful poet completes the circle by remaking the man through the art. (*Au* 273) Unsurprisingly, Yeats identified his poetic persona as a lover – indeed an unsatisfied lover: the poet's 'finest work,' he says, arises out of the 'tragedy' of his personal life, and, for Yeats, that tragedy was 'remorse, lost love or mere loneliness....' (*Id.*) The beloved is also someone intended, complete. She 'is Rosalind, Cleopatra, never The Dark Lady.'

Because poet and beloved are created in the poem from events in life, examination of the relationship between the life and the poetry is well calculated to expand understanding of both the poetry and the role of Yeats's Muses in its creation. The differing ways in which these distinctive and vibrant women contributed to Yeats's creativity provide instructive context for assessing what Elizabeth Butler Cullingford calls Yeats's apparent vulnerability to 'feminist criticism...as a love poet in a tradition that has stereotyped and silenced its female object.'[23] Yeats's Muses, it will appear, tended to be neither stereotypical nor silent. Rather, their volubility provides an interesting opportunity to hear the Muse herself comment on her role in the creative process.

1. Olivia Shakespear, from *Literary Yearbook*, 1897.

1
White Woman That Passion Has Worn: Olivia Shakespear

In 1896, as Yeats turned thirty-one, and a bit more than mid-way between his first proposal to Maud Gonne in 1891 and their 'spiritual marriage' of 1898, Olivia Shakespear introduced him to the real experience of what fascinated him so much as metaphor: the sexual union of man and woman. In the period just before and just after they began their sexual relationship, Yeats wrote poems to Shakespear that address her anonymously as 'white woman'. Read in light of his contemporaneous theory of symbolism, these poems suggest an important affinity between Shakespear and the White Goddess.

Shakespear and Yeats had met when she was seated opposite him at a dinner for *The Yellow Book* on 16 April 1894. He focused on her at once as 'a woman of great beauty' and 'incomparable distinction':

> At a literary dinner where there were fifty or sixty guests I noticed opposite me, between celebrated novelists, a woman of great beauty. Her face had a perfectly Greek regularity, though her skin was a little darker than a Greek's would have been and her hair was very dark. She was exquisitely dressed with what seemed to me very old lace over her breast, and had the same sensitive look of distinction I had admired in Eva Gore-Booth. She was, it seemed, about my own age, but suggested to me an incomparable distinction. (*Mem* 72)

The photographic evidence bears out this description. Mendelssohn's photograph of Shakespear's profile for the *Literary Yearbook* in 1897 (Plate 1) shows her, as Foster puts it, 'dark-haired and lovely,' looking 'slightly like a more reflective Maud Gonne.' (*Life 1*, 153) At the time of *The Yellow Book* dinner, Shakespear was about to publish the first of six novels. There is no record of Shakespear's formal education, and her biographer suggests that, like the women in her novels, she was privately tutored and given free access to large libraries.[1] Yeats quickly perceived that 'She had profound culture, a knowledge of French, English, and Italian literature, and seemed always at leisure.' (*Mem* 74)

This beautiful and accomplished daughter of an upper class military family was married to Henry Hope Shakespear, a London solicitor of whom our most salient knowledge consists of his wife's report that he 'ceased to pay court to me from the day of our marriage' (*Mem* 87–8) and the fact that the couple's daughter, Dorothy, was born nine months and five days after her parents' wedding. (OS 19) Ezra Pound, who would eventually marry Dorothy, thought Olivia 'the most charming woman in London.'[2]

Yeats was 'not introduced to [Shakespear], but learned that she was related to [his friend Lionel Johnson] and had asked my name.' (*Mem* 72) Shortly after *The Yellow Book* dinner, Shakespear attended a play, *The Land of Heart's Desire*, that Yeats had written at the request 'of a new friend,' Florence Farr. (*Id.*) Shakespear resolved, she later told Yeats, 'to write you if [I] could not meet you otherwise.' (*Mem* 74) Lionel Johnson ended the impasse with an introduction. Yeats responded to this extraordinary woman by telling her about Maud Gonne: 'I told her of my love sorrow, indeed it was my obsession, never leaving by day or night.' (*Id.*)

Fascinated by Shakespear's beauty, profound culture, and 'gentle and contemplative' nature (*id.*), Yeats took her description of her plight in a loveless marriage to be an invitation to a romantic relationship. They agonized over what course to pursue. A divorce by Shakespear would cost her custody of her daughter and the financial support of her husband. And then there was Yeats's obsession with Gonne. Both Yeats and Shakespear enlisted 'sponsors' to guide their thinking. Yeats's was likely Florence Farr. (*Life 1*, 154) After two years of sporadic meetings, in early 1896 Yeats decided to take the plunge. His reasoning, if not admirable, was simple: 'after all, if I could not get the woman I loved, it would be a comfort even but for a little while to devote myself to another.' (*Mem* 85) 'No doubt,' added Yeats, 'my excited senses had their share in the argument, but it was an unconscious one.' (*Id.*)

Yeats recounts how '[a]t last she came to me in I think January . . . and I was impotent from nervous excitement.' (*Mem* 88) The sympathetic Shakespear 'understood instead of, as another would, changing liking for dislike – was only troubled by my trouble.' (*Id.*) As a result, '[m]y nervousness did not return again and we had many days of happiness.' (*Id.*)

Yeats's prosaic reference to 'many days of happiness' does not do justice to the profound impact his belated introduction to sexual love must have had on his emotional life. One needs to examine the poems addressed to Shakespear to glimpse something of the intensity of that experience. Even in the poems, the underlying emotion is filtered through theories of symbolism that arose out of Yeats's decision to make magic, 'next to my poetry the most important pursuit of my life' – one that, by the time he met Shakespear, had become 'the centre of all that I do & all that I think & all that I write.'[3] His magical theories emphasized the ability of symbols to open the door to primordial storehouses of the imagination that he called the great mind and the great memory. His 1901 essay 'Magic' defines magic to include something very much like poetic inspiration – 'visions of truths in the depths of the mind when the eyes are closed' – and identifies three fundamental doctrines that assign a critical role to symbols in unlocking the door to inspiration:

(1) That the borders of our minds are ever shifting, and that many minds can flow into one another, as it were, and create or reveal a single mind, a single energy.
(2) That the borders of our memories are as shifting, and that our memories are a part of one great memory, the memory of Nature herself.
(3) That this great mind and great memory can be evoked by symbols. (*E&I* 28)

In his essay on Shelley, published a year earlier, Yeats had explained his understanding of how symbols could inspire the poet by granting access to a great Memory 'that renews the world and men's thoughts age after age' and 'is still the mother of the Muses, though men no longer believe in it.' (*E&I* 79, 91) His experience, like Jung's[4] pointed toward the existence of such a great Memory:

Any one who has any experience of any mystical state of the soul knows how there float up in the mind profound symbols, whose meaning, if indeed they do not delude one into the dream that they are meaningless, one does not perhaps understand for years. Nor I think has any one, who has known that experience with any constancy, failed to find some day, in some old book or on some old monument, a strange or intricate image that had floated up before him, and to grow perhaps dizzy with the sudden conviction that our little memories are but a part of some great Memory that renews the world and men's thoughts age after age, and that our thoughts are not, as we suppose, the deep, but a little foam upon the deep. (*E&I* 78–9)

Using the language he would later use to describe his own belief in inspiration, Yeats's essay argues that Shelley 'must have expected to receive thoughts and images from beyond his own mind...for he believed inspiration a kind of death; and he could hardly have helped perceiving that an image that has transcended particular time and place becomes a symbol, passes beyond death, as it were, and becomes a living soul.' (*Id.* at 80)

Convinced that symbols would magically open the door to inspiration from beyond his mind, Yeats had joined the Hermetic Order of the Golden Dawn, an occult society to which he was introduced by MacGregor Mathers, the imaginative force behind the blending of the Kaballah, alchemy, astrology, and Rosicrucianism that made up the Order's ritual and doctrine. Mathers himself instructed Yeats in the evocation of visions by the use of symbols. Mathers' wife, Moina, sister of the philosopher Henri Bergson and known within the Order as '*Vestigia Nulla Retrorsum*' ('No Traces Behind'), presided over Yeats's official initiation into the Isis-Urania Temple in March 1890. He took the Order name of *Demon Est Deus Inversus* ('The Demon Is An Inverted God'). Years later, in the dedication of the 1925 edition of *A Vision* to 'Vestigia,' he summed up the quest pursued by himself and his fellow students in the Golden Dawn: 'We all... differed from ordinary students of philosophy or religion through our belief that truth cannot be discovered but may be revealed, and that if a man do not lose faith, and if he go through certain preparations, revelation will find him at the fitting moment.' (*AVA* x) The Yeats who had his first experience of sexual love with Olivia Shakespear was waiting for revelation to find him.

In the summer following Yeats's sexual initiation, Shakespear and magic coalesced around a series of events that placed the White Goddess at the heart of his search for poetic inspiration. Believing that his style had become too elaborate and 'would not help me in that spiritualization of Irish imagination I had set before me,' he turned for advice to Shakespear, who 'was powerfully affected by my symbols.' (*Mem* 99–100) In response to questions posed while she was 'in a state of semi trance,' Shakespear 'obtained these sentences, unintelligible to herself: "He is too much under solar influence. He is to live near water and to avoid woods, which concentrate the solar power".' (*Mem* 100) Yeats understood this message to mean that he needed an influx of 'lunar power,' which he believed was 'the chief source of my inspiration.' (*Id.*)

He then departed on a trip to the west of Ireland, where he stayed at Edward Martyn's home, Tulira. After eight unsuccessful nights of invoking lunar power, on the ninth night, just as he was going to sleep, he invoked, as he reported in a letter to William Sharp, 'the spirits of the moon & saw between sleep & waking a beautiful woman firing an arrow among the stars.'[5] The woman was, he concluded, the Roman moon goddess, 'the symbolic Diana.' (*Id.*) The next morning, fellow guest Arthur Symons read a poem he had written about a dream of the preceding night in which he had been visited by a woman of great beauty. Yeats regarded Symons' dream as a shared vision, and thus thought that the opening line of Symons' poem – 'O source of the songs of all poets' – linked his own vision to the source of poetic inspiration. (*Mem* 101) Yeats later consulted an expert in Mediterranean antiquities, who advised him that the archer shooting the arrow was 'the Mother-Goddess... [who] is pictured upon certain Cretan coins of the fifth century B.C.....' (*Au* 576–8) The archer vision was a powerful experience for Yeats – one he spent a great deal of time and effort trying to understand and assimilate – and it pointed to Olivia Shakespear as a conduit for a message from the White Goddess to seek lunar inspiration.[6]

Yeats's familiarity with the Wisdom variation of the White Goddess tradition informed his perception of Shakespear as a priestess of the White Goddess. That tradition is encapsulated in Yeats's observation that his friend, the painter W. R. Horton, 'evidently thought that at full moon was Sophia & connected this with his beloved,' whom he saw as a link 'between man & something not themselves – a divine element.' (*YVP 1*, 213) Simon Magus' formulation of this doctrine was available to Yeats in his copy of Flaubert's *The Temptation of St. Antony*,[7] and in his friend G.R.S. Mead's compendium of writings about Simon Magus.[8] These sources recount that the 'First Thought' of the divine mind, 'the Universal Mother,' 'Ennoia,' or 'Wisdom,'[9] – 'the Muse-principle,' as Harold Bloom put it[10] – generated powers who created the world, and then, not wanting to be regarded as other than self-created, detained Ennoia and enclosed her in human flesh, within which she migrated for centuries in different female bodies. (*Id.*) Ennoia was thus a feminine incarnation of divine creativity and wisdom – someone whose relationship with Simon was likely to capture Yeats's attention.

Simon asserted that a woman called Helena whom he found in a brothel in Tyre was the latest incarnation of Ennoia. (*Id.*) She is represented as a harlot to 'show the depth to which the divine principle has sunk by becoming involved in the creation.' (*Id.*) Ennoia's incarnation in a living woman was profoundly important for Yeats because it provided an alternative to the Gaelic Muse, the Leanhaun Shee, who, as he recounted in his 1888 collection of Irish folklore, lives in the otherworld, sucking the life from the poets she inspires. 'She is the Gaelic Muse,' he wrote, 'for she gives inspiration to those she persecutes, and will not let them remain long on earth.'[11] The 'greatest of the Irish poets,' had belonged to her. (*Id.*) Her potential for mischief is apparent in Yeats's *Stories of Red Hanrahan (M 2005* 139*)*, in which a poet is bewildered and silenced by the pale and other-worldly Leanhaun Shee. Ennoia's incarnation in Helena, however, brought the Muse into the poet's world, and implied the possibility of a constructive relationship. Yeats accepted the tradition that Simon and Helena were married, and saw their union as an instance of his recurring theory that a man perfects himself in a union with his anti-self. (*Au* 481)

The Gnostic Muse's derivation from the Great Goddess figured in the moon throughout the archaic world (Gnostic Religion 108–9) is suggested by the facts that Helena was also called Selene (Moon) (*id.*), and was worshipped in the form of a statue of the moon goddess Minerva. (Simon Magus 10) In Flaubert's novel, Simon Magus makes this link explicit, telling St. Antony that Helena has been known by many names, including Helen of the Trojans, but 'she really is the Moon.' (Temptation 171–3) Like the Egyptian Isis, who was worshipped in the Greaco-Roman world as the Great Mother and regarded as the personification of Wisdom or *Sophia*,[12] the lunar Muse principle embodied in Helena has been known by the names of most of the moon goddesses, including Diana, Ceres, Hecate, and Minverva. (*Id.* at 121)

The poems addressed to Shakespear reflect her association with the White Goddess. In one of the three poems Yeats identifies in *Memoirs* as written to Shakespear during the period before they became lovers (*Mem* 86) – one eventually titled 'He gives His Beloved certain Rhymes' – the poet addresses a 'pearl-pale' woman whose kinship with the moon is suggested by the statement that stars '[l]ive but to light your passing feet' – an image that echoes a line of Symons' poem in which his dream woman unveils 'that white swiftness to the feet'.[13] Yeats's poem locates his pearl-pale woman amid the stars:

> Fasten your hair with a golden pin,
> And bind up every wandering tress;
> I bade my heart build these poor rhymes:
> It worked at them, day out, day in.
> Building a sorrowful loveliness
> Out of the battles of old times.
>
> You need but lift a pearl-pale hand,
> And bind up your long hair and sigh;
> And all men's hearts must burn and beat;
> And candle-like foam on the dim sand,

> And stars climbing the dew-dropping sky,
> Live but to light your passing feet. (*VP* 157–8)[14]

The 'pearl-pale' skin of this woman links her to Dante's Beatrice, who had

> ... that paleness of the pearl that's fit
> In a fair woman, so much and not more;
> She is as high as Nature's skill can soar.

(Rossetti Dante 60) In other words, she approximates the White Goddess as closely as mortal woman can. The subject of Yeats's poem is specifically identified as 'white woman' in a draft of an abandoned third verse in which the poet says 'I bring my sorrowful rhymes to you/ White woman with the braided hair.' (*WR MM* 90–1) The white woman's kinship with a White Goddess who demands the death of her suitor is apparent from the original context of the poem, a story in which the rhymes are sung by the severed head of a poet who is beheaded before he is able to sing to a young queen with an old husband. ('The Binding of the Hair', *VSR* 181) The reference to an old husband like Hope Shakespear emphasizes the dual role of the white woman as both goddess and priestess, a figure both in and out of the material world.

Despite the lunar inspiration of the Muse and the poet's willingness to sacrifice, the giver of these rhymes has not been spared the hard work involved in constructing them: his heart 'worked at them, day out, day in....' (*VP* 158) In the third of the poems mentioned in *Memoirs*,[15] 'A Poet to his Beloved,' the verses, which are explicitly addressed to a 'white woman,' seem more the product of an inspired, dream-like state:

> I bring you with reverent hands
> The books of my numberless dreams,
> White woman that passion has worn
> As the tide wears the dove-grey sands,
> And with heart more old than the horn
> That is brimmed from the pale fire of time:
> White woman with numberless dreams,
> I bring you my passionate rhyme. (*VP* 157)

Yeats's association of his beloved with the whiteness of the moon is explained both by the Wisdom tradition and by the exoteric explanation in his 1900 essay, 'The Symbolism of Poetry,' which sets out the theory underlying his poetic practice of the preceding decade. In his essay,

Yeats asserts that 'poetry moves us because of its symbolism,' and instances the 'white moon' as his first example of a symbol (*E&I* 163, 155), explaining: 'All sounds, all colours, all forms, either because of their preordained energies or because of long association, evoke indefinable and yet precise emotions, or, as I prefer to think, call down among us certain disembodied powers, whose footsteps over our hearts we call emotions....' (*E&I* 156–7)

Emphasizing that the moon is a particularly powerful symbol because it evokes both emotions and ideas, Yeats suggests the moon's association with the White Goddess by saying 'if I look at the moon herself and remember any of her ancient names and meanings, I move among divine people....' (*Id.* 161) As summarized above, the moon's ancient names were the names of Egyptian, Greek and Roman moon goddesses, and her meanings were expressive of the great mother as source of creativity and Wisdom. These associations are repeated in another 1900 essay, 'The Philosophy of Shelley's Poetry,' in which Yeats identifies the moon as 'mistress of the waters [who] governs the life of instinct and the generation of things,' and notes that Keats saw the moon as symbolic of Intellectual Beauty (*E&I* 91), which, as Yeats says in his essay on Spenser, is another name for Wisdom. (*Id.* 366)

Thus, when Yeats's poems to Shakespear identify her with the moon, he is linking her to the ancient tradition of the White Goddess as the source of the creative Wisdom impulse. This linkage is a particular instance of his general practice in the *The Wind Among the Reeds*, noted by Richard Ellmann, of using natural elements as symbolic of forces operating within the mind as well as in nature.[16] *The Wind Among the Reeds*, Ellmann says, 'set the method for the modern movement,' much as Wordsworth's and Coleridge's *Lyrical Ballads* had shaped the Romantic movement:

> Wordsworth's theme had been the renewal of man's bond to nature; Yeats's was the uncovering of a secret nature in which all outward things took their character from internal pressures. The mighty presence which for Wordsworth was outside man was for Yeats inside, and all the scenic elements, such as stars, sea, winds, and woods, became emblematic of forces operative within the mind as upon things. (*Id.*)

The moon, the scenic element and emblem *par excellence*, is evoked in 'He remembers Forgotten Beauty', Yeats's moving encomium to Olivia Shakespear as emblematic of beauty and wisdom long faded from the world but still capable of operating within the human mind through Shakespear's mediation as priestess of the White Goddess:

> When my arms wrap you round I press
> My heart upon the loveliness
> That has long faded from the world;
>   *   *   *
> For that pale breast and lingering hand
> Come from a more dream-heavy land,
> A more dream-heavy hour than this;
> And when you sigh from kiss to kiss
> I hear white Beauty sighing, too,
> For hours when all must fade like dew,
> But flame on flame, and deep on deep,
> Throne over throne where in half sleep,
> Their swords upon their iron knees,
> Brood her high lonely mysteries.   (*VP* 155–6)

This poem, which is alive with passion for a real woman, was published in *The Savoy* in January 1896. Read in the context of 'The Symbolism of Poetry,' the sighs of the passionate white woman are magical symbols in which the poet hears lunar 'white Beauty' sighing too, and the woman's loveliness is a sign of 'the loveliness/That has long faded from the world' and that the poet seeks to restore by praising Beauty's representative, his Muse. Nearly forty years later, when Yeats sent Shakespear a draft of a poem in which his beloved 'sings as the moon sings,' he knew that she would understand that its theme of all creation shivering at the moon's sweet cry was his 'central myth.'[17] The poem, 'He and She' (*VP* 559), is discussed in Chapter 6.

The dual aspect of his beloved as a real woman and a symbol of something spiritual was perfectly congenial to Yeats, whose approach to the world was premised on the fundamental belief behind all his magical studies that everything in the temporal world mirrors something in the eternal world: '[f]or things below are copies,' as he quoted the Hermetic 'Great Smaragdine Tablet' in 'Ribh Denounces Patrick' (*VP* 556). It was second nature for him to attribute meanings to symbols that, as Ellmann put it, 'flowed between the two worlds' (Discovering Symbolism 110–11), and thus to see Olivia Shakespear as both a beautiful woman and a symbol of forgotten Beauty.

The role of symbols in mediating between the material and spiritual worlds had particular importance for a would-be writer of love poetry because, as Yeats put it in his essay on 'The Symbolism of Poetry,' he doubted 'that love itself would be more than an animal hunger but for the poet and his shadow the priest....' (*E&I* 158) Invoking the nine angelic hierarchies as a model of the linkage between the terrestrial and celestial worlds, and quoting Blake, Yeats argued that '[s]olitary men in moments of contemplation receive, as I think, the creative impulse from the lowest of the Nine Hierarchies, and so make and unmake mankind, and even the world itself, for does not "the eye altering alter all"?' (*Id*. 158–9) In other words, the idea of love is created by poets, and their creations are the product of inspiration from the spiritual world. These theories are reflected in Yeats's poems to Shakespear, in which, in true Muse poet fashion, he tells the truth about his relationship with his Muse, and is inspired by his communion with her.

Yeats's essay, sounding a theme that Graves would later adopt, stresses the need for the poet to achieve an almost magical mastery of language if he is to succeed in evoking the Muse and creating a poem that outlives its author. Recognition of the role played by verbally constructed symbols in poetry would make it impossible, he argues, 'for anybody to deny the importance of form,' because:

> although you can expound an opinion, or describe a thing, when your words are not quite well chosen, you cannot give a body to something that moves beyond the senses, unless your words are as subtle, as complex, as full of mysterious life, as the body of a flower or of a woman. (*Id*. 163–4)

Yeats's poems to Shakespear reflect an intensely crafted use of language to open the door to the Beauty long faded from the world. These poems are products of what Graves would later call '[t]rue poetic practice,' which 'implies a mind so miraculously attuned and illuminated that it can form words, by a chain of more-than-coincidences, into a living entity – a poem that goes about on its own (for centuries after the author's death, perhaps) affecting readers with its stored magic.' (White Goddess 481) All his life, Yeats sought to write poems that would live forever in the collective memory, even going so far as to suggest to the sources of his wife's automatic writing that once the *Iliad* entered the collective mind, it could reappear centuries after all the books in the world had been destroyed and the poem had vanished from every living mind. (*YVP 2*, 479)

Yeats recognized that his poems to Shakespear were 'curiously elaborate in style' (*Mem* 86[18]), a result of their use of language in a manner that Helen Vendler, in her fascinating study of Yeats's lyric form, calls 'magical' because it implies the poet's belief 'that language has powers of its own, which are independent of the story it tells.'[19] Vendler's close study of another poem from *The Wind Among the Reeds*, 'The Song of

Wandering Aengus' (*VP* 149–50), identifies such magical techniques as using words that are contained within each other, anaphora, and the repetition of phrases, lines, and sounds. (Secret Discipline 107–08) These techniques show, as Vendler puts it, 'that magical, non-rational, non-etymological relations between the words are as important to Yeats as logical, semantic, or etymological connections....' (*Id.*)[20] A similar magical use of language is apparent in the Shakespear poems, particularly 'He remembers Forgotten Beauty,' which achieves an incantatory effect with repetitive rhyme sounds, such as fled/thread, cloth/moth, rose/close, hand/land, this/kiss, deep/sleep. The poem concludes with a rush of incantation:

> But flame on flame, and deep on deep,
> Throne over throne where in half sleep,
> Their swords upon their iron knees,
> Brood her high lonely mysteries.

Yeats's highly polished celebration of the White Goddess '[b]rood[ing] her high lonely mysteries' captured the attention of Joyce's Stephen Dedalus. Stephen, while attracted to Yeats's injunction to Fergus to 'no more turn aside and brood/Upon love's bitter mystery,'[21] criticizes 'He remembers Forgotten Beauty,' asserting that he would rather 'press in my arms the loveliness which has not yet come into the world' than 'the loveliness which has long faded from the world.'[22] Stephen's critique overlooks the role of the poet's Muse, the beautiful woman who, like Olivia Shakespear, mediates between the spiritual and material worlds by reintroducing a forgotten Beauty.

Such mediation is at the heart of 'The Travail of Passion' (*VP* 172). Published in *The Savoy* in January 1896, about the time Yeats and Shakespear became lovers, this vivid poem shows Beauty rushing into the world through an 'angelic door' thrown open by a sexual relationship. The perfumed and loose-haired women who bend over the poet introduce divinity to the world – 'immortal passion breathes in mortal clay' – an incarnation of passion analogized to the incarnation and passion of Christ:

> When the flaming lute-thronged angelic door is wide;
> When an immortal passion breathes in mortal clay;
> Our hearts endure the scourge, the plaited thorns, the way
> Crowded with bitter faces, the wounds in palm and side,
> The vinegar-heavy sponge, the flowers by Kedron stream;
> We will bend down and loosen our hair over you,

That it may drop faint perfume, and be heavy with dew,
Lillies of death-pale hope, roses of passionate dream.

The women who loosen their perfumed hair evoke the 'sinner' of Luke's gospel who washes Christ's feet with her tears, dries them with her hair, kisses them, and anoints him with balm from a jar.[23] Like Simon Magus' Helena, these fallen incarnations of 'immortal passion...in mortal clay' are divine Wisdom enshrouded in human form. In fact, the sinner of Luke's gospel was traditionally conflated with Mary Magdalene,[24] and, as Yeats would have known from Mead's *Simon Magus*, Mary Magdalene was one of the traditional embodiments of the Wisdom figure and stood in relation to Christ as Helen to Simon. (Simon Magus 39, 74–5) The passion that courses through Yeats's poem may be a travail, but it is electrifyingly real. The intensity of Yeats's passionate relationship with his Mary Magdalene figure, Olivia Shakespear, engendered an even more audacious use of Mary Magdalene than Petrarch's address to her as 'dear friend of God.'[25] In 'The Travail of Passion,' the passionate relationship of the Wisdom figures with the Christ-like poet reflects Yeat's perception of his sexual experience with Shakespear as an encounter with the White Goddess. The poet experiences Beauty, another name for Wisdom, but the price is death.

Even Allen Grossman, who generally regarded the poems of *The Wind Among the Reeds* as confined by, rather than expanding, the Wisdom tradition, recognized 'The Travail of Passion' as an exception. Grossman thought the idea of the Wisdom goddess a 'perverse transfiguration of the courtly convention' because '[t]he confrontation with the Wisdom figure involves the impossibility of the objective relation and leads to the loss of love.'[26] In 'The Travail of Passion,' however, the beauty of the Wisdom figure re-enters the world through the poet's passionate relationship with her human incarnation. Grossman conceded that 'The Travail of Passion' is the one occasion in *The Wind Among the Reeds* when the 'guarded door of the Supernal Eden does swing open,' but he was unwilling to recognize the same process of mediation between 'the upper and lower elements of reality' in the other poems addressed to Shakespear, perhaps because 'The Travail of Passion' is the only poem with respect to which he finds biographical reference to her pertinent. (*Id.* 96–7) Grossman's concluding comment on 'The Travail of Passion' implicitly recognizes its author's place in the tradition of the Gravesian Muse poet. 'The experience of love,' he says, 'is an agony, like the crucifixion, the end of which is death and consequent purification of the lover.' (*Id.*)

Under the Gravesian rubric, the author of these poems would fight to the death with his other self for the favor of Olivia Shakespear as priestess of the White Goddess. Yeats, however, could not escape the pull of his fixation on Maud Gonne as the true representative of the White Goddess. Thoughts of Gonne had nearly distracted him from the path to Shakespear. Just after he had locked himself out of his rooms when a critical meeting with Shakespear and her sponsor was about to take place, he had received a letter from Gonne telling him that his ghost had walked into her hotel sitting-room in Paris on the day of the lock-out and had 'brought her soul away' and they 'had wandered round the cliffs [of] Howth where we had been together years before.' (*Mem* 87) Yeats nonetheless managed to plunge ahead to the consummation with Shakespear, but that liaison lasted less than a year before he returned to pursuit of the unattainable. An invitation to dinner from Gonne was all that was needed to trigger the change. Soon after the dinner, Yeats recounts, 'one morning instead of reading much love poetry, as my way was to bring the right mood round, I wrote letters. My friend found my mood did not answer hers and burst into tears. "There is someone else in your heart", she said. It was the breaking between us for many years.' (*Mem* 89)

Yeats's account is consistent with the doctrine that the poet gives his life for the White Goddess, but reflects his unwillingness to let Shakespear displace Maud Gonne from her central role as the Muse to whom he must sacrifice himself. Yeats put it this way: 'All our lives long, as daVinci says, we long, thinking it is but the moon that we long [for], for our destruction, and how, when we meet [it] in the shape of a most fair woman, can we do less than leave all others for her? Do we not seek dissolution upon her lips?' (*Id.* at 88)

Significantly, it is Yeats – not daVinci – who equates attraction to the Muse with a longing for the moon. In the passage to which Yeats refers, and which he quotes in 'The Tables of the Law,' daVinci speaks of a constant longing for 'each new spring time, each new summer, each new month, each new year....'[27] Muse-poet Yeats adds the idea of longing for the moon.

Yeats tells the story of his parting from Shakespear matter of factly, and with little visible evidence of mourning, in 'The Lover mourns for the Loss of Love,' a poem whose easy conversational flow – Pound admired its being made 'of a single sentence with no word out of natural order'[28] – is at once its charm and an indictment of the seemingly cavalier attitude of its author:

> Pale brows, still hands and dim hair,
> I had a beautiful friend
> And dreamed that the old despair
> Would end in love in the end:
> She looked in my heart one day
> And saw your image was there;
> She has gone weeping away. (*VP* 152)[29]

Shakespear knew exactly what had happened. It was clear to her that Yeats was locked in thrall to an unattainable Muse. In a vision she related to him when their friendship resumed a few years later, Yeats appeared as a Greek prisoner-poet offering incense at the marble tomb of a beautiful woman. (*Life 1*, 174) As Yeats described Shakespear's vision in a notebook, his figure 'would have no living love... because he said that no living beauty was like that marble beauty....'[30]

The conflicting attractions of the attainable and unattainable Muse were a recurring source of fascination for Yeats. His 1903 story 'Red Hanrahan' (*M 2005*, 141) reflects his experiences of Olivia Shakespear and Maud Gonne as differing incarnations of the White Goddess. Hanrahan is a poet who is about to begin a journey to marry a woman, Mary Lavelle, who has accepted his proposal, but he is diverted by an old man playing at cards, who turns the cards into a hare and a pack of hounds. The hounds chase the hare and Hanrahan follows the hounds, who lead him to 'a woman, the most beautiful the world ever saw, having a long pale face....' (*M 2005*, 145) The beautiful, pale woman is Echtge, queen of the Tuatha De Danaan, the original inhabitants of Ireland who, having been defeated by the first human invaders, retreated, as Gould and Toomey recount, 'into burial mounds, becoming identified with the fairies or Sidhe.' (*M 2005*, 361 n. 9) Hanrahan wants to ask the beautiful pale woman a number of questions, but is so filled with awe and dread that he is unable to speak. After hearing her entourage describe him as weak and afraid, and hearing the queen give a great sigh, Hanrahan falls asleep. When he awakes, he wanders in a state of bewilderment for a year, then seeks Mary Lavelle, only to learn that she has married someone else and disappeared. Hanrahan's pursuit of the overwhelming presence of the White Goddess had cost him happiness with a living beauty.

Nearly thirty years after forsaking Shakespear's living beauty to pursue the unattainable Gonne, Yeats wrote a series of lyrics that reveal his regret at having left Shakespear's satisfying cup 'half-tasted,' and his belated recognition that it had been his fixation on Gonne as a moon-like Muse that had led him to pursue a form of his own destruction at the expense of a satisfying relationship with Shakespear. His reminiscence was stimulated when, as he told Shakespear in a letter dated 6 December 1926, 'I came upon two early photographs of you yesterday, while going through my file – one from "Literary Year Book." Who ever had a like profile? – a profile from a Sicilean coin. One looks back to one's youth as to [a] cup that a mad man dying of thirst left half tasted. I wonder if you feel like that.' (*CL InteLex* 4972) It is fair to think that Yeats's reference to Shakespear's profile as 'from a Sicilian coin' conflates her profile with that of the Mother-Goddess pictured on Cretan coins that he saw in the archer vision to which he had been led by Shakespear's mediumistic advice to seek lunar inspiration. Yeats sent Shakespear a draft of 'The Empty Cup'(*VP* 454), which makes use of the moving metaphor in the letter of the old man dying of thirst who remembers a cup 'left half tasted,' and attributes the craziness of his mistake to being 'moon-accursed':

> A crazy man that found a cup,
> When all but dead of thirst,
> Hardly dared to wet his mouth
> Imagining, moon-accursed,
> That another mouthful
> And his beating heart would burst.
> October last I found it too
> But found it dry as bone,
> And for that reason am I crazed
> And my sleep is gone.   (*VP* 454) (*Tower MM* 487)

The author of 'The Empty Cup' realizes that he was 'crazy' when, in 1896, 'all but dead of thirst' for a sexual relationship with a beautiful woman, he '[h]ardly dared to wet his mouth' with Olivia Shakespear, but, instead, cursed by the moon, imagined that another mouthful would cause his beating heart to burst. An earlier poem in the same series, 'First Love,' explains that the reason he feared his heart would burst was that the curse of the moon had hitched him to pursuit of the unattainable Gonne, and his heart would burst if he abandoned that pursuit. His 'First Love' was also a priestess of the White Goddess: she was 'nurtured like the sailing moon/In beauty's murderous brood' but had 'a heart of stone' that he nonetheless pursued 'For every hand is lunatic/That travels on the moon.' (*VP* 451)

The experience that informed Yeats's understanding of 1926 likely included more than one resumption of his affair with Shakespear. His widow told Ellmann that the affair resumed in 1903, after Gonne's marriage in February of that year (M&M 182), and Deirdre Toomey's analysis of the horoscopes Yeats calculated for Shakespear suggests that in June 1910 they either had a further 'affair or became very close emotionally in a way that paralleled the involvement of late 1895 and early 1896.'[31]

Whether or not the affair was revived, Yeats's 1890s relationship with Shakespear was a powerful life-long stimulus to creativity. When Yeats wrote the poem 'Friends' in January 1911 to praise '[t]hree women that have wrought/What joy is in my days,' Olivia Shakespear was so powerful a persona in his mind that she seems to hover over the description of the first two women, one of whom he initially intended to be Lady Augusta Gregory. The notion of a poem celebrating three friends is a characteristically Yeatsian gesture. It reflects a general practice captured in Graham Hough's observation that '[n]o poet in our day has written more about his family and his friends than Yeats, and no one has been more successful in enlarging them to heroic proportions' – a success achieved by using 'his very high sense of his own dignity to add to the dignity of his friends.'[32] The three eponymous friends of this poem are all women, and the poem's magnificent tribute is built around four recurring ideas central to Yeats's thinking about his creative process: joy, delight, ecstasy, and sweetness. He begins by declaring that all three friends contributed to his overall joy. The other three emotional states – delight, ecstasy, and sweetness – are distributed among the three friends:

> Now must I these three praise –
> Three women that have wrought
> What joy is in my days:
> One because no thought,
> Nor those unpassing cares,
> No, not in these fifteen
> Many-times-troubled years,
> Could ever come between
> Mind and delighted mind;
> And one because her hand

> Had strength that could unbind
> What none can understand,
> What none can have and thrive,
> Youth's dreamy load, till she
> So changed me that I live
> Labouring in ecstasy.
> And what of her that took
> All till my youth was gone
> With scarce a pitying look?
> How could I praise that one?
> When day begins to break
> I count my good and bad,
> Being wakeful for her sake,
> Remembering what she had,
> What eagle look still shows,
> While up from my heart's root
> So great a sweetness flows
> I shake from head to foot.

(*VP* 315–16) Each of the creatively productive emotional states engendered by the three friends has extensive denotations and connotations in the Yeatsian lexicon that bear on what 'Friends' is telling us about Shakespear's role as Muse.

The question 'What is joy?' that Yeats would later pose in 'Vacillation' (*VP* 500) was one that fascinated him all his life. The word has a rich history. The troubadours used it both to refer to a state of general happiness and to describe erotic pleasure, and Dante recounts in *La Vita Nuova* that when Love appeared to him in a dream, he seemed 'to rejoice inwardly.'[33] In his 1907 essay, 'Poetry and Tradition,' written in the wake of the emotional maelstrom surrounding the opening of the Abbey's production of Synge's *The Playboy of the Western World*, and Yeats's ensuing trip to Italy with Augusta and Robert Gregory, Yeats emphasized the importance of 'shaping joy' in controlling his tendency to anger and hatred, noting that it is 'only when we are gay over a thing, and can play with it, do we show ourselves its master, and have minds clear enough for strength.' (*E&I* 252–5) He returns to this theme in his touching 3 February 1913 letter to Mabel Beardsley, whose gaiety in the face of impending death from cancer affected him deeply. 'May blessed spirits – and I believe in spirits –,' he wrote, 'keep the gaiety of your soul – heroism it only is but a perpetual gaiety. What is personality, charm but a form of joy? And that is why we follow it to the worlds

end.' (*CL InteLex* 2081) All three friends brought Yeats joy, 'a perpetual gaiety,' an attitude he thought a prerequisite to creativity. As he said in 'Lapis Lazuli,' 'All things fall and are built again,
And those that build them again are gay.' (*VP* 566)

Yeatsian delight and sweetness are defined in 'A Prayer for my Daughter,' where he articulates his conviction that a soul that succeeds in freeing itself of hatred learns that it is 'self-delighting' and 'that its own sweet will is Heaven's will':

> Considering that, all hatred driven hence,
> The soul recovers radical innocence
> And learns at last that it is self-delighting,
> Self-appeasing, self-affrighting,
> And that its own sweet will is Heaven's will;
> She can, though every face should scowl
> And every windy quarter howl
> Or every bellows burst, be happy still. (*VP* 405)

This sense of delight is rooted in Neo-Platonism. Proclus, in the commentary on Plato's theology that Yeats knew in Taylor's translation (*NC* 243), explains that, whereas the vicious man sees his own baseness within, the worthy man 'is able to associate with, and love himself.'[34] Such a soul is self-delighting: '[t]he worthy man perceiving himself beautiful rejoices and is delighted, and producing in himself beautiful conceptions, gladly embraces an association with himself.'[35] In other words, the friend who was counterpoint to Yeats's delighted mind had helped him to perceive himself as beautiful, and to embrace an association with himself. For Dante, the act of creatively praising his beloved engendered an overflowing sweetness: in his sonnet 'Ladies that have intelligence in love,' sweetness flows over the poet when he praises his beloved.[36]

Per Amica Silentia Lunae explains that the last of the four creative states, ecstasy, is the word tradition offers 'for the awakening, for the vision, for the revelation of reality.' (*Myth* 331) It is 'some realization or fulfillment of the soul in itself, some slow or sudden expansion of it like an overflowing well.' (*Mem* 153) It is the poet's holy grail.

There has been broad agreement among readers of 'Friends' that the sweetness-engendering third friend is Maud Gonne, and that the two other friends are Olivia Shakespear and Lady Gregory. There is disagreement, however, as to which creatively productive emotional state is being assigned to Shakespear and which to Gregory. The conventional view, based on A. Norman Jeffares' influential *Commentary*, has been that the first friend – the partner in a duet of '[m]ind and delighted mind' – is Olivia Shakespear, and the second – the one whose hand had strength that could unbind youth's dreamy load until the poet lived labouring in ecstasy – is Gregory. More recently, both John Harwood and Deirdre Toomey have reversed the identifications. Harwood argues that the reference to 'her hand' suggests the 'erotic imagery of . . . the "lingering hand"' in 'He remembers Forgotten Beauty,' and thus the second friend is not Gregory, but Shakespear, whose hand released 'youth's dreamy load,' which Harwood reads as 'the burden of Yeats's virginity.' (OS 136) The trouble with this reading is that the poem does not praise some lingering manual dexterity, but a hand that '[h]ad strength.' The traditional connotation of a 'strong hand' as a firm guide accords perfectly with Gregory's role as a teacher and enforcer of strict work habits, as depicted, for example, in 'Coole Park, 1929,' which celebrates 'a woman's powerful character' that '[c]ould keep a swallow to its first intent.' (*VP* 489) Gregory's strong hand is apparent, too, in Yeats's accounts of how, when his 'nervous system was worn out' during his first visits to Coole, Gregory sent 'cups of soup when I was called' in the morning, then took him outdoors to collect folk beliefs. When he was in good health again, but 'indolent,' he asked her 'to send me to my work every day at eleven, and at some other hour to my letters, rating me with idleness if need be, and I doubt if I should have done much with my life but for her firmness and her care.' (*Mem* 125–6; *Au* 377) Gregory's 'firmness' is clearly evoked by the strong hand of the second friend. Her unbinding of 'youth's dreamy load' parallels Yeats's encomium in *Memoirs* that 'she brought to my wavering thoughts steadfast nobility.' (*Mem* 161)

Nonetheless, Toomey maintains that Gregory is the first friend rather than the second. She reasons that the poem's assertion that no thought could come between mind and delighted mind 'in these fifteen/Many-times-troubled years' identifies Gregory as the first friend because Yeats had known Gregory for fifteen years 'since 1896' and the friendship had been 'continuous.'[37] (*YA* 6 at 225) But 'Friends' was composed during January 1911 (*id.* at 224), and Yeats would not have known Gregory for fifteen years until August of that year.[38] Toomey argues that 'Yeats had known Shakespear for seventeen years at the time of writing the poem' (*id.* at 225), but if one accords Yeats the latitude of measuring from the commencement of a sexual relationship with Shakespear in January

1896, the fifteen years fits exactly.[39] Finally, Toomey argues that the 'continuous' nature of the Yeats-Gregory relationship should trump the three-year hiatus in the Yeats-Shakespear communion, but the poem does not assert that the relationship was 'continuous.' Rather, it asserts that no thought has come between mind and delighted mind during a fifteen-year period that was '[m]any-times-troubled' – a description that foreshadows Yeats's observation, upon Shakespear's death in 1938, that 'we have never had a quarrel, sadness sometimes but never a difference.'[40] Thus, the fifteen-year, many-times-troubled relationship points to Shakespear as the first of the friends. 'Friends' lauds her for leading Yeats to the sense of abounding, overflowing delight that he found necessary to releasing his creativity. A successful sexual relationship with a mediumistic woman who brought him a message of the need for lunar inspiration was a necessary part of the genesis of extraordinary poems like 'He remembers Forgotten Beauty' and 'The Travail of Passion.'

Despite Shakespear's status as the first of the friends, identification of the second friend remains problematic, even in the face of strong traces of Gregory, because of the difference between the final text of the poem and the draft Yeats sent to Gregory of what he described as 'certain lines about you.' (*ISW MM* 221) The enclosed lines, as corrected, were these:

> ...... Her hand
> Showed me how I could unbind
> The weight that none can understand
> Youths bitter burden, & would give
> Every gift that may be
> Could I copy her & live
> In a laborious reverie

Harwood argues that the 'bitter burden' in these lines refers to poverty, which Gregory's hospitality alleviated, and thus the poem's eventual gratitude for unbinding 'youth's dreamy load' – rather than its 'bitter burden' – must refer to a friend other than Gregory. However, there is ample basis for thinking that the 'bitter burden' that Gregory helped Yeats to shed included the burden of compelled labour, and that Gregory is thus referred to in both the draft and the final poem. Yeats identified Gregory's Coole with freedom from both poverty and compelled labour in a 1909 diary note on the composition of 'Upon a House Shaken by The Land Agitation.' 'Here,' Yeats said, referring to Coole, 'there has been no compelled labour, no poverty-thwarted impulse.' (*Mem* 226) Poverty and compelled labour were both a part of youth's bitter burden. Thus, a shift in the draft of 'Friends' from an escape from poverty to an absence of compelled labour is not a shift away from Gregory. Rather, the lines sent to Gregory mark the beginning of a process of finding how to merge the notion of Gregory as an enforcer of a work ethic with the Coole tradition of freedom from compelled labour. According to the lines sent to Gregory, the aspect that Yeats would 'copy' was that of living '[i]n a laborious reverie,' which describes a life that, while it may involve reverie, is nonetheless labourious. Yeats was painfully aware that labouring – 'stitching and unstitching,' as he said in 'Adam's Curse' – was as much a part of writing poetry as inspiration: 'It's certain there is no fine thing/Since Adam's fall but needs much labouring.' (*VP* 205) The second and third drafts of 'Friends' show Yeats making the brilliant revisions possible only to a master. The lines shifted from the notion of his 'copying' Gregory in laborious reverie to her teaching him, then to her 'changing him,' and the change progresses from laborious reverie to 'in labour & ecstasy,' to in labouring ecstasy, and, finally, to '[s]o changed me that I live/Labouring in ecstasy.' The notion of labouring in ecstasy is one of the great Yeatsian themes. Ecstasy – the visionary revelation of reality – can transform the writing of poetry from the 'much labouring' of Adam's Curse to the joyous state described in 'Among School Children' in which:

> Labour is blossoming or dancing where
> The body is not bruised to pleasure soul,
> Nor beauty born out of its own despair,
> Nor blear-eyed wisdom out of midnight oil.

(*VP* 445–6) Or, as said more simply in 'Friends,' a woman can lead the poet to transform the 'stitching and unstitching' of 'Adam's Curse' – what seems a bitter burden to a dreamy youth – into ' labouring in ecstasy.' 'Labouring in ecstasy,' with its evocation of the joyous dancer and dance of 'Among School Children,' is so significantly different from the laborious reverie of the lines sent to Gregory that it is fair to think that some of the delight Yeats associated with Shakespear informed his masterful revision of 'laborious reverie' to 'labouring in ecstasy.' In the final version of the poem, Shakespear and Gregory merge to represent both the delight of inspiration and the *techne* – 'the stitching and unstitching' – necessary to fashion inspiration into poetry.

The fact that Shakespear's delighted mind overflows into Yeats's praise of Gregory may be explained by the fact that, although Gregory's discipline and sense of order were essential enablers of Yeats's creativity, she was not a Muse. As discussed in Chapter 3, Yeats believed that the erotic passion of the courtly love poets was the source of their power, and would have agreed with Arlene Croce's definition of the Muse as 'that dream of eros which inspires art....'[41] There is no indication that Yeats was erotically attracted to Gregory. The role of Gregorian stability and order in his creative life can be understood in terms of his observation in a letter to W. T. Horton endorsing Blake's belief 'that the intellect must do its utmost before inspiration is possible. It clears the rubbish from the mouth of the sybils cave but it is not the sybil [sic].'[42] Gregory cleared the mouth of the Sibyl's cave, but despite all her marvelous contributions to Yeats's creative life, she was not a Muse.

Shakespear, who remained an erotic image in Yeats's psyche for decades, was the Muse Yeats needed to inspire magical poems like 'He remembers Forgotten Beauty' and 'The Travail of Passion.' Her erotic allure, generosity, beauty, and empathy with Yeats's occult interests were exactly the qualities required to symbolize the reemergence on earth of the Beauty that had long faded from the world, thereby breaching the barrier between the upper and lower worlds that Grossman identifies in *The Wind Among the Reeds*. While poems like 'He hears the Cry of the Sedge' (*VP* 165), and 'He thinks of his Past Greatness when a Part of the Constellations of Heaven' (*VP* 177) can be fairly characterized as 'the sexual act of the impotent man' (Grossman 163), the poems inspired by Shakespear are that rare Yeatsian achievement – memorable poems inspired by an attainable – and attained – Muse. The significance of Shakespear's contribution to these poems is not diminished by the fact that, as noted by Jahan Ramazani, her dark beauty necessarily gave way to the 'pearl-pale' and 'White Beauty' conventions of the Wisdom tradition.[43]

Although Shakespear's Musedom might be subject to the feminist critique of the Muse as a passive receptacle chosen by the poet –'*la demoiselle éleu,*' as Croce puts it, echoing Rossetti and Debussy (Croce 168) – the idea of a living woman as symbol and intermediary of timeless Beauty calls for a Muse of circumscribed dimension. Shakespear brought to the role exactly what it required. Moreover, her contribution to Yeats's creativity extended beyond particular poems of *The Wind Among the Reeds*. As reflected in 'Friends,' her generosity, sympathy, and delighted mind engendered self- delight in Yeats's conception of himself at a time when precisely that stimulus to creativity was sorely needed.

For better or ill, however, Shakespear ultimately did not adhere to either the courtly love rubric of unattainability or Graves' definition of the Muse as the task master who cannot be possessed. Yeats too readily won her, and thus lost her as Muse. Rather than exhibiting the distance that caused Petrarch to speak of Laura as his 'sweet enemy,'[44] Shakespear was, as Yeats said in *Memoirs*, 'too near my soul, too salutary and wholesome to my inmost being' for him to sacrifice himself as to a Muse, which he described as giving 'the love that was her beauty's right.' (*Mem* 88)

Nonetheless, the very nearness to Yeats's soul that disqualified Shakespear from classic Muse status transformed her into an icon of constructive love as friendship. Yeats's 1929 poem, 'After Long Silence' (*VP* 523), one of his most beautiful love poems, must surely be addressed to Olivia Shakespear. David Clark made a valiant effort to identify the addressee as Moina Mathers, one of Yeats's compatriots in the Golden Dawn, but there is no evidence of a love affair between Mathers and Yeats, and the conversation that occurred 'after long silence' with Moina Mathers referred to Yeats's treatment of her husband in his autobiography – not the supreme theme of Art and Song.[45] Moreover, the tone of 'After Long Silence' is so much of a piece with Yeats's contemporaneous correspondence with Shakespear – to whom he sent a prose draft of the poem in a letter of 16 December 1929 (*CL InteLex* 5327) – that this poignant poem must be taken as a timeless tribute to his first lover:

> Speech after long silence; it is right,
> All other lovers being estranged or dead,
> Unfriendly lamplight hid under its shade,
> The curtains drawn upon unfriendly night,
> That we descant and yet again descant
> Upon the supreme theme of Art and Song:
> Bodily decrepitude is wisdom; young
> We loved each other and were ignorant.

The poem's arresting opening immediately captures the reader's attention, and focuses it on a conversation about love, 'the supreme theme of Art and Song.' Significantly, Yeats at last finds the 'wisdom' that comes with bodily decrepitude in conversation with Olivia Shakespear, the 'white woman' of the wisdom tradition he immortalized in early poems before casting away her cup half-tasted in favor of Maud Gonne. Although the ignorant young poet had abandoned Shakespear as Muse, the older Yeats discovers at last that she was, after all, the white woman who showed the way to wisdom. Shakespear's role as Muse of the poem of friendship between lovers is enduring and unique.

2. Florence Farr in *A Sicilian Idyll*, 1890, courtesy of Senate House Library, University of London, MS 982/6/4.

2

Where the Blessed Dance: Florence Farr

In May 1890, approximately four years before he would meet Olivia Shakespear, Yeats was in the audience at the clubhouse in Bedford Park, the suburban London artists' colony to which his father had moved the family in 1888. He was there to see Florence Farr perform in a play, *A Sicilian Idyll*, that John Todhunter had written at his suggestion.[1] Farr was the daughter of William Farr and Mary Elizabeth Whittal of Shropshire. Her father had a distinguished career in London as Compiler of Abstracts for a new scheme for collecting vital statistics. He was a proponent of preventive medicine and a close friend of Florence Nightingale, who was likely the inspiration for his daughter's name.[2] Farr herself attended Queen's College, London but found it 'really damaging to the vital apparatus' and left to try her luck as an actress. (FF 18–19) She married a fellow member of a touring company, Edward Emery, in 1884, but they separated four years later and were divorced in 1895. (FF 21–4) In the May 1890 performance, Farr played a shepherdess-priestess, Amaryllis, who, suspecting her suitor of unfaithfulness, prays for his death to the Greek Moon Goddess Selene:

> Hear me, Selene, for to thee I sing!
> Calling on thee by thy most dreadful name,
> Hecate; thou who through the shuddering night
> Pacest where black pools of fresh-offered blood
> Gleam cold beside the barrows of the dead:
> Dread goddess, draw him dying to my feet![3]

There was thus a powerful impetus from the outset of their relationship for Yeats to see Farr as a priestess of the White Goddess.

In fact, Yeats analogized Farr's beauty to that of Demeter, one of the names of the White Goddess. 'She had three great gifts,' Yeats wrote, 'a tranquil beauty like that of Demeter's image near the British Museum

Reading-Room door, and an incomparable sense of rhythm and a beautiful voice, the seeming natural expression of the image.' (*Au* 121) These qualities suggested that Farr might become for Yeats the priestess of the White Goddess she portrayed in Todhunter's play. Moreover, the interest she shared with Yeats in magic led her to look to lunar goddesses as sources of wisdom. By June 1890, she had joined Yeats as a member of the Isis-Urania Temple of the Order of the Golden Dawn.[4] Her new Order name, *Sapientia Sapienti Dono Data*, 'Wisdom is Given as a Gift to the Wise,' reflected her life-long search for wisdom, and her 1894 essay on alchemy identified the 'Wisdom Goddess' as the source of 'the secret wisdom of the ages.'[5]

Through their work in the Isis-Urania Temple, both Yeats and Farr became familiar with the rites of the Egyptian goddess Isis, who was identified with both Demeter and Selene.[6] The name of the temple itself highlighted the role of Isis, giving only second billing to the Muse of astronomy. The prominent role of Isis in the temple's affairs is apparent from the fact that when W. T. Horton joined the Order, he sent Yeats a drawing of Isis, noting that he remembered 'what you told me about the "Priestess of Isis".'[7] In reply, Yeats suggested that Egyptian faces may 'very well come to you after your initiation, as the Order is greatly under Egyptian influence....'[8] Indeed, the temple's founder, MacGregor Mathers, was so devoted to Isis that, after he relocated to Paris in 1894, he conducted public rites in her honor. Yeats, who likely attended Mathers' rites of Isis at the Théâtre Bodinière, Rue Saint-Lazare, in March 1899, described such an occasion in the final version of his unpublished novel, *The Speckled Bird*. (*SB* 78–9[9]) The novel also shows that the makings of the idea that Farr was a reincarnation of a priestess of a moon goddess were ready to hand. The principal female character, Margaret, relates that the Mathers figure (Maclagan) believes that she 'was once a priestess in a temple of the moon in Syria. You know he believes that we live again and again....' (*SB* 22)

Farr's study of Egyptian magic and ritual led her to a vision in which she was addressed by a divinity akin to the White Goddess that Graves would later posit as the object of the true poet's quest. The divinity described in Farr's notebook for 10 November 1892 spoke to her as follows:

> I am the mighty Mother Isis; most powerful of all the world,
> I am she who fights not but is always victorious, I am that
> Sleeping Beauty whom men have sought, for all time; and

the paths which lead to my castle are beset with danger and illusionary influence – I am lifted up on high, and do draw men unto me, I am the World's Desire, but few there be who find me. (FF 75)

Farr's magical studies and beautiful rhythmic voice made her the perfect partner for Yeats in his efforts to construct a spoken poetry that could magically open the door to an influx of imaginative power from the Great Mind and the Great Memory. He would later articulate the basis for such a partnership in his essay on magic, which linked magicians and poets, saying that symbols are the greatest of all powers 'whether they are used consciously by the masters of magic, or half unconsciously by their successors, the poet, the musician and the artist.' (E&I 49)

Yeats's essay defined the poet's task in a way that required Farr's contribution: 'our life in cities,' he said, 'which deafens or kills the passive meditative life, and our education that enlarges the separated, self-moving mind, have made our souls less sensitive.' (E&I 41) Farr's enchanting voice would be critical to accomplishing the poet's duty to re-kindle the sensitivity of the soul: 'Have not poetry and music arisen, as it seems, out of the sounds the enchanters made to help their imagination to enchant, to charm, to bind with a spell themselves and the passers-by?' (Id. 43) Yeats's notion that sound could communicate at a spiritual level, thus enabling the poet's spoken word to unlock forces hidden in a collective unconscious, was not dissimilar to Eliot's notion of 'the auditory imagination,' a 'feeling for syllable and rhythm, penetrating far below the levels of conscious thought and feeling, invigorating every word' and fusing ancient and civilized mentalities.[10]

The idea of Farr as enchantress was percolating as Yeats watched her performance in *A Sicilian Idyll* in 1890. Writing in the *Boston Pilot*, he reported that Farr

> ...won universal praise with her striking beauty and subtle gesture and fine delivery of the verse. Indeed her acting was the feature of the whole performance that struck one most, after the verse itself. I do not know that I have any word too strong to express my admiration for its grace and power.[11]

As he said later in *The Trembling of the Veil*, he 'made through these performances a close friend and a discovery that was to influence my life.' (*Au* 120) The friend, of course, was Farr; the discovery was that 'in the performance of all drama that depends for its effect upon beauty of language, poetical culture may be more important than professional experience.' (*Id.* 121)

Farr seemed poised to assume the role of a unique kind of Muse whose functions would include reciting Yeats's poetry in a way that enchanted the listener. Indeed, Farr was described as Yeats's Muse by Mabel Dolmetsch, the wife of the musician and restorer of ancient musical instruments who created the stringed instrument, called a psaltery, that Farr eventually used to accompany her verse recitation.[12] Farr knew that her role as inspiring Muse could carry over from the stage into life. Onstage, in *A Sicilian Idyll*, Alcander implored her to be a 'perpetual priestess' who commands him to perform great deeds. (Idyll 36–7) Her answer – 'Can I inspire thee so?' – carried over into life when she so inscribed her alluring photograph from the production.[13] The inscription was apparently addressed to Todhunter (Fletcher 197), and there were at least two independent reasons why Farr did not immediately become Yeats's Muse. One was named Maud Gonne. Although Yeats had met Gonne in January 1889, his autobiography, with customary mastery over the Yeatsian myth, places that fateful event just *after* Farr's memorable performance in *A Sicilian Idyll*, so that Yeats's life narrative veers away from Farr and toward Gonne. (*Au* 123) In any event, there was an obstacle to Farr's being immediately available to play Yeats's Muse. The obstacle was George Bernard Shaw, who was also in the audience at the Bedford Park Clubhouse in May. He made her acquaintance shortly thereafter, he recalled, 'and had no difficulty in considerably improving it.'[14] If Farr was going to be a Muse, she would be Shaw's rather than Yeats's.

Shaw, however, was not the type to play the slave to Farr as Muse. He insisted on being master. Like Henry Higgins, he was soon drilling his new acquaintance in speech exercises, thus beginning a struggle, not so much for Farr's heart as for her soul, between Shaw, as a proponent of a modern realist theatre, and Yeats, as champion of theater as a form of oral poetry. In no time, the energetic Shaw was exhorting Farr by letter to

> persevere with the speaking... You have reached the stage of the Idiotically Beautiful. There remain the stages of the Intelligently Beautiful and finally of the Powerfully Beautiful, and until you have attained the last you will never be able to compel me to recognize the substance of that soul of which I was shown a brief image by Nature for her own purposes.[15]

Nature's purpose had been that Shaw fall in love with Farr. Even allowing for Shavian hyperbole, his correspondence betrays the fall. For example:

> This is to certify that you are my best and dearest love, the regenerator of my heart, the holiest joy of my soul, my treasure, my salvation, my rest, my reward, my darling youngest child, my secret glimpse of heaven, my angel of the Annunciation, not yet herself awake, but rousing me from a long sleep with the beat of her unconscious wings, and shining upon me with her beautiful eyes that are still blind.[16]

Perhaps the normally wary Shaw was thrown off guard by Farr's conviction of the equality and independence of women, which was perfectly in accord with what Shaw saw as the quintessence of Ibsenism – the duty of woman to throw off the role of the 'Womanly Woman' whose soul finds its supreme satisfaction in sacrificing for a lover, husband, or child. Shaw felt that he became '*persona grata*' with Farr when, under Ibsen's influence, 'I wrote somewhere that "home is the girl's prison and the woman's workhouse".'[17] At Shaw's urging, Farr played Rebecca West in Ibsen's *Rosmersholm* in February 1891, and, when asked in a post-performance interview for her view of Rebecca, answered in a voice that echoed Shaw: 'Rebecca West is attractive just because she is so thoroughly womanly, and if she is not womanly then I give up my claim to womanhood, and proclaim myself an abnormal development at the end of the century.' (FF 48) Perhaps the echo of Shaw is explained by the fact that, according to Shaw's most recent biographer, Farr and Shaw had 'almost certainly' become lovers in the winter of 1890–91. (Shaw 160)

Yeats's reaction to Farr's performance illustrates the depth of the chasm between Ibsen's theatre and Yeats's vision of Farr as a magical reciter of poetic drama. 'Florence Farr', he lamented, 'who had but one great gift, the most perfect poetical elocution, became prominent as an Ibsen actress and had almost a success in *Rosmersholm*, where there is symbolism and a stale odour of spilt poetry.' (*Au* 280) Yeats was convinced that Ibsen's dialogue – 'so close to modern educated speech that music and style were impossible' (*Au* 279) – was a vehicle designed to destroy Farr's one great gift and leave her perennially 'almost a success' (*id.* 280). Shaw, however, would not let Farr be a Muse-like ideal. He insisted on drilling her in stage technique. 'You are so real to me as a woman,' Shaw insisted, 'that I cannot think of acting being to you anything more than a technical accomplishment which I want to see carried to a high degree of perfection.'[18] Farr played the moody and violent Blanche Sartorius in *Widowers' Houses*, Shaw's first produced play, in December 1892. Less conventionally, she also contributed to the opening scene of Shaw's *The Philanderer*, which was based on the jealous Jenny Patterson's bursting into Farr's rooms on 4 February 1893 to confront Shaw. (Shaw 162–3)

Farr tried to make a different sort of contribution to Shaw's career when Annie Horniman,[19] the English heiress who would become the key financial backer of the Abbey Theater, offered to fund a theatrical project of Farr's choice. Farr used Horniman's gift to ask both Yeats and Shaw to write plays for a theatrical program to be organized by Farr. The generosity of Horniman and Farr enabled Yeats to write a play fueled by thoughts of Gonne. Farr, he recalled, 'asked me to write a one-act play that her niece, Miss Dorothy Paget, a girl of eight or nine, might make her first stage appearance, and I, with my Irish Theatre in mind, wrote *The Land of Heart's Desire*, in some discomfort when the child was theme, for I knew nothing of children, but with an abundant mind when Mary Bruin was, for I knew an Irish woman whose unrest troubled me.' (*Au* 280)

Because Shaw's play was incomplete when Farr's program opened on 29 March 1894, Yeats's *The Land of Heart's Desire* was paired with a new play by John Todhunter, *A Comedy of Sighs*. Although Aubrey Beardsley's poster for the double bill at the Avenue Theatre became a classic, and Yeats's curtain raiser was a moderate success, Todhunter's play was a disaster, both for its author and for Farr as leading lady. Yeats thought Farr 'had brought the trouble upon herself perhaps, for always in revolt against her own poetical gift, ... and against her own Demeter-like face in the mirror, she had tried when interviewed by the Press to shock and startle....' (*Au* 280–1) In a letter to Elizabeth Robins, Shaw called the performance a horrifying 'transformation of an amiable, clever sort of woman into a nightmare, a Medusa, a cold, loathly, terrifying, grey, callous, sexless devil.'[20]

Recognizing, as Jane Harrison would soon write, that the Medusa was a ritual mask[21] concealing Athena, Goddess of Wisdom (White Goddess 223–5), Farr would not resist characterization as a Medusa. Indeed, when she urged her readers to long for a glance from the Wisdom Goddess, she painted her Wisdom Goddess with the mask of the Medusa:

We have all been taught to look with horror upon Medusa's head with the serpents twisting round its face, the terror of which turned all to stone who gazed upon it. But we must, if we would learn the secret wisdom of the ages, learn to long for a glance from those wonderful eyes which will bestow upon us the gift of indifference to personal joys and sorrows... [and to draw] inspiration from the supernal light – that 'Wisdom Goddess' who wears the serpent crowned head upon her shield.[22]

Practical-minded Shaw did not want a Medusa playing the part of Raina in *Arms and the Man* that he had been writing for Farr. 'What madness led Todhunter to write her a part like that?', Shaw asked in his letter to Robbins, 'what idiocy has led me to do virtually the same thing in the play which I have written to help her in this hellish enterprise?' Shaw rushed *Arms and the Man* to completion, but convinced Farr to relinquish the part of Raina for that of Louka, the feisty and amorous servant girl.

Yeats's memorable account of the opening night is implicitly framed in terms of the struggle for Farr's allegiance. After loud applause and cries of 'Author' at the final curtain, Shaw strode on stage. In the ensuing silence, a single 'Boo' rang out. 'I assure the gentleman in the gallery... that he and I are of exactly the same opinion,' Shaw replied, 'but what can we do against a whole house who are of the contrary opinion?' (*Au* 282) From the moment of the crowd's ringing approval, Yeats thought, Shaw became 'the most formidable man in modern letters.' (*Id.*)

Yeats himself watched Shaw's play 'with admiration and hatred.' 'It seemed to me inorganic, logical straightness and not the crooked road of life, yet I stood aghast before its energy....' (*Au* 283) Farr and Yeats often walked part of the way home together, talking of Shaw, and of Yeats's preference for the illogic of poetry and the mysticism of the crooked road, as opposed to the inorganic logical straightness of Shaw. Farr seemed to share Yeats's 'hesitations', but he was left in doubt 'whether the cock crowed for my blame or for my praise.' (*Au* 284)

Shaw's influence is apparent in Farr's 1894 novel, *The Dancing Faun*, which weaves commentary on unequal treatment of women and Shavian paradox into its well constructed, if simple, plot.[23] Although Shaw and Farr seem to have ceased being lovers toward the end of 1894 (Shaw 174), a warm, bantering relationship still persisted two years later, as reflected in Shaw's letter to Farr warning 'mankind to beware of women with large eyes, and crescent eyebrows, and a smile, and a love of miracles and moonshees.'[24] Yet Yeats eventually succeeded in turning Farr's 'incomparable sense of rhythm and... beautiful voice' toward the two interests that commanded much of his attention during the last decade of the nineteenth century and the beginning of the twentieth: the study and practice of magic and the related use of the chanted human voice to enable the poet to create a sense of enchantment akin to that of the magician.

Farr devoted enormous time and effort to occult studies. She was an indefatigable participant in the affairs of the Isis-Urania Temple, writing rituals, leading others in pursuing visions, giving exams, and publishing books on her extensive and detailed research.[25] Like other contemporary women, Farr found the Golden Dawn more open to equal treatment of women than society at large, an attitude traceable to Mathers who, in his 'Historic Lecture to Neophytes G.D.,' called attention to the 'success of women in occult researches.'[26] Almost half the membership of the Isis-Urania temple were women. (YGD 12) Farr quickly advanced within the order, becoming the officer in charge of rituals (Praemonstratrix) by 1895 (*CL 1*, 485) and Mathers' London representative in 1897 (YGD 12). In fact, when Yeats sought to take an examination to advance to the 'second order' of the society, his examiner was Farr. (*CL 2*, 641) Given the similarity between theatre and the Golden Dawn's combination of ritual and incantatory speech, the Yeats-Farr collaboration logically led to a joint effort to create a theatre in which the wisdom pursued esoterically within the Golden Dawn could be imparted to a theatrical audience that would yet be 'like a secret society,' as Yeats later put it, 'where admission is by favour and never to many.' ('A People's Theatre' in *Ex* 244 at 254)

Farr was essential to this effort to create a poet's theatre because the entire idea hinged on actors who could recite lyrics in a way that created a sense of enchantment. As Yeats put it in a November 1899 letter to George Russell, his plays were 'really a magical revolution for the magical word is the chanted word.' (*CL 2*, 464) Thus, when Yeats set about to produce *The Countess Cathleen* in 1899, his first action was to appoint Farr as manager. (*Mem* 120) Farr organized the production, rehearsed the actors and played the role of Aleel, the Yeats-like poet who is crazed by his love for the Countess. Farr's performance, which Yeats kept among his 'unforgettable memories' after more than thirty-five years (*Au* 417), convinced him of the potential of his poetic theatre to restore poetry to its role as something that was spoken rather than read.

Although George Moore succeeded in deposing Farr as manager, her conduct of the rehearsals carried over to the performance in which, as

Yeats had explained in *Beltaine,* the lyrics were 'not sung, but spoken, or rather chanted to music, as the old poems were probably chanted by bards and rhapsodists.'[27] Yeats likely had in mind Plato's theory that *rhapsodes*, professional reciters of Greek poetry, became inspired as they recited.[28] James Joyce, who was in the audience, thought 'Who will go drive with Fergus now?' was 'the best lyric in the world,' and set it to music himself.[29]

Despite these successes, the Yeats-Farr partnership was threatened by Farr's organization of a selective group within the Isis-Urania Temple for the study of Egyptian symbolism and rituals. When Horniman sought to outlaw groups, Yeats backed Horniman, but, at a contentious council meeting of 1 February 1901, Yeats and Horniman were outvoted. (*CL 3*, 25 n. 2 & 29 n. 1) In the run-up to the council meeting, Yeats sent Farr a heavy-handed letter, complaining that she had backed out of a compromise solution he had negotiated with her, and threatening her with exclusion from a contemplated 'theatre of art' in London:

> I shall await your reply with considerable anxiety as much will depend upon it. If you will keep faith with me – and I cannot suppose that you mean to do anything else – we can do much together. The G.D. is only part of a much greater work – work that may bring you greater opportunities (I am [*remainder of letter in WBY's hand*] {unable to tell you all about the theatrical project, as it concerns the secret of others, but I tell you now, in strict confidence, that I have been approached by a group of writers & artists with a view to a theatre of art.}) We can make a great movement & in more than magical things but I assure you that if (through week vitality, through forgetfulness or through any other cause) you make it difficult for us to relay upon one another perfectly you make everything impossible. (*CL 3*, 26–7)

Signing the letter 'yrs fratny, DEDI,' Yeats added 'I am very sorry to have to write you a letter like this.' And so he should have been. It was a bullying letter. Farr, however, was not to be bullied. At the council meeting, Farr responded to Yeats's speech against groups by asking 'Who and what are *you* in the Order?' or words to that effect.[30] It was no small matter to dispute Yeats on a matter relating to the Order of the Golden Dawn. As he said in a letter to the membership on the subject of groups, 'We who are seeking to sustain this great Order must never forget that whatever we build in the imagination will accomplish itself in the circumstance of our lives.' (*CL 3*, 40) Nevertheless, to the credit of both Yeats and Farr, neither let this dispute deter them from what they saw as the all-important work of popularizing the rhythmic chanting of poetry.

Throughout the first decade of the twentieth century, Yeats and Farr developed and demonstrated this art in a way that captured, as Farr said in the essay she wrote at the end of the decade, 'the inherent melody' of the poem.[31] After an initial attempt with Farr plucking a single-stringed homemade lyre on 16 February 1901, Arnold Dolmetsch designed the first modern psaltery for Farr, and instructed her and Yeats in its use. By 1902, Yeats was in a position to write in his essay 'Speaking to the Psaltery': 'I have just heard a poem spoken with so delicate a sense of its rhythm, with so perfect a respect for its meaning, that if I were a wise man and could persuade a few people to learn the art, I would never open a book of verses again....' (*E&I* 13)

Farr recited the poems '[w]ithin the limits of an octave of semitones,' and speaking 'as I would without music,' indicated the drift of her voice on the vibrating strings of the psaltery. (*Music* 16–17) Musician and magician, she believed in the power of sound, arguing that 'matter concerns us for a little time but style concerns us for all time. And style...is the appreciation of phrases as *melodies*, not merely as the expression of thought.' (*Id.* 21) Echoing Yeats's argument in 'Magic' that it was the artist's duty to reawaken the soul that had been deadened by life in cities, Farr suggested that the 'mystery of sound' could overcome 'the din of the traffic of the restless' and restore 'the peace of those who are listening for the old magic, and watching till the new creation is heralded by the sound of the new word.' (*Id.*)

Yeats was equally committed to what he called 'this great work,' and was convinced it could change 'the substance and manner of our poetry.'[32] In the opening speech of King Guaire in his 1904 play *The King's Threshold*, he described the effect he was seeking as mastery of

> ...how to mingle words and notes together
> So artfully that all the Art's but Speech
> Delighted with its own music.... (*VPl* 257)

The key to the whole process was Farr herself, who, as Yeats said in 'Literature and the Living Voice,' 'divined enough of this older art' of the minstrel that she could discover the 'recurring pattern of sound' within poetry and declaim it in speech 'regulated by notes.' (*Ex.* 219) 'I do not think,' he argued, 'Homer is ever so moving as when she recites him to a little tune played on a stringed instrument not very unlike a lyre.' (*Id.*) Farr's demonstrations, he said, showed 'that ordinary men and women take pleasure in it and sometimes say they never understood poetry before.' (*Id.*)

Importantly, Farr's chant-like recitation released poetry from its domination by music in song, and her notations, made in conjunction with the poet, allowed him a measure of control over how the poetry would be recited. As stated in a handbill for one of his performances with Farr, 'only when declamation is regulated and recorded can it become an art perfecting itself from generation to generation.'[33]

Yeats threw himself into the project, explaining in a July 1901 letter to Robert Bridges, 'I shall be altogether content if we can perfect this art for I have never felt that reading was better than an error, a part of the fall into the flesh, a mouthful of the apple.' (*CL 3*, 92) Yeats's letter to Bridges suggests his awareness of the Muse-like character of Farr's role. Yeats tells Bridges that one of the most successful of Farr's recitations is Bridges' poem 'Muse and Poet.' Significantly, the poem was, in fact, entitled 'Will love again awake?', and 'Muse and Poet' reflected Yeats's perception of Farr's performance. (*CL 3*, 91 n. 5) As Bridges' poem opens, the poet is receiving a complaint from a 'lady fair/Whom once he deigned to praise.'[34] The lady fair's kinship to the moon is clear:

> Her beauty would surprise
> Gazers on autumn eves, who watched the broad moon rise
> Upon the scattered sheaves.

The 'Lady Fair' is more than fair: she is a Muse, the bearer of the moon's wisdom:

> Her eyes men Beauty call
> And Wisdom is her name.

For his joint performance with Farr at London's Clifford's Inn on 10 June 1902, Yeats wrote the charming poem, 'The Players ask for a Blessing on the Psalteries and on Themselves,' in which the poet asks for a blessing on Farr, 'the hands that play':

> O kinsmen of the Three in One,
> O kinsmen, bless the hands that play.
> The notes they waken shall live on
> When all this heavy history's done;
> Our hands, our hands must ebb away. (*VP* 213)

Yeats's 3 June 1902 letter to Arnold Dolmetsch refers to the poem, then in draft form, as 'Prayer to the Seven Archangels to bless the Seven

Notes,' thus making clear that the 'kinsmen of the Three in One,' are the archangels, kinsmen of the trinity, who are invoked as intermediaries between the divinity and the players. (*CL 3*, 194) The significance that Yeats attached to Farr's 'hands that play' can be gleaned from his later assertion of his belief in 'the tradition stated for the last time explicitly in Swedenborg & in Blake, that [God's] influence descends to us through hierarchies of mediatorial shades & angels.'[35] In other words, rhapsodic Farr was an essential link in transmitting inspiration from eternity.

Contemporaneously with launching poetry readings accompanied by the psaltery, Farr was co-authoring two plays expressive of her researches into Egyptian magic. Her co-author was Olivia Shakespear, to whom Yeats had introduced her in August 1894 and with whom she probably conducted discussions as Yeats's proxy as to how Yeats and Shakespear should proceed with their affair in the mid 1890s. (*Life 1*, 154) Needing to raise money to pay the difference between the £10 cost of the psaltery and the £4 she had planned to pay for it, Farr decided to stage and appear in the two plays, an idea that, once again, brought Farr, Yeats and Shaw together in a theater, this time Victoria Hall for the performance on 16 November 1901 of *The Beloved of Hathor*, a play centered on Hathor – an aspect of the moon goddess Isis[36] – and her priestess, played by Farr, who accompanied her chanting with the psaltery. (*CL 3*, 121)[37] Yeats reviewed both plays, which were performed together in January 1902. (*UP 2*, 265–7) His review was generally unenthusiastic about the plays themselves, but found that Farr and her niece performed 'always with that beauty of voice, which becomes perhaps the essential thing in a player when lyrical significance has become the essential thing in a play.' (*Id.*) When Farr and Paget delivered their ritual adoration of the gods 'copied or imitated from old Egyptian poems,' Yeats sensed that they spoke 'as one thinks the Egyptian priestesses must have spoken them.' (*Id.*) As at the clubhouse in Bedford Park in May 1890, Farr stood before Yeats as a priestess of the White Goddess.

The second play, *The Shrine of the Golden Hawk*, seemed to have planted a seed in Yeats's mind on the theme of the poet's sacrifice to his Muse. His review said that 'neither play stirred in me a strictly dramatic interest' with the exception of 'one final dramatic moment when a priestess, who has just been shrinking in terror before her God, the Golden Hawk, dances in ecstasy before his image....' (*Id.*) That moment was likely in Yeats's mind when he wrote *The King of the Great Clock Tower* more than thirty years later. The poet in that play had praised the Queen in songs sung by '[h]ard-hearted men that plough the earth and sea' (*VPl* 995) – the achievement Yeats had sought for himself and Farr when, in an essay written in connection with the opening of the Abbey Theatre, he said he sought poetry 'set for the speaking voice, like songs that sailors make up or remember....' (*Ex* 202, 217) In *The King of the Great Clock Tower*, the poet pays a price for such success – the King severs his head – but the Queen dances before the severed head and kisses it as it sings. Yeats's Notes to the play in the 1934 Cuala Press edition reveal that, as he wrote the play, he was thinking about both Farr and the connection between the Muse and 'the old ritual of the year: the mother goddess and the slain god' – the archetype that Graves would later place at the core of Musedom. (*VPl* 1009–10) Taken together, these verbal traces suggest that the queen's dance before the singing head in Yeats's play may have originated in the ecstatic dance that caught his attention in Farr's *The Shrine of the Golden Hawk*.

At the time Yeats was first watching Farr's plays, the stage seemed set for her to take on the role of Muse. The only missing element was a romantic relationship with the poet. Yeats's 16 June 1905 letter, however, bears traces of the onset of romance. 'I was very glad to get your letter,' he wrote, '– a dip into the river of life changes even an old handwriting and gives it a new and meaning face.' (*CL 4*, 114) This exhilarating 'dip into the river of life' had been foreshadowed in Yeats's 11 June letter, in which he asked Farr to 'send me your horoscope... at once' because he wanted to 'tell you about some of the aspects I saw in my hasty glance in London & to look up some aspects between it & mine.' (*CL 4*, 112–13) Yeats and Farr worked closely together that summer as Farr produced his *The Shadowy Waters* in London for the convention of the Theosophical Society, and played the lead role of Dectora. (*Life 1*, 336–7)[38] In August, after Lady Gregory had arranged a gift of the Kelmscott Chaucer for Yeats's fortieth birthday, he was suggesting to Farr that they take a bicycle trip and, his 'imagination full of Chaucer,' follow 'the journey of the Canterbury pilgrims....' (*CL 4*, 151) 'I do not see why we should not go,' he added, 'with some harmless person to keep up appearances.' (*Id.*)

The frequency and tone of these letters bears out George Yeats's reports that Yeats and Farr became lovers.[39] For better or ill, however, a consummated relationship can be inimical to Musedom. It is fatal to the relationship in the courtly love tradition, and can have the same effect in the realm of the White Goddess if it leads the poet to think his

Muse is his for the asking. Thus Yeats's January 1906 letter to Farr, while one of his most joyous and least guarded, also contains elements that are inconsistent with the relationship of poet and Muse: he finds it too easy to talk to her, and not because, as with a Muse, 'all is wisdom,' but because he feels 'unrestrained, one's own self.' Most importantly, she is not, like a Muse, his master, but rather 'an equal':

> I want to see you very much now and it will always be a great pleasure to be with you... You cannot think what a pleasure it is to be fond of somebody to whom I can talk – as a rule any sort of affection annihilates conversation, strikes one with a silence like that of Adam before he had even named the beasts. To be moved and talkative, unrestrained, one's own self, and to be this not because one has created some absurd delusion that all is wisdom, as Adam may have in the beast's head, but not in Eve, but because one has found an equal, that is the best of life. All this means that I am looking forward to seeing you – that my spirits rise at the thought of it. (*CL 4*, 327–8)

This revealing letter suggests that, like Shakespear, Farr might have been too near Yeats's soul to function effectively as a Muse, and that he would thus abandon her. Nonetheless, it seems that it was Farr who abandoned Yeats. His widow gave two accounts of his explanation for the end of the romance with Farr. George Yeats told Ellmann that her husband said the affair ended with Farr remarking 'I can do that for myself.'[40] Ellmann's notes of the interview do not show the context of this remark, but Farr's entire life is testimony to her pride and confidence in going it alone. Her belief in the solitary life, shielded by her Medusa mask, is reflected in her comment on Molly Allgood's engagement, as reported in Yeats's letter to Gregory: 'they will only meet now & again like sensible people. That is the only endurable kind of marriage.'[41] The other explanation appears in George Yeats's essay in a volume of Yeats's and Shaw's letters to Farr, where she wrote that the Yeats-Farr affair was a brief one that ended because Farr 'got bored.' (*A Forward* 43) Although this explanation is consistent with Farr's observation in *Modern Woman: Her Intentions* that '[d]ivorce is always brought about because of the weariness and boredom one human being causes another,'[42] Yeats's letters suggest that they were simply quite different personalities. Even as early as February 1906, Yeats, hoping to be 'forgiven for my too great preoccupation with your self,' commented that both he and Farr had changed and were moving in fundamentally different directions. He found that, in public speaking, he could now 'move people by power not merely – as the phrase is – by "charm" or "speaking beautifully"....' The change extended, he felt, 'into the personal relations of life – even things seemingly beyond control answer strangely to what is within...' As for Farr, 'I think you have changed too,' he said '...is it that those Eastern meditations have freed you....' In other words, Yeats sees himself becoming more involved in the world and Farr withdrawing more and more from it, a contrast emphasized when Yeats closes by saying that he, too, has begun eastern meditation of Farr's sort, 'but with the object of trying to lay hands upon some dynamic and substantializing force as distinguished from the eastern quiescent and supersentualizing state of the soul – a movement downwards upon life not upwards out of life.' (*CL 4*, 334–6.) The perceptive and fatalistic Farr would have recognized this fundamental difference and not tried to change it. As she later wrote John Quinn about the rupture in his friendship with Yeats, 'it is impossible to find any relationship that goes quite smoothly,' and the 'feeling we have that other people ought to behave according to our own ideals leads to nearly all our unhappiness and a desire for a false kind of progress.'[43]

The independent Farr distanced herself from sexual involvement with Yeats so promptly that she ran little risk of losing Muse status by being 'always his for the asking.' Indeed, in another February letter Yeats sent Farr some revealing lines of verse implying that she retained her power to inspire, but that her fickleness cast her more as witch than Muse. Yeats's letter says that the lines – part of 'a choral ode about witches' – were 'suggested in some vague way' by a letter from Farr that has not survived. The lines, slightly revised, were published in *The Shanachie* under the title 'Against Witchcraft.' The subject of the poem enchants the poet with desire, but meets his desire with hate as often as love:

> Or, they hurl a spell at him
> That he follow with desire
> Bodies that can never tire
> Or grow kind, for they anoint
> All their bodies joint by joint
> With a miracle working juice,
> That is made out of the grease
> Of the ungoverned unicorn;
> But the man is thrice forlorn
> Emptied, ruined, wracked and lost
> That *they* follow, for at most
> They will give him kiss for kiss

> While they murmur 'After this
> Hatred may be sweet in the taste.'
> Those wild hands that have embraced
> All his body can but shove
> At the burning wheel of love
> Till the side of hate comes up.   (*CL 4*, 341–2)[44]

Yeats ended his letter 'Yours always, shall I say affectionately or would that arouse too much scorn?' (*Id*.) By mid-November 1906, he was complaining '[i]t is a long time since I heard from you,' and seeking to reclaim her as Muse by telling her that the first musician in his play *Deirdre* 'was written for you – I always saw your face as I wrote very curiously your face even more than your voice and built the character out of that.' (*CL 4*, 517–19)

Yeats and Farr considered a joint lecture and psaltery tour in the United States, but New York lawyer John Quinn, who had helped arrange Yeats's 1903–4 tour, advised Yeats that '[i]t wouldn't do for you and Miss Farr to come here together. This is after all a provincial people.'[45] Quinn told Yeats that he was known in the most dignified way in America 'and can lecture here again, especially at the Women's Colleges. But coming here with a woman would be entirely different.' In the event, Farr toured America on her own for four months in 1907, lecturing on 'speaking to the psaltery.' Yeats implicitly staked a claim to Farr in a letter to Quinn early in her journey, noting that 'she & Lady Gregory are my closest friends' and 'I have seen a great deal of her of late especially....'[46] Nonetheless, Quinn likely became Farr's lover during her solo tour, while Yeats wrote Farr from Florence, which he was visiting with Augusta and Robert Gregory, lamenting her silence and finding 'it very hard to find out how to write to you. I want you too [sic] understand that I am sorry you are away & I am afraid to say it, because you get cross if one says such things & yet after all I shall be very glad when you return.'[47]

The tour was a critical and financial success for Farr, and spurred further solo performances. In the spring of 1908, she was in the south of France, where she received favourable reviews of her recitation of the Provencal poets. Yeats plainly missed her. Adverting to her activities in the Monte Carlo casino (where she hoped to earn the cost of her travels) he inquired, in early April, 'When do you return? Have you lost all yet?'[48] By 21 April, he was again asking 'When do you return?' and this time lamenting that 'London is unendurable when you are not in it.'[49]

He did manage to see her in Liverpool in October when she played Clytemnestra to Mrs. Campbell's Electra in Arthur Symons' translation of Hugo Von Hofmannsthal's *Electra*. Writing for the *Liverpool Courier*, Dixon Scott praised Farr's voice, which 'surged and moaned like the wind in the trees..., like an old wind wandering among eternal pines; and when it fell a little or drooped towards tenderness, it was but to provoke that strange, desirable terror which comes upon men when they hear lost winds chattering dreadfully among the last year's leaves.'[50] Meanwhile, Farr's dedication to the psaltery was unabated. Ezra Pound wrote to his father in August 1909 that he was working at psaltery settings with Farr for some of his poetry.[51]

As the first decade of the century turned to the second, two of Yeats's letters reflect Farr's un-Muselike propensity to be his equal. In December 1910, he mentions to Gregory, who often read to him because of his poor eyesight, that 'Mrs. Emery has asked 20/- a week for four evenings reading out to me – she was leaving town & was to let her rooms for that amount.' No doubt remembering Gregory's frequent unremunerated performance of the same task, he quickly added, 'I have told her I shall reduce her to 15/- presently. It is a good deal but somebody is necessary.'[52] A month later, Yeats asked Farr to come to Dublin to play the first musician in an Abbey production of *Deirdre*, but offered to pay only her expenses, explaining that 'we of course have very small profits....'[53] Farr responded, according to Yeats's letter to Mabel Dickinson, by 'demanding an increase of pay because of the watchfulness she will have to keep up at Euston & Hollyhead to keep the railway porters from breaking the psaltery.'[54]

Watching Farr perform the role he wrote for her was an emotion-laden experience for Yeats. His reaction vacillated from finding that 'the lyrics when Mrs. Emery does them are most living and bea[u]tiful & seem to make the whole play more bea[u]tiful,' to finding that 'Miss Farr lost her head and was exceedingly bad,' to reporting that she had improved and that he had received a letter from Professor Brown stating 'I never want to see Dierdre without her.'[55]

Shortly after the close of *Deirdre*, Yeats and Farr returned to London for a performance at the Little Theatre on 16 February 1911, the tenth anniversary of their first joint program with the psaltery. It would be their final psaltery lecture and performance. At almost precisely this time, Yeats was writing 'Friends,' his beautiful tribute to the 'Three women that have wrought/What joy is in my days.'[56] (*VP* 315) One might expect that the poem, which first appeared in *The Green Helmet and Other Poems*, published in October 1912, would include Farr in this select group: she had been his lover, his compatriot in occult studies, and his co-venturer in the 'great work' that promised to change 'the substance and the manner of our poetry.' (*Ex* 220) He had not previously hesitated to acknowledge her importance. He had, for example, dedicated *In the Seven Woods* (1906):

> TO FLORENCE FARR
> The only reciter of lyric poetry
> who is always a delight, because
> of the beauty of her voice and
> the rightness of her method. (*VP* 850)

Such praise was almost routine. He had ended the 1906 preface to Volume II of *The Poetical Works of William B. Yeats* with praise for her work in attempting to 'restore the whole ancient art of passionate speech' (*VPl* 1294), had dedicated *The Land of Heart's Desire* in the same series to her, and had insisted that her music for his plays be included in the series as 'essential to the completeness of my record....'[57]

Moreover, Farr understood the role of Yeatsian Muse so well that her 1912 novel, *The Solemnization of Jacklin*,[58] involves a 'worshiper of "the goddesses of the crossways"' who, imagining he is 'learning the mysteries of Hekate and Artemis', observes that '[i]f I give all I am to a woman she is transfigured and becomes the Symbol of the Beauty which is beyond all visible beauty.' (Jacklin 40, 26) Nonetheless, Farr is absent from 'Friends.' Yeats was straightforward enough about this in his autobiography, calling his relationship with Farr 'an enduring friendship that was an enduring exasperation....' (*Au* 122) Believing that she had never reached her full potential as an actress, he referred to her as 'that accomplished speaker of verse, less accomplished actress (*Au* 396), and commented to Sturge Moore that she was '"a chalk egg" he had been sitting on for years.'[59] Most exasperating of all, she refused to play the Muse: 'she would dress without care or calculation as if to hide her beauty and seemed contemptuous of its power.' (*Au* 122) Nor would she stand on a pedestal as an object of adoration: '[i]f a man fell in love with her she would notice that she had seen just that movement upon the stage or had heard just that intonation and all seemed unreal.' (*Id.*) Yeats summed up his enduring exasperation in 'The Trembling of the Veil':

I used in my rage to compare her thoughts, when her worst mood was upon her, to a game called Spillikins which I had seen played in my childhood with little pieces of bone that you had to draw out with a hook from a bundle of like pieces. A bundle of bones instead of Demeter's golden sheaf! Her sitting-room at the Brook Green lodging-house was soon a reflection of her mind, the walls covered with musical instruments, pieces of Oriental drapery, and Egyptian gods and goddesses painted by herself in the British Museum. (*Au* 122–3)

The written record does not show whether or when Farr was aware of her exclusion from 'Friends' or whether she and Yeats discussed the subject. We do know that Farr wrote to John Quinn in June 1912 that 'I may be off to Ceylon before the end of the year to end my days in the "society of the wise" as the Vedantist books say one should.'[60] In fact, she left England on 5 September 1912 to accept an offer from Sir Ponnambalan Ramanathan to become the Principal of his Buddhist College for Girls on the Jaffna Peninsula in Ceylon. Before leaving, she had discussed her reasons for the move over dinner on 17 July with her good friend H.W. Nevinson, who wrote in his journal that '[s]he goes for meditation & old age, being 52.'[61] There is no record of what discussion Farr and Yeats had when they dined and attended the theatre on June 29th or when they worked together in preparation for Farr's reading of Rabindranath Tagore's poetry from a manuscript prepared by Yeats.[62]

On 18 July 1912, Yeats was in the audience at Clavier Hall when Farr gave her final psaltery performance. (Kelly Chronology 157) Harold Monro's account in *Poetry Review* reported that the audience was 'spellbound.' He noted London's regret at its 'loss of so fine an artist,' and hoped that there were others 'who have sufficient restraint and self-surrender to submit themselves, after her manner, to the cadence and rhythms of poetry, becoming for the time being, a sensitive medium for their conveyance to an audience, rhapsodist rather than exponent, instrument rather than representative.'[63] Before her departure, as recounted in Yeats's 18 March 1935 letter to Arnold Dolmetsch, Farr gave Yeats the 'particularly fine psaltery' that Dolmetsch had made for her.[64]

Ezra Pound bid her a public farewell in his fascinating 'Portrait d'une Femme.'[65] The poem takes off from Dorothy Shakespear's comment that Farr's recent novel, *The Solemnization of Jacklin*, was '[*s*]*uch* a Sargasso Sea muddle,' with '[e]verybody divorced several times, & in the end going back to their originals....'[66] Pound transforms the Sargasso Sea into an image of Farr's ability to retain her unique identity while collecting the jetsam of London's cultural life and the flotsam of the great minds that swirled about her:

> Your mind and you are our Sargasso Sea,
> London has swept about you this score years
> And bright ships left you this or that in fee:
> Ideas, old gossip, oddments of all things,
> Strange spars of knowledge and dimmed wares of price.
> Great minds have sought you – lacking someone else.
> You have been second always. Tragical?
> No. You preferred it to the usual thing:
> One dull man, dulling and uxorious,
> One average mind – with one thought less, each year.
> Oh, you are patient. I have seen you sit
> Hours, where something might have floated up.
> And now you pay one. Yes, you richly pay.
> You are a person of some interest, one comes to you
> And takes strange gain away:
> Trophies fished up; some curious suggestion;
> Fact that leads nowhere; and a tale for two,
> Pregnant with mandrakes, or with something else
> That might prove useful and yet never proves,
> That never fits a corner or shows use,
> Or finds its hour upon the loom of days:
> The tarnished, gaudy, wonderful old work;
> Idols and ambergris and rare inlays,
> These are your riches, your great store; and yet
> For all this sea-hoard of deciduous things,
> Strange woods, half-sodden, and new brighter stuff:
> In the slow float of the differing light and deep,
> No! There is nothing! In the whole and all,
> Nothing that's quite your own.
> Yet this is you.

Rachel Blau Du Plessis argues that Pound's poem presents Farr as a Muse, but marginalizes her by showing 'a dehistoricized, unspecified female figure' – a 'semi-adequate' inspirer 'whom the speaker must treat elegiacally, regretfully and from a position of farewell.'[67] Du Plessis rests her assertion that Pound presents Farr as a Muse on the three lines in which he describes Farr as 'a person of some interest' who 'richly pay[s]' and from whom one 'takes strange gain away.' Nothing in these lines of typical Poundian fascination with the concept of interest identifies Farr as a Muse, as opposed to a generous friend. In fact, the poem focuses on engaging aspects of Farr's personality that accompanied her refusal to accept the role of Muse. If she was 'second always,' Pound makes clear that he is addressing her preference for independence rather than 'the usual thing:/One dull man, dulling and uxorious/ One average mind....' Finally, Du Plessis' castigation of the note of farewell overlooks the fact that the poem is not a dismissal, but an *adieu* to Farr, who was about to leave England for Ceylon, leaving Pound wondering if she would see her portrait before she goes.[68]

Farr was not Pound's Muse. Was she Yeats's? At a minimum, she was a *rhapsode*, an inspired reciter of Yeats's poetry. Moreover, as in the courtly love tradition discussed in Chapter 3, she inspired a career of amelioration, stirring Yeats to heroic efforts to create a poetic theater, and was the subject of Yeats's romantic pursuit. Nonetheless, Yeats wrote no great poetry in praise of Farr as an adjunct to his pursuit. She was not a Muse in the Gravesian or courtly love sense of a superior force to whom the poet is subject. Quite the contrary, as Yeats said in his January 1906 letter to her, she was 'an equal' – exactly the wrong status for a Muse. Rather than idealizing her, Yeats saw her as she was. Thus, in an 11 June 1908 letter to Mabel Dickinson, Yeats, fresh from an evening with the famous beauty Mrs. Patrick Campbell, confided that:

Florence Farr was there – really a more beautiful woman – but nothing beside Mrs. Campbell. You do not really look at Mrs. Campbell – you think you are but in reality it [is] a vague impression, a sort of fiery light that dazzles you. Florence Farr has less personality & so you look at her & and nothing mortal quite bears being looked at.[69]

Farr was a 'mortal' – not a goddess, as required for a Muse.

Farr would not have had it any other way. The first actress to play Ibsen's characters in England, and a sympathizer with Shaw's interpretation of Ibsen, she undoubtedly agreed with Shaw that Ibsen showed 'that the sacrifice of the woman of the Stone Age to fruitful passions which she herself shares is as nothing compared to the wasting of the modern woman's soul to gratify the imagination and stimulate the genius of the modern artist, poet and philosopher.'[70] Farr's agreement with Shaw is apparent in her *New Age* article on Ibsen's Hedda Gabler, when she says that Hedda almost becomes 'of one kin with the goddesses who demanded not love but great deeds from their heroes: the goddesses created in an age before woman had learned to be abject and amorous, when instead she was half-mother, half-lover, with a touch of the patron saint.'[71]

Neither Farr nor Yeats's treatment of Farr in his writings is vulnerable to the feminist criticism that Muses are passive creatures who 'do not choose to be Muses' but are chosen. (Croce 166) Farr refused to be cast in the role of a passive Muse, and appears as a vigorous participant in Yeats's life narrative.

Farr's departure from London was not an exit from Yeats's life or work. Their surviving correspondence contains no evidence of any rupture in a genuine friendship built around a series of important shared interests. Yeats wrote to her in February 1913 that '[y]our letters have interested me very deeply,' adding '[y]ou have probably found the thing we have all been looking for.'[72] Promising to send her a volume of Tagore's poetry, some of which she had read from manuscript at one of Pound's Tuesday evenings in London,[73] he tells how he has 'been deeply moved by Tagore,' who has 'given me a great desire to get away from controversies everything but the minds daily caprice.' (*Id.*) When he sends Tagore's *Gitanjali* on 12 June 1913, it is clear that he is attracted to her life of contemplation. 'Your letters are charming & make me long for a like life,' he writes. 'Perhaps I too in a few years may drift into Asia.'[74] Still, he wonders about the attractions of her past life: 'do you long for your psaltery?' he asks.

His letter of 4 October 1914 is redolent of their years of joint pursuit of spiritual truth. He asks if she remembers 'the old GD prophesies' and tells her of his work on the essay that would be published as 'Swedenborg, Mediums and Desolate Places,' confiding that 'I do not give any of my personal proofs of the survival of the soul....'[75]

In August 1916, he writes to say that he is in France 'staying with Maud Gonne,' and adds that '[t]he death of her husband has made no difference in our relations. She belongs now to the Third Order of St. Francis & sighs for a convent.' As to their own relationship, '[y]es,' he says, '– when the war is over if it has not too greatly impoverished me (& it has halved my income) & I shall hope to get to India and Ceylon ... & if I do I shall remember your "separate front door".' He tells her that he has finished the first draft of 'Memoirs,' which 'are not to be published till after my death.' Warning that '[i]t is a very candid book & will be quite unpublishable unless the world grows more free spoken,' he asks 'Do you want to go in over a nom-de-plume or not?'[76]

In November 1916, Farr was diagnosed with cancer of the left breast. She underwent a mastectomy in early December. Although she confided to Shaw that she had 'galloping cancer with a vengeance,'[77] she kept this news from family and others, advising Yeats, with typical cheer and resolve, that the tumor was not malignant and its removal left her side 'a beautiful slab of flesh adorned with a handsome fern pattern made by a cut & 30 stitches....'[78] Yeats's 5 March 1917 response to Farr's letter notes his great distress at the news of her illness and wonders if it is a result of the climate.[79] Given the jaunty tone of her letter, he may perhaps be forgiven this, but not the closing observation that Maud Gonne's daughter, Iseult, 'is now a tall beauty very mystical & subtle.'

Farr died on 29 April 1917. Her final letter to Yeats had ended with a poem she described as expressing 'Fechtner's [sic] idea of our being senses & thoughts.'[80] It is likely that Yeats and Farr had discussed Theodor Fechner's idea that, as Yeats expressed it in his 28 March 1915 letter to Mabel Beardsley, '[a]re we perhaps the senses of a whole invisable world? Perhaps the angels & devils can read the books we only glance at in passing....'[81] It is unclear which of the two introduced Fechner to the other. In *The Solemnization of Jacklin*, Farr attributes to Fechner the idea that '[l]iving creatures are the sense organs of the earth.' (Jacklin 94) Yeats owned, and extensively annotated, the 1914 edition of Fechner's *On Life After Death*,[82] and, in a discarded draft of *A Vision*, referred to Fechner's view that 'the dead are the thoughts of the living.'[83]

Fechner posited that the human spirit exists in three phases, one prior to birth, one after birth, and one after death.[84] The individual's mind, he argued, is 'simultaneously his own property, and the property of those higher spirits [in the life after death]; and whatever comes to pass in it, equally belongs to both sides....' (*Id.* 46) According to Fechner, the spirits of the living and the dead meet often, sometimes both sides being conscious of it, and sometimes only one. (58)

In assertions that may have planted the germ of Yeats's moving invocation of Farr in 'All Souls' Night,' Fechner wrote that there is 'one means of meeting consciously for the living and the dead,' namely 'the memory of the living for the dead.' (*Id.*) 'If you think of a dead person earnestly and intensely,' Fechner argued, 'not only the thought of him or her, but the dead person himself will be in your mind immediately' (61) '[T]o every song celebrating their noble acts,' the dead listen, said Fechner, and – in an observation pregnant with meaning for Yeats – 'here is a vital germ for a new phase of art.' (63)

Farr's poem – written with Fechner in mind – is a tribute to her stoicism in the face of encroaching death and an expression of her belief that her 'wild ghost' would yet be heard reverberating through time:

The Earth & We

We are the eyes, the sense, the vision of Earth
And she is just a Kerub face that floats
Dancing and laughing round the sun. In mirth
She hides in cloaking masks of night and gloats
In shadows ov'r her aureol of beams
Like coloured feathers in St. Michael's wings.
When we are dead she makes thoughts of our dreams;

And if we are remembered when she sings
Her song to the sun; t'is [sic] because our wild ghosts
Clamour within her, till she suddenly screams
Tragic notes – wakening tremendous strings,
Reverberating, calling Fames' starry hosts.

Farr's death-bed poem bequeathed Yeats a marvelous source of poetic inspiration – the notion that 'if we are remembered' after death, our dreams are made thoughts that can still be heard. Yeats hears Farr's thoughts, and gives them voice, in 'All Souls' Night,' a poem situated in Oxford at midnight on a night when, as Paul Muldoon emphasized in his inaugural lecture as Oxford Professor of Poetry, the veil between the living and the dead is particularly thin.[85] Yeats – the recipient of Farr's death-bed suggestion that her 'wild ghost' will clamour – sets the scene dramatically, and predicts that '[a] ghost may come.'

Then, believing with Fechner that he can commune with the dead by invoking their spirits, and knowing from Farr's poem that she is awaiting his call, Yeats summons three ghosts, the first W.R. Horton, who 'loved strange thought'; the last MacGregor Mathers, his and Farr's leader in the Golden Dawn; and, placed between them, Farr herself:

On Florence Emery I call the next,
Who finding the first wrinkles on a face
Admired and beautiful,
And knowing that the future would be vexed
With 'minished beauty, multiplied commonplace,
Preferred to teach a school
Away from neighbour or friend,
Among dark skins, and there
Permit foul years to wear
Hidden from eyesight to the unnoticed end.

Before that end much had she ravelled out
From a discourse in figurative speech
By some learned Indian

> On the soul's journey. How it is whirled about,
> Wherever the orbit of the moon can reach,
> Until it plunge into the sun;
> And there, free and yet fast,
> Being both Chance and Choice,
> Forget its broken toys
> And sink into its own delight at last.   (*VP* 472–3)

The second of these stanzas summarizes the wisdom that Farr had achieved in Ceylon and communicated to Yeats by letter on a subject, the soul's journey after death, that captivated them both. The poem's reference to the soul's plunge from the orbit of the moon into the sun reflects that Yeats had learned, as he told a correspondent, 'from the letters of a friend who died in Ceylon,' that 'the Cingalese have a precisely similar symbolism' to that of a 'a very important dialogue by Plutarch describing the passage of souls from the lunar to the solar influence.'[86] The poem speaks in language shared by Farr and Yeats when it tells how, following the soul's plunge, it would 'Forget its broken toys/And sink into its own delight at last.' In one of her letters from Ceylon, Farr had confessed to reading English newspapers, and said that such commerce with the 'society of the unwise' had 'delayed my attainment of real saintliness by some years,' but that 'Mr. Ramanathanan assures me I am "all right" and my mind has lost its hold on most of the *malams* or evils which cause a soul to subject itself to birth & death.'[87] Farr would have understood perfectly the poem's description of her soul's escaping the cycle of birth and death as 'forgett[ing] its broken toys.' Writing to Farr of Mabel Beardsley's joy in the face of death, as exemplified by her playing with dolls dressed like people out of her brother Aubrey's drawings, Yeats had said that '[t]o turn the world into a box of toys is one of the ways of conquering it & ones self.'[88]

When Yeats sums up these shared beliefs by declaring that Farr had found a path for her soul to sink into its own delight, he was bestowing his supreme encomium. Self-delight was the state he wished for his daughter in 'A Prayer for my Daughter,' a poem that, as he said in a letter to Ezra Pound, was 'much the same sort of thing' as 'All Soul's Night.'[89] In 'A Prayer for My Daughter,' he wishes his daughter what Farr had already achieved amid the clamoring of wild ghosts:

> Considering that, all hatred driven hence,
> The soul recovers radical innocence
> And learns at last that it is self-delighting,

>   Self-appeasing, self-affrighting.
>   And that its own sweet will is Heaven's will;
>   She can, though every face should scowl
>   And every windy quarter howl
>   Or every bellows burst, be happy still.   (*VP* 405)

There is thus little room for doubt that the second of the two stanzas about Farr in 'All Soul's Night' celebrates Farr's achievement as a student of the soul's journey. The first is more troubling. Jahan Ramazani argues that Yeats's description of Farr's reasons for leaving London, including the reference to wrinkles on her beautiful face, suggests a 'botched' life and that her portrait in the poem 'calls more attention to the botched life than to any knowledge of a life beyond that life.' (Poetry of Death 37) Certainly the poem can be faulted for overemphasizing what Dorothy Paget described as her aunt's desire to avoid the 'withering of the leaf before an audience.'[90] Yeats gave a slightly more balanced narrative, which took into account Farr's desire to join 'the society of the wise', in the Dedication to the 1925 edition of *A Vision*, in which 'All Souls' Night' appeared as an epilogue. There, he recalled that Farr, 'coming to her fiftieth year, dreading old age and fading beauty, had made a decision we all dreamt of at one time or another, and accepted a position as English teacher in a native school in Ceylon that she might study oriental thought and had died there.' (*AVA* ix–x) Given the poem's emphasis on Farr's success in achieving wisdom, its mention of her wrinkles – contrasted with Horton's penchant for 'that sweet extremity of pride/That's called platonic love' – may be taken as an appreciation of Farr's success in enabling Yeats to see a woman as she really is, rather than as a platonic image. Certainly the poem does not, in Ramazani's phrase, occlude the woman to the form of the Muse poem. Yeats's portrait of Farr is not susceptible to the feminist critique that the feminine subject of the love poem is a stereotypical, featureless beauty. (Gender and History 5, 22)

Nor does the poem describe Farr's life as 'botched.' To the contrary, it lauds her deep and hard-won knowledge of life beyond this life, and enacts the process of her transmittal of that knowledge through the marvelous thing the poet has to say, namely that he bears thoughts from his dead companion in the search for meaning in life and death:

>   I have mummy truths to tell
>   Whereat the living mock,
>   Though not for sober ear,

> For maybe all that hear
> Should laugh and weep an hour upon the clock.
> Such thought – such thought have I that hold it tight
> Till meditation master all its parts,
> Nothing can stay my glance
> Until that glance run in the world's despite
> To where the damned have howled away their hearts,
> And where the blessed dance;
> Such thought, that in it bound
> I need no other thing,
> Wound in mind's wandering
> As mummies in the mummy-cloth are wound. (*VP* 474)

Much as Yeats would return to Olivia Shakespear for the wisdom of bodily decrepitude in 'After Long Silence,' when he seeks the wisdom of the dead in 'All Souls' Night,' it is another compatriot in the pursuit of the wisdom tradition, Florence Farr, wrinkles and all, that he summons. Farr had been excluded from 'Friends,' but in 'All Souls' Night,' that magnificent poem about the ability of the dead to inspire the living poet, she not only inspires, but lives 'where the blessed dance.' The unique nature of her mode of inspiration is captured in Yeats's observation that the poem was written in a moment of 'exaltation.' (*AVA* xii)

3. Maud Gonne, c.1890–92, from Lucien Gillain, *Heures de Guéirte. Poésies d'un Dragon*, 1893.

3

The Apple on the Bough Most Out of Reach: Maud Gonne

On 30 January 1889, some fifteen months before Yeats would watch Florence Farr perform in *A Sicilian Idyll*, and about five years before he would be seated across from Olivia Shakespear at *The Yellow Book* dinner, Maud Gonne heeded the suggestion of the Fenian leader John O'Leary that she call on the Yeats home in Bedford Park, where both father and son shared political ideas similar to those that attracted Gonne to O'Leary's movement. Gonne, then 22, was the daughter of a British army officer of independent means who was making a name for herself as a fiery orator supporting Irish nationalist causes. Yeats was 23 and still living at home with his family. His narrative poem *The Wanderings of Oisin* had been widely reviewed, and he was beginning to make a reputation in Dublin and London.

From their initial meeting through the last of his many proposals in the summer of 1917, and even until the end of his life, Yeats wrote poem after poem to or about Maud Gonne – the most sustained and fully developed tribute to a Muse in the history of literature in English. The poetry is remarkable for its majestic but unsparing portrait of Gonne, for the poignancy of what its author called the 'barren passion' of his twenty-eight year pursuit of 'that monstrous thing/Returned and yet unrequited love,' and, most of all, for the sheer ingenuity and persistence with which Yeats found the stuff of poetry in every aspect of his often troubled relationship with his Muse.

The tenacity of Yeats's pursuit of Maud Gonne cannot be understood apart from her role as a Muse of the courtly love tradition, who is unattainable by definition. That tradition, which had originated in Europe near the beginning of the Twelfth Century,[1] found its way to Yeats through Malory's *Morte d'Arthur*, Rossetti's translations of Italian poets who had been influenced by the troubadours, and Rossetti himself. Yeats admired the depiction of the courtly tradition in *Morte d'Arthur*, and thought the 'Arthurian Tales' one of the great achievements of the eleventh and twelfth centuries. (*AVA* 198)[2] The core of courtly love, as summarized by Bernard O'Donoghue, was that '[t]he lover sings the song; he is the lady's inferior and her adoring votive; his love inspires and refines him; above all, he is totally possessed by love, and all he does is in response to it.'[3]

Love inspired the troubadours in both direct and indirect ways. Indirectly, the lover was inspired to embark upon what Frederick Goldin calls 'a life-long career of amelioration' so that '[i]n longing and service, he becomes more skillful at arms, more graceful in song, more generous, more decorous, more humble, more noble.'[4] As discussed below, Yeats constructed his beautiful poem to Gonne, 'Adam's Curse' (*VP* 204), around the idea that the courtly poet is inspired to improve his craft, or *techne*. The courtly beloved's direct inspiration was figured in the troubadours' adoption of the Ovidian conceit that a woman stimulated her admirer into action by transmitting her beauty like an arrow through the lover's eyes into his heart.[5] Yeats may not have known the poems by Chrétien de Troyes and Arnaut Daniel that Maurice Valency cites for the proposition that the poet's song was inspired by 'unswerving contemplation of the image thus imposed on the poet's heart and soul' (*Id.* at 109), but he was likely familiar with Rossetti's translations of Guinicelli's and Cavalcanti's poems in which a glance from the lady pierces the poet's heart like an arrow and spurs him to song.[6] Yeats applied this theory of the Muse in 'The Arrow,' in which a 'wild thought' engendered by the beauty of his beloved pierces his marrow and gives birth to a poem.[7]

The intensity of this form of inspiration was heightened by the courtly code's tenet that the lover is destined never to possess the object of his pursuit, whose unavailability stirs his passion. As Denis de Rougemont says, the beloved is, by definition, 'that which indeed incites to pursuit, and rouses in the heart ... an avidity for possession so much more delightful than possession itself.' She is 'the woman-from-whom-one-is-parted: to possess her is to lose her.' (*Western World* at 284) Yeats's image of himself as a part of this tradition is apparent, for example, in his account of how he consoled himself during long periods of celibate waiting for Maud Gonne by repeating Lancelot's confession: 'I have loved a queen beyond measure and exceeding long' (*Mem* 125), a creative misquotation of Malory's 'I have loved a queen unmeasureably and out of measure long.'[8]

The courtly lover's passion for his absent beloved impressed Yeats as the defining element of the tradition because it was the lover's source of power and strength. It was not lost on Yeats that Parsifal, 'seeing nothing before his eyes but the image of his absent love, overcame knight after knight....' (*AVA* 197–8) He attributed the origin of the courtly lover's passion to 'something [that] must have happened in the courts and castles of which history has perhaps no record,' some 'forgotten reverie [or] initiation' that 'separated wisdom from the monastery and, creating Merlin, joined it to passion.' (*AVA* 196–7) Courtly love, he thought, had 'come back from the first Crusade or up from Arabian Spain or half Asiatic Provence and Sicily.... (*Id.*) Anticipating de Rougemont's theory that the eastern passion of the courtly lover planted an unsettling idea at the heart of western society (Western World 107, 136–7), he contrasted the passion found in the tales of the *Arabian Nights* with '[a] certain Byzantine Bishop [who] had said upon seeing a singer of Antioch, "I looked long upon her beauty, knowing that I would behold it upon the day of judgment, and I wept to remember that I had taken less care of my soul than she of her body...."' In the *Arabian Nights*, however, when 'Harun Al-Raschid looked at the singer Heart's Miracle, and on the instant loved her, he covered her head with a little silk veil to show that her beauty "had already retreated into the mystery of our faith".' The Bishop, Yeats concluded, 'saw a beauty that would be sanctified but the Caliph that which was its own sanctity and it was this latter sanctity... that created romance.'

The ensuing tradition had its greatest impact on Yeats through Dante, whose love for an unattainable woman – 'the suffering of desire,' as Yeats memorably called it (*Au* 273) – inspired Dante to become, as Yeats put it in another lapidary phrase, the 'chief imagination of Christendom' (*VP* 368). Dante concisely summarized this conception of the Muse in his reply to the Luccan poet Bonagiunta who, upon encountering Dante in purgatory, inquired whether he was the one who 'drew forth' the new rhymes beginning '*Donne ch'avete intelletto d'amore.*' Dante's reply – in the Shadwell verse translation that Yeats read (*Myth* 329) – is a Muse poet's articulation of the idea that Blake would express by saying 'the authors are in eternity':

> I am the one who hark
> To Love's inspiring, and I mark,
> As he within doth teach
> To utter forth my speech.[9]

The rhymes beginning 'Ladies who have intelligence in love' had come to Dante, as he recounts in *La Vita Nuova*, in a flash of inspiration while he was reflecting on the relationship between his poetry and his pursuit of Beatrice. Yeats crystallized the idea of the unattainable woman as the source of inspiration by defining Dante in terms of his 'hunger for the apple on the bough/Most out of reach' (*VP* 368), and specifically identified himself as a follower of the courtly love tradition – the 'old high way of love' – in 'Adam's Curse' (*VP* 204), one of the many poems he wrote to Maud Gonne. Viewed as an imitation of Dante's pursuit of Beatrice, Yeats's long quest for Gonne seems almost normal. Certainly, Gonne had the two qualities that Arlene Croce posits as necessary for a Muse: beauty and mystery. (Croce 164) Yeats's biographer Roy Foster sums up the former: '[She] was majestic, unearthly, appealing all at once; and her classic beauty came straight out of epic poetry. Immensely tall, bronze-haired with a strong profile and beautiful skin, she was a *fin de siècle* beauty in Valkyrie mode: both her appearance and her character represented tragic passion.' (*Life 1*, 88) No one captured her beauty in words better than Yeats, who saw her as 'Pallas Athena in that straight back and arrogant head' (*VP* 578), with

> ... beauty like a tightened bow, a kind
> That is not natural in an age like this,
> Being high and solitary and most stern[.]   (*VP* 256–7)

Moreover, Gonne's frequent sojourns in France, where she was secretly the mistress of French politician and journalist Lucien Millevoye, contributed mightily to the necessary air of mystery, and also brought her squarely into the tradition of Dante's Beatrice and Petrarch's Laura by making her, in Denis de Rougemont's phrase, 'the woman-from-whom-one-is-parted.' (Western World 284) A sense of apartness lay at the core of Gonne's identity. Her mother died when she was four, and her father when she was nineteen. She was brought up between London, France and her father's military postings in Ireland, with her education in the hands of governesses.[10] Foster suggests that she identified with Ireland 'as the one fixed point in her unhappy early life.' (*Life 1*, 91) She insisted that her family's roots could be traced to Ireland.[11]

Yeats's retrospective account of his initial meeting with Gonne reflects his desire to cast her in the image of Beatrice to his Dante. In fact, Yeats goes Dante one better. Whereas Dante is visited by Love upon first seeing Beatrice, Yeats is stirred even before he sees Gonne; he experiences 'premonitory excitement' upon first reading her name. (*Mem* 40) Her initial appearance, when, as Yeats put it, 'the troubling of my life began,' was momentous: 'a sound as of a Burmese gong, an overpowering tumult that had yet many pleasant secondary notes.' (*Id.*) Yeats's account of the event uses 'the Virgilian commendation "She walks like a goddess"' (*Au* 123), thus echoing Dante's comment on first seeing Beatrice – 'of her might have been said those words of the poet Homer, "She seemed not to be the daughter of a mortal man, but of God".' (Rossetti Dante 31)

What was it that made Gonne so overwhelmingly attractive to Yeats? A clue lies in the fact that his first autobiographical reference to her mentions that she was 'a beautiful girl who had left the society of the Viceregal Court for Dublin nationalism.' (*Mem* 40) This conjunction of a beautiful woman, the Anglo-Irish Ascendancy that governed Ireland, and a penchant for Irish nationalism meshed perfectly with Yeats's goal of creating a national literature that would define a new Irish consciousness.[12] Agreeing with Arnold that the Celts were 'passionate' and 'turbulent'[13], Yeats thought the Irish imagination manifested itself in 'the bragging rhetoric and gregarious humour of O'Connell's generation and school....' and wanted his poetry to further what he saw as an emergent tendency for Ireland to turn away from O'Connell 'and offer herself to the solitary and proud Parnell as to her antiself....' (*Au* 195) What was needed, he thought, was 'philosophy and a little passion.' (*Id.*) Gonne's amalgam of beauty, Ascendancy pedigree, and nationalist politics made her a perfect subject for passionate poems that would help define Ireland in the Anglo-Irish image of the 'solitary and proud Parnell.' It was no accident that Yeats praised her beauty as being 'high and solitary and most stern.' (*VP* 257) Nor is it surprising that he saw Gonne as the equivalent of the idealized lady of the courtly love tradition. Just as the courtly lyrics were 'created to serve as a model for the rest of society to imitate,' thus establishing the 'moral and aesthetic purpose' of the courtly society, its reason for being, (Mirror 66–7), Yeats's poems about Gonne would be calculated to define a new Irish mentality.

Both Yeats and Gonne immediately recognized their usefulness to each other. She spoke of 'her wish for a play that she could act in Dublin,' and he promptly offered to write for her the play he eventually called *The Countess Cathleen*, a story of an aristocratic beauty who sells her soul to save the starving people in the west of Ireland. Yeats knew exactly what he was doing. He told Gonne that 'I wished to become an

Irish Victor Hugo,' thinking 'it was natural to commend myself by claiming a very public talent, for her beauty as I saw it in those days seemed incompatible with private, intimate life.' (*Mem* 41) The notion that public celebration of Gonne's Anglo-Irish beauty would help Yeats define Ireland underlies his comment that 'there was much patriotism and more desire for a fair woman' (*Id*. 59) in his early efforts to create an Irish national literature. He so firmly attached his poetic enterprise to the task of moulding a new Irish consciousness that, as Seamus Heaney put it, he became the 'pre-eminent theorist, visionary and exemplar of a literature based on the category of nationality.'[14]

Gonne's utility in creating a new Irish consciousness was enhanced by the fact that she shared Yeats's belief in a spiritual world that was accessible by dream and occult symbol. These beliefs were so fundamental to each of them that, as appears from their letters and autobiographical writings, it was a matter of course for them to speak of meeting each other in dreams or on 'the astral plane,' a realm somewhere between the material and the spiritual, first identified by Paracelsus and popular among theosophists.[15] The combination of shared commitments to Irish nationalism and occult practices was a potent cocktail. By the mid-1890s, Yeats had developed '[a]n obsession more constant than anything but my love itself' for developing 'mystical rites – a ritual system of evocation and meditation – to reunite the perception of the spirit, of the divine, with natural beauty.' (*Mem* 123) Believing that '[c]ommerce and manufacture had made the world ugly' and that 'all lonely and lovely places were crowded with invisible beings and that it would be possible to communicate with them,' Yeats planned to initiate Irish youth into an order that united Christianity with the truths of an ancient world. (*Id*. 124) He contemplated a holy island devoted to a Temple of Heroes of the Celtic Order and wanted Gonne to be his partner in this great work. 'There would be', he thought, 'a spiritual birth from the soul of a man and a woman.' (*Id*. 125) He and Gonne would attain a revelation 'from the memory of the race itself' through symbol and myth.' (*Id*.)

It was their shared belief in the power of dreams that precipitated Yeats's proposal to Gonne in the summer of 1891, after she had written him a letter telling of a dream in which '[s]he and I had been brother and sister somewhere on the edge of the Arabian Dessert, and sold together into slavery.' (*Mem* 46) Gonne's letter defined the terms that, with one brief exception, would govern their relationship until its end. Yeats saw the 'brother and sister' dream as the sign of a special relationship; Gonne saw it as the hallmark of a non-sexual one. Yeats responded to the letter by asking Gonne to marry him. Her answer confirmed her role as the woman who is lost by possession: 'No, she could not marry – there were reasons – she would never marry; but in words that had no conventional ring she asked for my friendship.' (*Id.* 46)

Gonne had already made her debut as a Muse in the exciting months after their first meeting, during which Yeats began writing *The Countess Cathleen* as part of an effort 'to create an Irish Theatre.' (*Au* 200) Although Gonne declined to play the role of the countess, and Yeats read the play to Florence Farr for a theatrical opinion (*Life 1*, 97), the published version of the play was dedicated to 'Maud Gonne, at whose suggestion it was planned out and begun....' (*VPl* 2) In addition, the forces she set at work led to another play, *Cathleen ni Houlihan*, in which the title character, an old woman who represents the mystical figure of Ireland, invites a young man to follow her to 'help her in her time of troubles.' Gonne agreed to play the lead role in *Cathleen ni Houlihan* and her performance in April 1902 was an iconic moment that defines her to this day. As she led the young man away, she was revealed to be 'a young girl... with the walk of a queen.' Her last lines evoked the essence of the Fenian tradition:

> They shall be remembered for ever,
> They shall be alive for ever,
> They shall be speaking for ever,
> The people shall hear them for ever.   (*VPl* 229)

Mary Colum remembered that 'people's hearts stopped beating' at her 'marvelous beauty, her height and the memories of her militant patriotism.'[16] The young actress Marie Nic Shiubhlaigh thought Gonne's beauty was 'startling,' 'the most exquisitely-fashioned creature' she had ever seen, and that '[i]n her the youth of the country saw all that was magnificent in Ireland.'[17]

The dramatic form readily accommodated Yeats's ideas about Gonne as Muse and symbol of Ireland, but he had more difficulty finding the right lyric mode to express a Muse whose distinctive qualities he sought to emphasize as expressive of the national consciousness. For example, although Gonne maintained that the Rose in the poems collected under that heading in *Poems* (1895) alluded to her, and through her to Ireland (NC 23), there is nothing in those poems to distinguish their subject from any other woman. Indeed, the epigraph of the volume – St. Augustine's 'Too late I loved you Beauty so old and so new. Too late

I loved you' – suggests that the poems are addressed to a platonic form of Beauty. This impression is reinforced by Yeats's note asserting that 'he has found, he believes, the only pathway whereon he can hope to see with his own eyes the Eternal Rose of Beauty and of Peace.' (*VP* 846) Looking back from the vantage point of 1925, Yeats conceded the Rose's similarity to 'the Intellectual Beauty of Shelley and of Spenser,' but thought it differed from its predecessors in that he had 'imagined it as suffering with man and not as something pursued and seen from afar.' (*VP* 842)

Yeats's early lyric efforts to focus on Gonne's individuality frequently sound one of the three notes that Adrienne Rich finds common to many Muse poems, the presentation of the woman as 'beautiful, but threatened with the loss of beauty, the loss of youth – the fate worse than death.'[18] 'When You are Old' (1891)[19] is such a poem, but it goes beyond the traditional pattern by focusing on Gonne's 'pilgrim soul':

> When you are old and grey and full of sleep,
> And nodding by the fire, take down this book,
> And slowly read, and dream of the soft look
> Your eyes had once, and of their shadows deep;
>
> How many loved your moments of glad grace,
> And loved your beauty with love false or true,
> But one man loved the pilgrim soul in you,
> And loved the sorrows of your changing face;
>
> And bending down beside the glowing bars,
> Murmur, a little sadly, how Love fled
> And paced upon the mountains overhead
> And hid his face amid a crowd of stars.   (*VP* 120–1)

The attribution of a 'pilgrim soul' refers to Gonne's status as fellow-voyager on a quest for occult wisdom. At Yeats's urging, she was initiated into the Order of the Golden Dawn on 2 November 1891, taking the order name *'Per Ignem Ad Lucem'* (*'Through Fire to Light'*). (Int. to *G-YL* 21)[20] At the time Yeats was praising her 'pilgrim soul,' she was seeking occult knowledge of a most intimate kind from him and George Russell (AE) following the death of her two-year-old son by Millevoye, whom she described to Yeats and AE as adopted. AE's advice – that a deceased child could be reincarnated in a child conceived at the grave of the deceased – would lead to the birth of Gonne's daughter, Iseult.

Another early poem reflects the second traditional theme identified by Rich, that of a beautiful woman who dies young. (On Lies 39) The poem, originally entitled 'Epitaph,' and collected as 'A Dream of Death,' grew out of a rumour that Gonne had died. This 1891 poem reflects that, almost from the beginning of his relationship with Gonne, Yeats thought of himself as her memorialist:[21]

> I dreamed that one had died in a strange place
> Near no accustomed hand;
> And they had nailed the boards above her face,
> The peasants of that land,
> Wondering to lay her in that solitude,
> And raised above her mound
> A cross they had made out of two bits of wood,
> And planted cypress round;
> And left her to the indifferent stars above
> Until I carved these words:
> *She was more beautiful than thy first love,*
> *But now lies under boards.* (*VP* 123)

The forced comparison to the poet's 'first love' – his distant cousin Laura Armstrong, who was already engaged when she inspired the character of the enchantress in Yeats's early play *The Island of Statues*[22] – bears traces of Yeats's struggle to assume the role of lover as his poetic identity. Gonne recovered from her illness and was 'greatly amused' when Yeats sent her the poem. (SQ 147)

Yeats returned to the traditional theme of the Muse's threatened loss of beauty in 'The Lover pleads With his Friend for Old Friends,' published in July 1897. In a departure from the traditional poem of this sort, however, Gonne's beauty takes a back seat to a description of her successes as a political organizer and orator. By the time Gonne first met Yeats she had already campaigned successfully in support of evicted tenants in Donegal, and similar efforts followed in Galway. (Int. *G-YL* 18–19) The poem refers to the 'shining days' of her stirring oratory, which included speeches protesting against a Dublin celebration of sixty years of Victoria's reign and in support of a commemoration of the 1798 rebellion. Yeats, who thought Gonne's politics 'my one visible rival' (*Mem* 63), recounts her success, reminds her that only he – and not the crowds – will be permanently attracted to her beauty, and passes over in silence her likely future as an orator and political organizer:

> Though you are in your shining days,
> Voices among the crowd

> And new friends busy with your praise,
> Be not unkind or proud,
> But think about old friends the most:
> Time's bitter flood will rise,
> Your beauty perish and be lost
> For all eyes but these eyes.   (*VP* 172–3)

Gonne seemed unperturbed at the potential loss of her beauty. She wrote Yeats thanking him 'for the beautiful little poem,' and observed 'I am not the least inclined to forget old friends.'[23] Nonetheless, Gonne's political success evoked an unusual response in a poem published in 1898, 'He wishes his Beloved were Dead':

> Were you but lying cold and dead,
> And lights were paling out of the West,
> You would come hither, and bend your head,
> And I would lay my head on your breast;
> And you would murmur tender words,
> Forgiving me, because you were dead....   (*VP* 175)

The wish encapsulated in the title of this poem would be shocking if it did not accord so perfectly with the aesthetic of Yeats and his contemporaries of 'The Tragic Generation' of the 1890s, as reflected, for example, in Villiers de l'Isle-Adam's *Axël*, in which the lovers jointly commit suicide as the only way to perfect their love.[24] When Yeats read the play he knew 'that here at last was the sacred book I longed for' (*Au* 320), and his attendance at a five-hour performance of the play in Paris in 1894 with Gonne – one of the profound experiences of his life – gave rise to his recurring fondness for Axël's dying observation that 'As for living, our servants will do that for us.'

Yeats's review of the play in *The Bookman* of April 1894 is essential context for reading 'He Wishes His Beloved Were Dead.' The review quotes Verlaine's description of 'a type of woman' common in Villiers de l'Isle-Adam's work, a summary that Yeats may have quoted with Gonne in mind:

Villiers conjures up the spectre of a mysterious woman, a queen of pride, who is mournful and fierce as the night when it still lingers though the dawn is beginning, with reflections of blood and of gold upon her soul and her beauty. (*UP 1* 323–4)

The heroine of the play, Sarah, 'a woman of this strange Medusa-like type,' comes to the castle of Count Axël, who 'lives in the Black Forest studying magic with Janus, a wizard ascetic of the Rosy Cross.' (*Id.*) Yeats's review focuses particularly on 'the last great scene' in which Axël proposes to kill Sarah, because 'the knowledge that she is in the world will never let him rest.' (*Id.*) This

... marvelous scene prolongs itself from wonder to wonder till in the height of his joyous love Axel remembers that this dream must die in the light of the common world, and pronounces the condemnation of all life, of all pleasure, of all hope. The lovers resolve to die. They drink poison, and so complete the fourfold renunciation – of the cloister, of the active life of the world, of the labouring life of the intellect, of the passionate life of love. The infinite alone is worth attaining, and the infinite is the possession of the dead. Such appears to be the moral. Seldom has the utmost pessimism found a more magnificent expression.

Yeats's longing for the perfection of such an extraterrestrial union with Gonne explains his wish that his beloved were dead. Remaining unanswered are Elizabeth Butler Cullingford's questions: 'For what must the woman forgive the speaker? Have they quarreled? Has he murdered her?' (Gender and History 48) The answers are not far to seek. Yeats explains in *Memoirs* that, in the summer preceding publication of this poem, Gonne berated him by letter for making her do 'the most cowardly thing I have ever done in my life.'[25] She was referring to his having locked her inside the National Club to prevent her from joining the crowd during a police charge that followed her Dublin address protesting the celebration of Queen Victoria's Jubilee. The speeches had been part of Gonne's 'shining days,' but Yeats's actions, she thought, darkened her achievement. Gonne's letter pointed to a fundamental difference in their natures: '... I was born to be in the midst of a crowd,' she said, but 'you have a higher work to do' and should not involve yourself 'in the *outer* side of politics....' (*Id.*; emphasis in original)

Two other poems of 1898 show Yeats struggling to control the image of himself and Gonne not only contemporaneously, but for future generations as well. 'He thinks of those who have Spoken Evil of his Beloved' (*VP* 166) addresses the serious threat posed to his poetic enterprise by a parade of slanderous gossip about the proud and solitary woman he would celebrate as an emblem of Irish consciousness. His poetry will be more powerful than the gossip: 'weigh this song with the great and their pride,' he challenges, and the result will be that '[t]heir children's children shall say they have lied.' 'The Fish' (*VP* 146) reminds the Muse that the poet can control her reputation for his own purposes. He laments that the fish constantly escapes his net, and urges her to remember that the people of coming days will think she is hard and unkind, '[a]nd blame you with many bitter words.'

As 1898 drew to a close,[26] chastened by Gonne's reproaches over the Victoria Jubilee, Yeats wrote 'He wishes for the Cloths of Heaven,' a memorable indication of his subservience to his Muse:

> Had I the heavens' embroidered cloths,
> Enwrought with golden and silver light,
> The blue and the dim and the dark cloths
> Of night and light and the half-light,
> I would spread the cloths under your feet:
> But I, being poor, have only my dreams;
> I have spread my dreams under your feet;
> Tread softly because you tread on my dreams.   (*VP* 176)

As suggested by his frequent lecture observation that 'He wishes for the Cloths of Heaven' was the way 'to lose a lady,'[27] Yeats knew that he needed to find a new footing as Muse-poet. Suddenly, before there was time for a natural evolution in his poetic practice, a crisis in his relations with Gonne erupted on a December morning in 1898, nine years after their first meeting. When Yeats told Gonne of a dream that morning in which she kissed him, she replied with news of a dream the previous night in which their spirits were married: 'When I fell asleep last night I saw standing at my bedside a great spirit. He took me to a great throng of spirits, and you were among them. My hand was put into yours and I was told that we were married. After that I remember nothing.' (*Mem* 132) '[T]hen and there' Yeats recounted, 'for the first time with the bodily mouth, she kissed me.' (*Id.*)

Gonne then poured out the story of her life: how she had fallen in love with Millevoye, become his mistress and borne him a son, who had already been born at the time of Yeats's first proposal, and a daughter, who had been conceived in an effort to reincarnate the deceased son. Gonne seemed to be inviting talk of marriage: she was drawing Yeats into the most intimate details of her life, introducing sexual passion into their relationship, and relating to him a message from the spiritual world that they were married. Yeats's reaction seems designed to maintain Gonne's usefulness as Muse by preserving her unattainability inviolate. He later referred to these events of December 1898 as the beginning of a 'spiritual marriage,'[28] but he steadfastly eschewed the physical: '[I]n all that followed I was careful to touch [her] as one might a sister. If she was to come to me, it must be from no temporary passionate impulse, but with the approval of her conscience.' (*Mem* 133) In retrospect, Yeats recognized that his 'high scruple' masked more complicated feelings: 'Many a time since then, as I lay awake at night, have I accused myself of acting, not as I thought from a high scruple, but from a dread of moral responsibility, and my thoughts have gone round and round, as do miserable thoughts, coming to no solution.' (*Id.*)

Deirdre Toomey makes a convincing case that Gonne's outpouring to Yeats and revelation of her vulnerability was, in effect, an invitation to marriage to which Yeats failed to respond because of 'psychic impotence,' perhaps brought on by seeing '[a] woman [he had] viewed as essentially, supernaturally, virginal... dragged down into sexuality and motherhood.'[29] More than a quarter century after the event, Yeats lodged a similar charge against himself in 'The Tower's' moving admonition to

> admit you turned aside
> From a great labyrinth out of pride,
> Cowardice, some silly over-subtle thought
> Or anything called conscience once[.]   (*VP* 413)

A few days after Gonne's 1898 revelations, she told Yeats she heard a voice saying 'You are about to receive the initiation of the spear.' (*Mem 134*) Then: 'We became silent; a double vision unfolded itself, neither speaking till all was finished. She thought herself a great stone statue through which passed flame, and I felt myself becoming flame and mounting up through and looking out of the eyes of a great stone Minerva.' (*Id.*) In this remarkable shared vision, Gonne appears as the White Goddess Minerva[30] but she is cast in stone, a permanent reminder of her unattainability. Yeats got the message. When he spoke vaguely of marriage on the eve of Gonne's departure from Dublin at the end of the 1898 crisis, her reply was: '"No, it seems to me impossible" and then, with clenched hands, "I have a horror and terror of physical love".' (*Id.*)

The revelation that the subject of his poetry of celibate yearning was, in fact, the mother of a deceased son and a young daughter was fundamentally unsettling to Yeats's poetic enterprise. 'My whole imagination has shifted its foundations,' he wrote to Lady Gregory, '& I am not yet used to the new foundation.' (*CL 2*, 329) He felt as though 'the seas & the hills' had 'been upheaved.' (*Id.*) He wrote no love poetry after the December 1898 revelations until 1901.

A draft 'Subject for lyric,' probably written following a visit from Gonne in London about two years after her startling revelations of 1898, shows Yeats at an imaginative impasse.[31] The first section laments that his Muse is unmoved by the songs she engenders:

> Subject for lyric
>
> I
>
> O my beloved you only are
>   not moved by my <sorrows> songs
> which you only understand
> You only know that it is
>   of you I sing when I tell
>   of the swan on the water
>   or the eagle in the heavens
>   or the faun in the wood
> Others weep but your eyes
>   are dry.

In the second section, Yeats sees his poetry as but 'play[ing] with images of the life you will not give to me' while Gonne, who had broken with Millevoye in 1900, began an alliance grounded in a common interest in political action with Major John MacBride, who had led an Irish Brigade against the British in the Boer War and, living in Parisian exile, turned to Gonne for help in writing the lectures he planned to give on a fundraising tour of America. (*Lucky Eyes* 201–3) Gonne's life of action is background to Yeats's deprecation of his life as a poet:

> II
>
> O my beloved. How happy
> I was that day when you
> Came here from the
> railway, & set your hair
> aright in my looking glass
> & then sat with me at
> my table, & <then> lay resting
> in my big chair. I am
> like the children, O my
> beloved & I play at
> <life &> marriage. I play
> <at> with images of the life
> you will not give to me O
> my cruel one.

In the third section, Yeats says, in effect, that he is turning his back on the courtly love tradition – 'put[ting] away all the romances' – and retreating to the woods:

> III
>
> I put away all the romances,
> how could I read of queens
> & of noble women, whose
> very dust is full of sorrow.
> Are they not all but my
> beloved whispering to me.
>
> I went into the woods. I
> heard the cry of the birds
> & the <cry> of the deers, <?&I>
> & I heard the winds among the
> reeds, but I put my hands
> over my ears for were not
> they my beloved whispering to
> me. O my beloved, why do
> you whisper to me of sorrow
> always.

In the last section Yeats returns to Gonne's necessity as Muse – verses are nothing to him '[i]f you were not there to listen' – but laments her refusal to be moved by his poetry:

> IIII
>
> O my beloved what wer verses to me
> If you <are> were not there to
>   listen
> & yet all my verses a little t you.
> Your eyes set upon far
>   magnificence
> upon impossible heroism
> have made you blind and have
>   made you deaf
> you gave your country a flame
> <I fear> you hav no thing bu
> the s verses that ar but like
> <?rushes> & leaves in the
> middle of
>   a wood.
> Other eyes fill with tears but
>   yours are dry

Dante had pointed the way out of such an impasse in *La Vita Nuova*, which tells how, after Beatrice had denied him the salutation that had been his chief source of happiness, he focused his poetry inward to his emotional reactions to Beatrice. In response to a question by her friends as to the purpose of his love, he explained that, Beatrice's salutation having being taken from him, Love, his Master, 'hath placed all my beatitude where my hope will not fail me,' namely 'In those words that do praise my lady.' (Rossetti Dante 57) Realizing that his poetic practice did not accord with his purpose, he 'resolved that thenceforward I would choose for the theme of my writings only the praise of this most gracious being.' (*Id.* 58)

Dante then recounts an experience that would be of great interest to a searcher after inspiration like Yeats. As Dante passed along a path beside a stream of clear water, 'there came upon me a great desire to say something in rhyme' and as he wrestled with how to do so, 'I declare that my tongue spake as if by its own impulse, and said, "Ladies that have intelligence in love". (*Id.*) Dante promptly adopted these inspired words as the first line of his *canzone 'Donne ch'avete intelletto d'amore.'* Dante's experience told Yeats that praising his beloved would open the door to inspiration.

In 'The Arrow,' written in 1901, and 'The Folly of Being Comforted,' published in January 1902, Yeats, Dante-like, turned away from the introspection of the draft 'Subject for lyric' in favor of a poetry of praise. Both poems employ the classic 'Muse poem' theme of the ageing beloved but add a strong measure of Dantean praise. 'The Arrow' also transforms the courtly conceit that the Muse stimulates the poet into song by transmitting her beauty like an arrow through the lover's eyes into his heart. (In Praise of Love 151, 219–20) In Yeats's poem, it is not Gonne's beauty itself, but a 'wild thought' engendered by it, that pierces his marrow and gives birth to the poem:

> I thought of your beauty, and this arrow,
> Made out of a wild thought, is in my marrow.
> There's no man may look upon her, no man,
> As when newly grown to be a woman,
> Tall and noble but with face and bosom
> Delicate in colour as apple blossom.
> This beauty's kinder, yet for a reason
> I could weep that the old is out of season.   (*VP* 199)

'The Folly of Being Comforted' (*VP* 199) also transcends the usual contours of the poem to the ageing Muse. Whereas the traditional poem, according to Rich, threatens the Muse with loss of beauty, Yeats insists on the permanence of Gonne's beauty, and fulfills his prophecy by immortalizing in verse its continuing renewal. Although Yeats would eventually concede that, in the case of Eva Gore Booth and Constance Markieweicz, '[t]he innocent and the beautiful/Have no enemy but time' (*VP* 476), he insists here that '[t]ime can but make [Gonne's] beauty over again':

> One that is ever kind said yesterday:
> 'Your well-belovèd's hair has threads of grey,
> And little shadows come about her eyes;
> Time can but make it easier to be wise
> Though now it seems impossible, and so
> All that you need is patience.'
>
> Heart cries, 'No,
> I have not a crumb of comfort, not a grain.
> Time can but make her beauty over again:
> Because of that great nobleness of hers
> The fire that stirs about her, when she stirs,
> Burns but more clearly. O she had not these ways
> When all the wild summer was in her gaze.'
>
> O heart! O heart! if she'd but turn her head,
> You'd know the folly of being comforted.

These beautiful poems did nothing to advance Yeats's courtship. Gonne had joined MacBride on his American lecture tour in February 1901 and, having resisted his marriage proposals, returned home in May in a state of exhaustion. When Yeats joined her on a visit to her sister Kathleen, Gonne interpreted his compliments to Kathleen as criticism of her life of political agitation that was diminishing her beauty. (SQ 317–18) Kathleen's observation that it is 'hard work being beautiful' (*id.*) set Yeats thinking about the hard work – Plato's *techne* – of writing poetry. The result was the touching 'Adams Curse' (*VP* 204), in which Gonne's exhaustion and a hollow moon symbolize a similar entropy in Yeats's career as a courtly love poet. In a flowing form that embodies its substance, the poem begins with Yeats's commentary on the hard work of writing poetry:

> I said: 'A line will take us hours maybe;
> Yet if it does not seem a moment's thought,

> Our stitching and unstitching has been naught.
> Better go down upon your marrow-bones
> And scrub a kitchen pavement, or break stones
> Like an old pauper, in all kinds of weather;
> For to articulate sweet sounds together
> Is to work harder than all these, and yet
> Be thought an idler by the noisy set
> Of bankers, schoolmasters, and clergymen
> The martyrs call the world.'

After reframing Kathleen's comment as 'we must labour to be beautiful,' Yeats concludes at the dead end to which the courtly love tradition – 'the old high way of love' – has brought him:

> I said: 'It's certain there is no fine thing
> Since Adam's fall but needs much labouring.
> There have been lovers who thought love should be
> So much compounded of high courtesy
> That they would sigh and quote with learned looks
> Precedents out of beautiful old books;
> Yet now it seems an idle trade enough.'
>
> We sat grown quiet at the name of love;
> We saw the last embers of daylight die,
> And in the trembling blue-green of the sky
> A moon, worn as if it had been a shell
> Washed by time's waters as they rose and fell
> About the stars and broke in days and years.
>
> I had a thought for no one's but your ears:
> That you were beautiful, and that I strove
> To love you in the old high way of love;
> That it had all seemed happy, and yet we'd grown
> As weary-hearted as that hollow moon.

Rather than being the source of a Muse's wisdom, the moon is worn, hollow, and weary-hearted.

In her autobiography, Gonne recalls that the conversation immortalized in 'Adam's Curse' took place following another Yeats proposal. (SQ 318–19) In response to his suggestion that he could make a beautiful life for her among artists and writers who would understand her, Gonne insisted that he was happier without her, and focused sharply on the importance of her unattainability to the role she was playing as Muse: 'you make beautiful poetry out of what you call your unhappiness and you are happy in that. Marriage would be such a dull affair. Poets should never marry.' (*Id.*)

Nine years later, she would express a similar thought in a letter to Yeats in which she breaks the usual Muse mode by laying claim to the role of father of the poems to which he gave birth. While the Muse notion has been criticized for turning the Muse into a passive vehicle to be used by the active male poet,[32] Gonne insists that she is the driving force behind the poems – their father: 'Our children were your poems of which I was the Father sowing the unrest & storm which made them possible & you the mother who brought them forth in suffering & in the highest beauty & our children had wings....' (*G-YL* 302)

Following the conversation reflected in 'Adam's Curse,' Gonne apparently had more unrest and storm in mind for Yeats. In a June 1902 letter to her sister, Gonne explained that, although '[m]arriage I always consider abominable,' she had decided to 'make that sacrifice to convention' and marry MacBride for the sake of Iseult.[33] Gonne disclosed that she would become a Catholic in connection with the marriage, and explained further that she was 'getting old and oh so tired and I have found a man who has a stronger will than myself....' (*Id.*) 'As for Willy Yeats,' she said, 'I love him dearly as a friend but I could not for one minute imagine marrying him.' (*Id.*)

Gonne seems to have waited until early in 1903 to impart to Yeats the news that the subject of his very public love poetry was about to marry someone else. Yeats wrote three letters trying to dissuade Gonne; only one of them survives and it is in draft. (*G-YL* 164–6) The letter is fascinating, both for what it contains and for what it omits. Yeats starkly laments, not the loss of a lover, but the death of the public person he had created in his poetry. 'Maud Gonne is about to pass away,' he wrote, and her death would destroy the 'great work' that they were to do together. (*G-YL* 164–5) Yeats's revealing letter reflects a remarkable kinship between his poems about Gonne and the courtly love lyrics whose function was to define and validate the society that produced them.[34] Yeats argues that Gonne's solitariness was part of her political appeal: 'the people' have admired and looked up to you, he wrote, because of your 'proud solitary haughty life which made [you] seem like one of the Golden Gods.' The unspoken thought behind this belief – that Gonne's attraction was allied to her Parnell-like Anglo-Irish solitary strength and pride – carries the subtext that her status as a Muse was tied to her remaining solitary, i.e., unattainable.

Worse still, Yeats argues, Gonne is about to lose not only her solitariness, but her status as a member of the Protestant Ascendancy as well. He argues that, by marrying the Catholic MacBride, she would thrust her soul down 'to a lower order of faith' and thrust herself 'down socially' as well, thereby losing the people's admiration for 'a superior class, a class whose people are more independent, have a more beautiful life, a more refined life.' Building on a detailed reference to their mystical marriage of 1898 and the projected Celtic order, Yeats emphasizes that marriage to MacBride will bring an end to 'our work,' which had been 'to teach a few strong aristocratic spirits... to believe the soul was immortal & that one prospered hereafter *if one laid upon oneself* an heroic discipline in living,' and then send 'them to uplift the nation.' (*Id.*) Again, carrying on the 'great work' with Yeats required that she not marry him, but follow the 'heroic discipline in living' of the mystical marriage. Unsurprisingly, the letter was not successful. Gonne and MacBride were married on 21 February 1903.

If, as Yeats had predicted in his letter, the marriage constituted the passing away of 'Maud Gonne,' it would simultaneously bring about the death of the courtly poet whose function was to sing her praises. Were Yeats debarred from glorifying Gonne, his voice as poet would be silenced. As Goldin says, since 'the lover's proclaiming of his consecration to the lady before the whole courtly society is an act that defines him,' 'to cease to sing is to cease to *be*.' (Mirror 101) In fact, Yeats wrote almost no lyric poetry for the next five years. The narrative poem 'The Old Age of Queen Maeve,' published in April 1903, implicitly praises Gonne as it describes Maeve's 'lucky eyes and a high heart,/And wisdom that caught fire like the dried flax' (*VP* 181), but Yeats's praise then fell silent.

He wondered to his journal in 1909 whether 'the heterogenous labour of these last few years'... had left him 'any lyric faculty.' (*Mem* 171–2) Part of that labour had involved assisting Gonne in extricating herself from the marriage to MacBride that turned out to be a disaster. After receiving a report from Gonne's cousin in early 1905, Yeats wrote to Gregory recounting what Foster calls 'the catalogue of MacBride's crimes: violence, sexual abuse, threats to the children.' (*Life 1*, 331) He was soon writing Gregory again after hearing details of MacBride's seduction of Gonne's seventeen-year-old half-sister and his molestation of the ten-year-old Iseult, 'the blackest thing you can imagine.'[35]

H.W. Nevinson's August 1906 journal reflects Florence Farr's fascinating commentary on the effect of these traumatic events on

Yeats's relationship to his Muse. Nevinson's journal recounts that Farr had told him of how Gonne had borne two children fathered by Millevoye, how she married MacBride to keep Millevoye away from the house, and how MacBride 'in drunkenness ravished the servants & even the little girl.' ('An Attendant Lord', *YA* 7 at 113.) Nevinson further reports that 'Yeats is rather disgusted now at her past. For 10 years he possessed the romantic love – now he shudders at it & is terrified lest it come again. Yet it was the secret of his power.' Both agreed, Nevinson concluded, 'the artist must never marry....' (*Id.*)

Yet Yeats could not resist the allure of Gonne's need for his help. Noticing a change in an aspect of his beloved that had always captivated him, he reported to Gregory that her 'will seems to be gone.'[36] He immersed himself in the practical business of retaining counsel and assembling proof for a separation hearing. This more self-confident Yeats dismissed the report that a jealous MacBride had threatened to shoot him, observing that his erstwhile rival's 'revolver... is probably empty.'[37] Gonne obtained a judicial separation under French law in August 1906, but appellate proceedings lasted until January 1908. (*G-YL* 251)

In June 1908, Yeats visited Gonne in Paris. Sensing that it was a momentous occasion, he made notes in the vellum notebook that Gonne gave him during the visit, and that, using the acronym of her Golden Dawn name, he called his 'P.I.A.L. Notebook.'[38] It records that, the day after his arrival, Gonne said something that 'blotted away the resent past & brought all back to the spiritual marriage of 1898.' (P.I.A.L Notebook.) The 'something' that Gonne said was likely that, as Nevinson recounted in his journal the following December after another meeting with Farr, 'Gonne had at last given in & told him she had really loved him all these 15 years.' ('An Attendant Lord,' *YA* 7 at 114) Soon after the Paris meeting, Gonne was writing to Yeats about a meeting in 'the astral.' 'We went somewhere in space I don't know where,' she wrote:

> You had taken the form I think of a great serpent, but I am not quite sure. I only saw your face distinctly & as I looked into your eyes (as I did the day in Paris you asked me what I was thinking of) & your lips touched mine. We melted into one another till we formed only *one being, a being greater than ourselves* who felt all & knew all with double intensity....[39]

She then fell asleep and dreamed that she and Yeats were in Italy together where, discussing this vision, Yeats said that 'it would tend to increase physical desire.' Gonne's response was very clear: 'there was nothing physical in that union – Material union is but a pale shadow compared to it.' (*Id.*)

Even so, by December 1908, she and Yeats had at last become lovers. (*Life 1*, 394) Her letter of that time suggests both a consummation and her conviction that the physical relationship could not continue, but needed to be replaced by a return to 'the spiritual love and union I offer':

> You asked me yesterday if I am not a little sad that things are as they are between us – I am sorry & I am glad. It is hard being away from each other so much there are moments when I am dreadfully lonely & long to be with you, – one of these moments is on me now – but beloved I am glad & proud beyond measure of your love, & that it is strong enough & high enough to accept the spiritual love & union I offer –
>
> I have prayed so hard to have all earthly desire taken from my love for you & dearest, loving you as I do, I have prayed & I am praying still that the bodily desire for me may be taken from you too. I know how hard & rare a thing it is for a man to hold spiritual love when the bodily desire is gone & I have not made these prayers without a terrible struggle a struggle that shook my life though I do not speak much of it & generally manage to laugh.
>
> That struggle is over & I have found peace. I think today I could let you marry another without losing it – for I know the spiritual union between us will outlive this life, even if we never see each other in this world again.
>
> Write to me soon.
>
> Yours
> Maud   (*G-YL* 258–9)

Ellmann suggested that the long-deferred consummation of 1908 is referred to in Yeats's boast in 'A Man Young and Old' (1926–27) that '[t]he first of all the tribe lay there' in the ageing man's arms

> And did such pleasure take –
> She who had brought great Hector down
> And put all Troy to wreck –
> That she cried into this ear,
> 'Strike me if I shriek.'   (*VP* 455)

Ellmann buttressed his conclusion by reporting that George Yeats confirmed its accuracy. (M&M xxii) That George Yeats was in a position to know is apparent from the transcripts of her collaboration with her husband in the process of automatic writing on which *A Vision* is based. That collaborative project involved, among other things, a searching analysis of Yeats's relationships with women – an inquiry that led him to the conclusion that his life had been governed by six critical moments when the spiritual world intervened directly in his own life. (*MYV 2*, 228–38) George's communicators agreed with Yeats's suggestion that, in the case of subjective people like himself, there is always sex at critical moments (*YVP 2*, 231) and Yeats identified one of his critical moments as an event with Gonne in Paris in 1907 or 1908. (*YVP 3* 193, 240)

The second half of 1908 was a dizzying roller coaster ride in Yeats's emotional life. His Muse had gone from the unattainable, to the attained, and then reverted to the unattainable. The foundations of his imaginative life were shaken as fundamentally as they had been with the revelations and spiritual marriage of December 1898. The surprising turns in Yeats's relationship with Gonne pose an interesting question in the theory of Musedom. Did his tasting of the 'apple on the bough/Most out of reach' vitiate Gonne's power as Muse? Gonne preempted consideration of this question by her prompt insistence on returning to a strictly spiritual relationship. By letter of 13 January 1909, she reminded Yeats of the necessity of her unattainability, supporting her view with historical precedent: 'Raphael bowed down to sex till it killed him when he was only 30,' she wrote, and 'his painting is the essence of prettiness,' but 'Michael Angelo denied the power of sex, *for a year* while he was painting the marvel of the Sistine Chapel ... & yet the passion of his work is terrible & makes Raphael's sink away into insignificance....' (*G-YL* 261–2) In Gonne's view, imperfection of the life – at least sexual life – is necessary to creating passion in the work.

Less convinced of the necessity of Gonne's unattainability, Yeats approached the question obliquely, focusing more generally on the effect of the relationship on his poetic enterprise. Once again, he found the resilience to write his way to a new kind of love poetry. By 22 January he had written the moving 'Words' (*VP* 255), a meditation on his understanding that the turmoil engendered by his Muse powered his poetic engine and that, were it not for the turmoil there might have been no poetry – he might have 'thrown poor words away/And been content to live':

> I had this thought a while ago,
> 'My darling cannot understand
> What I have done, or what would do
> In this blind bitter land.'
>
> And I grew weary of the sun
> Until my thoughts cleared up again,

> Remembering that the best I have done
> Was done to make it plain;
> That every year I have cried, 'At length
> My darling understands it all,
> Because I have come into my strength,
> And words obey my call';
> That had she done so who can say
> What would have shaken from the sieve?
> I might have thrown poor words away
> And been content to live.

His diary captured the same thought in prose:

Today the thought came to me that P.I.A.L. never really understands my plans, or nature or ideas. Then came the thought, what matter? How much of the best I have done and still do is but the attempt to explain myself to her? If she understood I should lack a reason for writing, and one can never have too many reasons for doing what is so laborious. (*Mem* 141–2)

Reflecting on the recent twists and turns in his relationship to his Muse, Yeats must have re-read her letter of the previous June, which was pasted into his P.I.A.L. Notebook, in which she gingerly criticized him because, owing to his belief that 'as a great writer' he should be above & apart from various 'petty quarrels & little animosities' of Irish politics, he was 'often very unjust to our people' and had taken up 'old class prejudices which are unworthy of you' and made him 'say cruel things which *sound* ungenerous....'[40] The intensity and volatility of Yeats's relationship to his Muse at this time is reflected in his journal entry for the day after he wrote the poem 'Words.' In apparent response to Gonne's June letter, and revealing something of the disgust that Farr had mentioned to Nevinson, he wrote:

> My dear is angry that of late
> I cry all base blood down
> As though she had not taught me hate
> By kisses to a clown. (*Mem* 145)

This Petrarchan enmity between poet and Muse[41] – the 'Odi et amo' of Catullus[42] – will lurk beneath Yeats's poetry about Gonne until it bursts into the open in 'A Prayer for My Daughter' (*VP* 403) in 1919. Yeats was no stranger to the way in which strongly felt opposing emotions could flicker into each other. Indeed, he is a textbook example of Anthony Storr's observation 'that creative people are distinguished by an exceptional degree of division between opposites, and also by an exceptional awareness of this division.'[43] Yeats might have been speaking of himself when he said of Synge, 'He could not have loved had he not hated....'[44] Yeats's poetry, however, continued to follow the courtly tradition, in which the poet's love makes him more generous, decorous, and noble.

The continuing courtly tone of Yeats's poetry was the result of a painstaking analysis of Gonne's unattainability and the conflicting emotions it engendered. His P.I.A.L. Notebook entry for 21 June 1909 shows him grappling with these questions. Noting that she 'will not divorce her husband and marry because of her church,' and that 'the old dread of physical love has awakened in her,' he concludes that he must escape from thralldom to his Muse: 'I was never more deeply in love, but my desires, always strong, must go elsewhere if I would escape their poison.' (NLI MS 36, 276) No doubt thinking of his aborted relationships with Olivia Shakespear and Florence Farr, he writes that Gonne, 'always a dream of deceiving hope, has all unknown to herself made other loves but as the phoenix nest, where she is reborn in all her power to torture and delight, to waste & to ennoble.' (*Id.*) Now, however, her power as Muse is waning: 'Of old she was a phoenix and I feared her, but she is my child more than my sweetheart.' (*Id.*) 'She would be cruel,' he concludes, if she were not a child, who can always say "you will not suffer because I will pray".' (*Id.*)

Yeats's rumination shows that he had managed to escape from the 'association of desire, religion, and cruelty' that Mario Praz, quoting Novalis, finds at the heart of the tradition of the 'Beauty of the Medusa,' derived from Flaubert, Baudelaire, and Moreau's paintings, and 'beloved by the Romantics,' especially Keats and Shelley.[45] Yeats's strong commitment to a Dantean poetry of praise steered him away from this tradition. So did his decision to 'go elsewhere' with his desires in order to 'escape their poison.' Specifically, in June 1908, as Yeats was visiting Gonne in Paris and receiving her invitation to renew the mystical marriage, he was writing to Dublin actress, medical gymnast and masseuse, Mabel Dickinson, with whom he had begun what George Yeats later called a 'purely amorous'[46] affair in April 1908. (*Life 1*, 384–6) He told Dickinson that 'the things that delight me this year at the Louvre are the big classic pictures by David & by some of the men of the seventeenth century for the moment I am tired of modern mystery & romance, & can only take pleasure in clear light, strong bodies bodies having all the measure of manhood.'[47] Reflecting his escape from the romantic agony of Baudelaire, Flaubert and Moreau, he tells Dickinson that he went to see Moreau's pictures, and that 'I used to delight in him, but now I am all for David & above all Ingres whose Perseus is all classic romance – the poetry of running feat & clear far sighted eyes – of a world where you would be perfectly happy & have enumerable pupils.' (*Id.*) Reiterating his escape from the romantic agony, he concludes: 'Ten years ago when I was last in Paris I loved all that was mysterious and gothic & hated all that was classic & severe. I doubt if I should have like you then – I wanted a twilight of religeous mystery in everybodies eyes.'

In contrast to the many poems he wrote to Gonne during his unsuccessful pursuit, Yeats wrote no poems to Dickinson during their 'purely amorous relationship,' although he did write an interesting lyric, 'The Mask' (*VP* 263), based on an idea he attributed to her.[48] The poem suggests that what matters is the Muse's mask, not what lies behind it, so long as 'there is but fire/In you, in me.' He eventually broke with Dickinson in 1913 after a pregnancy scare that, based on automatic writing from Elizabeth Radcliffe, he thought may have been deceptive (*Life 1*, 488), but this rupture came five years after Dickinson had helped him escape the lure of romantic agony.

Freed from fear, and seeing his former Muse more as his child, Yeats had been able to address in poetry the traumatic events of early 1903, when his Muse dealt a blow to his poetic enterprise by forsaking spiritual marriage with him to marry MacBride. One might have expected this to be the occasion for poems of Adrienne Rich's third category of Muse poem, those in which 'the woman was like Maud Gonne, cruel and disastrously mistaken, and the poem reproached her because she had refused to become a luxury for the poet.' (On Lies 39) Although Gonne is not immune from Yeatsian criticism, the general thrust of his poetry does not support Rich's characterization. To the contrary, Yeats wrote eight poems in the period 1908 through 1910 that continued his practice of praising Gonne, and seemingly accepted her proposal of a renewed spiritual marriage. His acceptance is apparent, both in the text of certain of the poems, and in the fact that these eight poems are linked under the title 'Raymond Lully and his wife Pernella' in the Cuala Press edition of *The Green Helmet and Other Poems* (1910). Yeats had intended to refer to Nicholas and Pernella Flamel, a fourteenth century couple devoted to mystical studies who assertedly discovered the philosopher's stone and continued to live, according to Waite's *Lives of Alchemystical Philosophers*, 'a philosophic life, sometimes in one country, sometimes in another' long after their apparent deaths.[49] Yeats was clearly aware of the Flamels' afterlife; in one of the drafts of *The Speckled Bird*, the Yeats-like figure hopes to find the Elixir, disappear to Arabia, and find 'Nicholas Flamel and his wife there.' (*SB* 163) Gonne, with whom Yeats had discussed a life modeled on the Flamels early in their relationship (*Mem* 49), advised Yeats of his mistaken reference to Lully (*G-YL* 294–5) and he issued an *erratum*.

One of the poems in the Nicholas and Pernella Flamel series, 'King and No King' (1909), wonders aloud whether Flamel-like eternal life as a couple awaits the poet and his Muse:

> And I that have not your faith, how shall I know
> That in the blinding light beyond the grave
> We'll find so good a thing as that we have lost?
> The hourly kindness, the day's common speech,
> The habitual content of each with each
> When neither soul nor body has been crossed. (*VP* 258)

'Reconciliation,' written in September 1908, both reflects Yeats's success in escaping the tradition of blaming the cruel Muse, and betrays the extent to which he defined Gonne as an occasion for poetry: the poet's concern over Gonne's marriage is not the loss of a lover, but the prospect that he will have '[n]othing to make a song about':

> Some may have blamed you that you took away
> The verses that could move them on the day
> When, the ears being deafened, the sight of the eyes blind
> With lightning, you went from me, and I could find
> Nothing to make a song about but kings,
> Helmets, and swords, and half-forgotten things
> That were like memories of you – but now
> We'll out, for the world lives as long ago;
> And while we're in our laughing, weeping fit,
> Hurl helmets, crowns, and swords into the pit.
> But, dear, cling close to me; since you were gone,
> My barren thoughts have chilled me to the bone. (*VP* 257)

'Reconciliation' expresses a corollary to the suggestion in 'Words' that Yeats's poetic engine might have stalled had Gonne married him – he 'might have thrown poor words away/And been content to live.' The corollary is that Gonne could not marry anyone else. Her marriage to MacBride left him with 'Nothing to make a song about.' His poetic enterprise required that Gonne remain solitary so that, like the object of the courtly lover's pursuit, she authorized 'a state of perpetual desire.' (In Praise of Love 167)

By 1910, Yeats had again found a way to 'make a song about' his Muse. In fact, 'A Woman Homer Sung' (*VP* 254) explains how the Muse's inspiration works. 'I dream,' Yeats says,

> ... that I have brought
> To such a pitch my thought
> That coming time can say,
> 'He shadowed in a glass
> What thing her body was.'
>
> For she had fiery blood
> When I was young,
> And trod so sweetly proud
> As 'twere upon a cloud,
> A woman Homer sung,
> That life and letters seem
> But an heroic dream.

Concentration on Gonne brings Yeats's thought 'to such a pitch' that his consciousness is open to the influx of the image of Gonne as Helen of Troy, treading on a cloud with such force of reality that life seems but a dream. This characterization of Gonne's functioning as Muse would later be repeated in 'A Bronze Head,' where, nearing the end of his life, he remembers how 'Propinquity had brought/Imagination to that pitch where it casts out/All that is not itself....' (*VP* 619).

Yeats returned to the blame question with 'No Second Troy' (*VP* 256), a fascinating poem, both biographically and artistically. Biographically, Yeats plunges directly into the emotional tinderbox of the occasion in 1897 when Gonne blamed him for barring her from joining the crowd during the police charge that followed her speech. When writing 'He wishes His Beloved Were Dead' in 1898, he had been the plaintive courtly lover prepared to seek his beloved's forgiveness once she was dead. In 1910, he is the master of the situation, someone who could 'blame her' for hurling 'the little streets upon the great,' but chooses not to do so:

> Why should I blame her that she filled my days
> With misery, or that she would of late
> Have taught to ignorant men most violent ways,
> Or hurled the little streets upon the great,
> Had they but courage equal to desire?

> What could have made her peaceful with a mind
> That nobleness made simple as a fire,
> With beauty like a tightened bow, a kind
> That is not natural in an age like this,
> Being high and solitary and most stern?
> Why, what could she have done, being what she is?
> Was there another Troy for her to burn?

Yeats justifies Gonne's incitement of violence by suggesting that something in her beauty – as in Helen of Troy's – inexorably sowed the seeds of violence. The conjunction of Gonne, Helen and violence cannot be read apart from 'Leda and the Swan' (1923), in which Yeats suggests that Zeus's rape of Leda led not only to the birth of the beautiful Helen, but to the violent sack of Troy and even the murder of Agamemnon:

> A shudder in the loins engenders there
> The broken wall, the burning roof and tower
> And Agamemnon dead. (*VP* 441)

By analogizing Gonne to Helen, whose name was a variant of Selene, the Moon Goddess,[50] and who was inhabited by the Wisdom principle,[51] Yeats at once casts Gonne as a White Goddess and links her penchant for violence with her unnatural beauty and the divine violence that engendered Helen's birth.

There is a temptation to see Gonne's attraction to violence as only oratorical and Yeats's justification of it as only theoretical, casting Leda's rape as a metaphor for the violence attendant upon the periodic influxes of the divine into history described in *A Vision*. But by the time of 'No Second Troy,' Gonne had sought to further an Irish Republican Brotherhood plot to blow up British troop ships during the Boer war and had acquiesced in MacBride's aborted plan to assassinate King Edward VII during their honeymoon in Gibraltar. (SQ 282–5; Int. to *G-YL* 31) Whereas Helen seems to have played at most a passive role in the destruction of Troy, Gonne's affinity for violence was not only active, but part of her appeal. Indeed, Yeats remembered nothing of her speech on the momentous occasion of their first meeting 'except that she vexed my father by praise of war....' (*Mem* 40)

Still – and this is part of the enigma of Yeats – the poem has a compelling grandeur. Pound, always quick to monitor Yeats's development as a poet, observed in a letter to Harriet Monroe, 'He is in transit I think from the "*dolce stile*" to the "*stile grande*"....'[52] The language and structure of 'No Second Troy', like its subject, is high and solitary and stern. In 'Peace' (1910), Yeats maintains the '*stile grande*', praising 'All that sweetness amidst strength,' and – contrary to the bravado of 'The Folly of Being Comforted' – finds peace at last 'when Time had touched her form.' (*VP* 259)

In 'Against Unworthy Praise' (1910), the last of the Nicholas and Pernella Flamel poems, Yeats restores the status quo that existed before Gonne deserted their spiritual marriage of two proud aristocrats (or would-be aristocrats). He proclaims that it has all been worthwhile because she has renewed his strength and thus been good for his poetry:

> O heart, be at peace, because
> Nor knave nor dolt can break
> What's not for their applause,
> Being for a woman's sake.
> Enough if the work has seemed,
> So did she your strength renew,
> A dream that a lion had dreamed
> Till the wilderness cried aloud,
> A secret between you two,
> Between the proud and the proud.   (*VP* 259)

In this mood of reconciliation, Yeats was ready to deal with Gonne when cataloguing the women 'that have wrought/What joy is in my days' in the great 1911 poem 'Friends' (*VP* 315). His answer to the question 'How could I praise that one that took/All till my youth was gone/With scarce a pitying look' was stark and simple:

> When day begins to break
> I count my good and bad,
> Being wakeful for her sake,
> Remembering what she had,
> What eagle look still shows,
> While up from my heart's root
> So great a sweetness flows
> I shake from head to foot.

Cullingford aptly notes that 'Yeats is able to overcome the self-pity of the disappointed passionate lover without losing the emotional intensity that links him with Gonne....' (Gender and History 100) On its face, Cullingford's further suggestion that '"Friends" climaxes with an image of orgasm' (*id.*) seems a stretch in the context of the retrospective look of 1911, when Yeats was resigned to a marriage that was spiritual at best. However, Yeats reported an erotic dream about Gonne to his P.I.A.L. Notebook in August 1909, and, as late as 1915, in 'A Deep-sworn Vow,' ceded primacy to Gonne among his Muses in lines that could support Cullingford's conclusion:

> Others because you did not keep
> That deep-sworn vow have been friends of mine;
> Yet always when I look death in the face,
> When I clamber to the heights of sleep,
> Or when I grow excited with wine,
> Suddenly I meet your face. (*VP* 357)

Even so, the 'sweetness' that flows in 'Friends' is less speculatively explained in terms of Dante's use of the same word to describe the emotion engendered in the poet by the creation of poetry in praise of his beloved.[53] Such a reading is consistent with Yeats's use of the word sweetness to describe the form of joy that arises when bitterness is replaced by self-delighting alignment of one's own will with heaven's will,[54] and his use of the same word in 'A Dialogue of Self and Soul' (1927) (*VP* 477) to describe the emotion that flows over him when he casts out remorse. It is no exaggeration to think of such sweetness as leaving the poet shaking from head to foot. As Pound remarked, Yeats knew 'what violent emotion really is like' and could 'see from the centre of it.'[55]

The powerful emotion beneath the closing lines of 'Friends' is akin to that which animates 'The Cold Heaven,' a 1912 poem in which Yeats transcends the traditional rubric of the Muse poem by finding inspiration, not in blaming his beloved, but in accepting blame himself. In so doing, he describes how Gonne functions as Muse:

> Suddenly I saw the cold and rook-delighting heaven
> That seemed as though ice burned and was but the more ice,
> And thereupon imagination and heart were driven
> So wild that every casual thought of that and this
> Vanished, and left but memories, that should be out of season
> With the hot blood of youth, of love crossed long ago;
> And I took all the blame out of all sense and reason,
> Until I cried and trembled and rocked to and fro,
> Riddled with light. Ah! When the ghost begins to quicken,
> Confusion of the death-bed over, is it sent

> Out naked on the roads, as the books say, and stricken
> By the injustice of the skies for punishment? (*VP* 316)

In this riveting poem Yeats takes the simple path Graves dictates for the true Muse poet: he tells the truth about himself and his beloved. The drafts of the poem show an extraordinary ability to find just the right words that have kept the poem alive long after its author's death. Starting with notes about an experience while idling in a railway carriage, they show Yeats focusing on the 'cold passionate fire' of the evening sky. (*ISW MM* 230–43) The conjunction of cold and passion – which Yeats may have found in a character in one of Olivia Shakespear's novels, and would later use to fuel his boast in 'The Fisherman' that he would write a poem 'as cold/And passionate as the dawn' (*VP* 348) – is gradually transformed into a metaphor for his relationship with his Muse. The drafts show how Yeats came to see the sky – one in which it 'seemed as though ice burned and yet was but the more ice' – as symbolic of a profound sense of passionate desolation that accompanied acceptance of responsibility for the failure of a relationship that, by definition, required a certain coldness in his Muse to fire his passion.

The poem tells how its author's intense focus on Gonne drove 'every casual thought of that and this' out of his mind and permitted him to concentrate in that state of 'wise passiveness' that Wordsworth said is the precursor of inspiration.[56] The creative process Yeats describes in 'The Cold Heaven' is very much akin to that recounted by Wordsworth in the 1802 preface to *Lyrical Ballads*:

> I have said that Poetry is the spontaneous overflow of powerful feelings: it takes its origin from emotion recollected in tranquility: the emotion is contemplated till by a species of reaction the tranquility gradually disappears, and an emotion, kindred to that which was before the subject of contemplation, is gradually produced, and does itself actually exist in the mind. In this mood successful composition generally begins, and in a mood similar to this it is carried on...

(Wordsworth 611) Idling in a railway carriage, Yeats realizes that his tranquil musing – 'every thought of that and this' – has disappeared and been replaced by a powerful emotion engendered by acceptance of responsibility.

Seamus Heaney's fascinating essay 'Sixth sense, seventh heaven' posits that there are three stages in the process of a poem's creation, the first being 'the lived experience that precedes the business of writing: "the emotion", as [Wordsworth] calls it, whatever has gathered up in the poet's mind and body and assumed an unaccounted-for significance, the whole complex that produces a sense that there's something in there needing expression, ready to reveal itself as something else' – what has traditionally been called inspiration.[57] At the second stage, there is a sense of 'a need for expression' and 'the process of searching for equivalence is underway....' (*Id.* at 202) The third stage is the writing itself.[58]

Heaney suggests that the three steps 'probably occur within the poet as a simultaneity.' (*Id.* 203) Certainly, in the 'The Cold Heaven,' the first two steps seem to overlap. The desire to express the emotion follows very quickly upon its emergence. This compression of the first two stages is the norm in Yeats's Gonne-inspired poems. For example, in both 'The Arrow' and 'A Woman Homer Sung,' the poem flows directly from the emotion: in the former, the thought flies from Gonne into the poem; in the latter, the poem emerges from the excited pitch to which Yeats is moved by thinking about his Muse.

'The Cold Heaven' anticipates the 'First Principles' Yeats entered in a manuscript book he began in the year of the poem's publication:

Not to find one's art by the analysis of language or amid the circumstances of dreams but to live a passionate life, and to express the emotions that find one thus in simple rhythmical language. The words should be the swift natural words that suggest the circumstances out of which they arose.[59]

'The Cold Heaven' and the principles it reflects are a microcosm of Gonne as Muse. From the start, Yeats had been attracted to her as the source of the 'passion' that, when added to 'a little philosophy,' could define a new Irish consciousness. Even though, as he would soon write, the passion was 'barren' in terms of human offspring (*VP* 270), she had provided the stuff of 'a passionate life' and the consequent emotions to be expressed in poetry. Yeats's passion – and Gonne's power of inspiration – had survived many serious disputes. Among the more significant were disagreement over Gonne's activist politics and Yeats's efforts to block her from joining the crowd at the 1897 demonstration in Dublin; a fundamental difference over the role of politics in art, which led to Gonne's walking out of a performance of Synge's *The Shadow of the Glen* and her resignation from the National Theatre Society in 1903;[60] and Gonne's rejection of Yeats and his 'great work' of a mystical union in favor of marriage to MacBride. The disputes themselves became part of the passionate life whose emotions found expression in poetry.

A new kind of poetry would be required by Yeats's acceptance of the failure of his relationship with Gonne. His lyrics about Gonne from 'The Cold Heaven' forward are celebration or interrogation of the past rather than the work of a poet pursuing his Muse. For example, 'When Helen Lived' (1913), which, read in conjunction with Yeats's journal, identifies Gonne as his Muse, is more commentary than pursuit. His journal asks: 'Why should we complain if men ill-treat our Muses, when all they gave to Helen while she lived was a song and a jest?' (*Mem* 225) The poem thus claims Gonne as Muse, but the claim is retrospective:

> We have cried in our despair
> That men desert,
> For some trivial affair
> Or noisy, insolent sport,
> Beauty that we have won
> From bitterest hours;
> Yet we, had we walked within
> Those topless towers
> Where Helen walked with her boy,
> Had given but as the rest
> Of the men and women of Troy,
> A word and a jest. (*VP* 293)

Three poems about Gonne written at Stone Cottage in January 1915 are in the memoralist mode of recording the past. 'Her Praise' (*VP* 350) tells how Yeats seeks to bring the conversation around to the 'foremost of those that I would hear praised.' In 'His Phoenix' (*VP* 353), Yeats compares himself happily with various exemplars of worldly success because 'I knew a phoenix in my youth, so let them have their day.' 'The People' (*VP* 351) echoes Gonne's insistence that she was 'the voice, the soul of the *crowd*' in response to Yeats's effort to dissuade her from marrying MacBride on the ground that she should remain above the crowd.[61] The poem presents what seems almost a direct quote from Gonne's conversations and letters in which she refused to blame the Irish people for booing her at the Abbey Theatre and otherwise turning on her after her separation from MacBride:

> 'The drunkards, pilferers of public funds,
> All the dishonest crowd I had driven away,
> When my luck changed and they dared meet my face,
> Crawled from obscurity, and set upon me
> Those I had served and some that I had fed;

Yet never have I, now nor any time,
Complained of the people.'

Gonne's letter to Yeats thanking him for a copy of 'The People' reviews her career as Muse: 'You have often tried to defend and protect me with your art,' she wrote, '– & perhaps when we are dead I shall be known by those poems of yours.'[62] Gonne was belatedly articulating what she had likely realized for some time, and Yeats had hoped from the outset.

Throughout it all, Gonne had been an effective Muse. She expanded the first of the two ways in which the objects of courtly love poems inspired their lovers: not only did her beauty stir Yeats to song, but the emotion she generated concentrated his mind and left it open to an influx of inspired reflection on the experience. She also inspired in the indirect manner of the courtly beloved by stirring Yeats to pursue a life of amelioration as both man and poet. Adherence to the courtly tradition propelled him, as he said in the 1907 essay 'Poetry and Tradition,' to subject his bouts of anger and hatred to the 'shaping power' of style in art and courtesy in life. (*E&I* 252–5) At the same time, his pursuit of Gonne inspired him to search for the words that might win her. The journal entry that gave rise to 'Words' sums up this aspect of the ameliorating tendency of courtly love: '[h]ow much of the best I have done and still do is but the attempt to explain myself to her?' (*Mem* 142) Significantly, the Muse to whom Yeats explained himself was an articulate partner in an intellectual exchange over specific ideas about life, politics and art. Gonne's Musedom is thus not subject to the criticism that it fosters an 'essentialist' notion of the Muse as a 'passive' 'feminine' figure.[63] Indeed, Gonne maintained vigorously that she was the driving force behind Yeats's poetry, the father of his poems. Rather than being the passive subject chosen by the poet, Gonne insisted upon retaining her status as an unattainable Muse figure, opposing marriage on the ground that her unattainability was necessary to Yeats's creativity.

Gonne transcends the typical courtly Muse in another way as well. Her detailed portrait in the poetry differs from the classic courtly lyric, which, as Julia Kristeva points out, had 'no object – the lady is seldom defined and, slipping away between restrained presence and absence, she simply is an imaginary addressee, the pretext for the incantation' in a poem that 'refers to its own performance.' (Tales of Love 287) No featureless or stereotypical[64] portrait of idealized beauty, Gonne has threads of grey in her hair, shadows about her eyes, and 'small hands

[that] were not beautiful.'[65] Nor is she the voiceless projection of the poet's ideals.[66] She is a successful orator who hurls the little streets upon the great and speaks in her own voice in disagreement with Yeats in 'The People.'

At the same time, she was an earthly goddess. 'A Thought From Propertius' builds from the Roman poet's question 'Why does such beauty linger on earth among mortals?'[67] This is a question Yeats had been pursuing at least from the time of the 'white woman' poems addressed to Olivia Shakespear. In this November 1915 poem, Yeats finds Gonne a fit companion for Wisdom Goddess Pallas Athena and simultaneously breaks what may be new ground for the Muse poet by lauding Gonne's 'great shapely knees.' (*VP* 355) Still, the mood of 1915 was elegiac. In 'Broken Dreams', he was ready to tell Gonne that 'Your beauty can but leave among us/Vague memories, nothing but memories.' (*VP* 356)

The subdued mood of 1915 was the result of forces crystallized by Yeats's reaction to extracts from George Moore's *Vale*, published in the January and February 1914 issues of the *English Review*, which satirized Yeats as a bourgeois with aristocratic pretensions who had never consummated his love for Gonne and was the subject of Dublin conversations as to 'why Yeats had ceased to write poetry.'[68] Yeats confronted Moore directly in the prefatory and concluding rhymes to *Responsibilities*, published in 1914. After first presenting the case for his family lineage, Yeats moves quickly in the prefatory rhymes to the intertwined questions of his unconsummated passion and his allegedly stalled creativity. He seeks the pardon of his 'old fathers' for not having extended the family line, but is quick to point out that his unrequited passion for his Muse has, in fact, engendered a body of poetry:

> *Pardon that for a barren passion's sake,*
> *Although I have come close on forty-nine,*
> *I have no child, I have nothing but a book,*
> *Nothing but that to prove your blood and mine.* (*VP* 270)

As to his future poetic career, the concluding rhymes insist that there is more to come, but perhaps in a different key. His Muse will still sing, but her voice, at least at the moment, is that of a '*reed-throated whisperer/ Who comes at need, although not now as once/A clear articulation in the air,/But inwardly,....*' (*VP* 320) His Muse, rather than the White Goddess, is Syrinx, a Diana look-alike who, pursued by Pan, was rescued by friendly nymphs who turned her into a reed beside a stream so that, as Ovid told it, 'while [Pan] sighed the moving winds began/to utter plaintive music in the reeds....'[69] As of the publication of *Responsibilities* in 1914, it was unclear to Yeats who was speaking to him in the reed-throated whisper. Events across the sea in Normandy would provide an answer.

4. Iseult Gonne, *c* 1918, courtesy Christina Bridgewater.

4
The Living Beauty: Iseult Gonne

In August 1912, while staying with Maud Gonne and her daughter Iseult at their summer home near Colleville in Normandy, Yeats wrote three poems that reflect a fundamental shift in his relationship to his Muse. The process set in motion that month culminated in October 1917, when Yeats abandoned the courtly love tradition and embarked on an entirely different pathway to the Muse. The last two years of this period witnessed so profound a transition in Yeats's creative process that Harold Bloom, writing in 1970, urged that 'Future and still better-informed criticism of Yeats than we have should focus itself on the two years from late 1915 to late 1917, for these were the most important in Yeats's imaginative life.'[1] Iseult Gonne stands at the center of this ferment.

In the first of the August 1912 poems, 'Fallen Majesty' (*VP* 314), Yeats consigns Maud Gonne to the past:

> Although crowds gathered once if she but showed her face,
> And even old men's eyes grew dim, this hand alone,
> Like some last courtier at a gypsy camping-place
> Babbling of fallen majesty, records what's gone.

The poet is no longer a vigorous practitioner of the 'old high way of love,' but is reduced 'to some last courtier' whose song has turned to babbling. Rather than building a new Irish consciousness, he merely records what's gone.

The second poem, 'A Memory of Youth' (*VP* 313), is a capsule summary of Maud Gonne's career as both a wisdom-conferring priestess of the White Goddess and the beloved of the courtly love tradition. The first stanza emphasizes the importance Yeats attached to love as a source of wisdom. He had enjoyed 'the wisdom love brings forth,' but the moon, the source of a Muse's wisdom, was obscured by a cloud:

> The moments passed as at a play;
> I had the wisdom love brings forth;

> I had my share of mother-wit,
> And yet for all that I could say,
> And though I had her praise for it,
> A cloud blown down from the cut-throat North
> Suddenly hid Love's moon away.

The second stanza chronicles Yeats's efforts as Muse poet – 'I praised her body and her mind' – and the last stanza asserts that Love would have died, were it not that a 'little bird' tore the clouds from the moon, the source of inspiration:

> Believing every word I said,
> I praised her body and her mind
> Till pride had made her eyes grow bright,
> And pleasure made her checks grow red,
> And vanity her footfall light,
> Yet we, for all that praise, could find
> Nothing but darkness overhead.
>
> We sat as silent as a stone,
> We knew, though she'd not said a word,
> That even the best of love must die,
> And had been savagely undone
> Were it not that Love upon the cry
> Of a most ridiculous little bird
> Tore from the clouds his marvellous moon. (*Id.*)

The little bird who opened the door to the wisdom of the marvelous moon suggests the arrival in Yeats's imagination of Iseult Gonne, the child who was conceived at the grave of her brother following her mother's conversations with Yeats and George Russell about the possibility of reincarnating the deceased child. (*Life 1*, 115–17) She is the subject of the third August 1912 poem, 'To a Child Dancing in the Wind':

> Dance there upon the shore;
> What need have you to care
> For wind or water's roar?
> And tumble out your hair
> That the salt drops have wet;
> Being young you have not known
> The fool's triumph, nor yet
> Love lost as soon as won,
> Nor the best labourer dead
> And all the sheaves to bind.
> What need have you to dread
> The monstrous crying of wind? (*VP* 312)

Iseult Gonne, who turned eighteen in the month this poem was written, was no longer a child, and was too old, by four years, to qualify as a nymphet as defined by Nabokov's Humbert Humbert. As will be seen, however, she did partake of what Humbert called the 'demoniac' quality of nymphets, their 'fey grace, the elusive, shifty, soul-shattering, insidious charm'[2] upon which, according to Lionel Trilling, 'the Greeks based their idea of the disease of nympholepsy' and others their conceptions of White Goddesses.[3]

At eighteen, Iseult Gonne also shared a quality attributed to the nymphet by Jenefer Shute, who points out that, whereas in Western culture generally, 'to be a woman is to be viewed,' '[i]n the case of Nabokov's nymphets, however, the girl-woman has not yet constituted herself as an object of visual consumption, and it is the male viewer who, like an artist or a magician, must create from this recalcitrant material a landscape of desire.'[4] In Shute's terms, 'To a Child Dancing in the Wind' could be said to describe the 'initial unconsciousness' of the body, which is ultimately constituted the 'object of desire.' (*Id.*)

A quarter century after Yeats pictured Iseult dancing in the wind, the memory of the occasion that prompted the poem was still a powerful image of unconscious energy: 'My imagination goes some years backward,' Yeats wrote in the 1937 edition of *A Vision*, 'and I remember a beautiful young girl singing at the edge of the sea in Normandy words and music of her own composition. She thought herself alone, stood barefooted between sea and sand; sang with lifted head of the civilisations that there had come and gone, ending every verse with the cry: "O Lord, let something remain".' (*AVB* 219–20) Iseult's emergence as Muse is apparent in Yeats's assertion 'that the Upanishads – somebody had already given her the Pyramids – were addressed to the girl.' (*Id.*)

The tension between Yeats's semi-paternal relationship with Iseult and her nascent role as Muse simmers beneath the surface of 'To a Child Dancing in the Wind.' In the absence of Iseult's father, who was not married to Gonne and lived apart from her from the time of Iseult's birth (*Mem* 133), and her stepfather, who had reportedly molested her, and been separated from her mother, by the time she was fourteen (*Life 1*, 330–1), Yeats, her mother's long-time suitor, assumed a paternal role. Iseult's need for a familial anchor was exacerbated by the fact that her mother – whom she called Amour (or Moura outside the family) – called her 'a charming girl I had adopted' or 'an adopted niece' or a 'cousin.'[5] Yeats's paternal role was so strong that Gonne would eventually maintain that Yeats was Iseult's father, because, as Yeats put it in a letter to Gregory, 'she was full of my ideas' when Iseult was born.[6] The situation was clear to Iseult. In January 1918, after Yeats's marriage, she inquired, in a postscript, 'Isn't uncle nicer than father?'[7]

From an early stage, the relationship between Yeats and Iseult Gonne extended beyond the paternal. Iseult, who was raised in France and was, as Jeffares put it, '*serieuse*' (IG 212), found an intellectual companion in Yeats. Even when she was 'not quite fourteen,' Yeats was writing to Gregory that Iseult had declared the *Iliad* her favorite book and that they agreed about plays, Iseult liking *Julius Caesar* and Goethe's *Iphigenia*. There is a third thread in the relationship: Yeats notes that '[s]he is tall, very tall & slight, & will be very beautiful I think.'[8] The Muse in Iseult had already begun to emerge. Ella Young recounts that, when Iseult was 'a beautiful dark-eyed dark-haired girl of twelve or thirteen,' Yeats, while visiting Paris, came to the house daily, instructing Iseult in art, poetry, and literature, and 'teaching her to chant verse as he thinks it should be chanted.'[9] Thoughts of Florence Farr could not have been far away. As Young reports, Yeats was 'desirous of chanting verse to the sound of a plangent string, a note now and then for accompaniment or emphasis.' *(Id.)* There was more than a little rapport between pupil and teacher. During a visit in 1910, when she was not quite 16, Iseult suggested that Yeats marry her. Yeats declined, citing too much Mars in her horoscope.[10] The seriousness and beauty of the young Iseult coalesce in a concise report of the occasion to Gregory that omits reference to the proposal, disclosing only that Iseult has 'taken to St. John of the Cross' and is 'very tall & pretty....'[11]

Yeats began formal construction of Iseult as object of desire in the poem 'Two Years Later' (*VP* 312), probably written in December 1913. In the interim since 'To a Child Dancing in the Wind,' Iseult had spent June through August 1913 in London with her aunt Kathleen, during which time Yeats introduced her to Rabindranath Tagore, and wrote to Tagore describing her as 'the start of a strong personality & of a very beautiful woman....'[12] Iseult had begun learning Bengali, taking lessons from Tagore's nephew, Divabrata Muckerjee (IG 227–8), and in September 1914, Yeats asked Tagore to consider giving Iseult and Muckerjee the translation rights to certain of his poems, telling Tagore that he thought 'very highly of Iseult's literary gift so much so that... I offered to edit a little book of prose poems of hers in English and French.'[13] 'I know that the girl has a delicate feeling for words despite her youth,' Yeats wrote, '& she has what may grow into very great literary talent.' Yeats's attraction to the beautiful Iseult during her visit to London did not escape the notice of Ezra Pound, who wrote to Dorothy Shakespear that 'the Eagle' was 'burning tapers to some new scion or scioness of the house of Gonne.' (EP-DS Letters 338) 'Two Years Later' defines Iseult as an object of desire who stands so squarely in the shoes of her mother that she will 'suffer as your mother suffered':

> Has no one said those daring
> Kind eyes should be more learn'd?
> Or warned you how despairing
> The moths are when they are burned?
> I could have warned you; but you are young,
> So we speak a different tongue.
>
> O you will take whatever's offered
> And dream that all the world's a friend,
> Suffer as your mother suffered,
> Be as broken in the end.
> But I am old and you are young,
> And I speak a barbarous tongue.

'On Woman (*VP* 345)', written in May 1914 (*WSC MM* 135), provides a glimpse of Yeats's state of mind as he began to construct Iseult into his Muse. A prose draft of the poem reflects the intensity of his longing for a woman in whom 'our minds and our bodies [might] find rest.' (*Id.* 429) He prays 'O God, grant... for my gift... that I shall love some woman so that every passion, pity, cruel desire, the affection that is full of tears, the abasement as before an image in a savage tent, hatred even it may be, shall find its prey.' (*Id.*) The poem itself first addresses the poet's hope that his Muse, unlike Maud Gonne, will be someone with whom he can enjoy the supportive conversational rapport he was finding with Iseult:

> May God be praised for woman
> That gives up all her mind,
> A man may find in no man
> A friendship of her kind
> That covers all he has brought
> As with her flesh and bone,
> Nor quarrels with a thought
> Because it is not her own.

> Though pedantry denies,
> It's plain the Bible means
> That Solomon grew wise
> While talking with his queens, . . .

The second part of the poem yearns for the kind of sexual satisfaction Yeats never found more than fleetingly with Maud Gonne, the passion of Solomon and Sheba, the

> Harshness of their desire
> That made them stretch and yawn,
> Pleasure that comes with sleep,
> Shudder that made them one.

Vendler, perhaps proleptically, suggests that 'On Woman,' which uses the Solomon and Sheba construct that Yeats would later apply to George Yeats after his marriage, was written to George Hyde-Lees. (Secret Discipline 188) Saddlemeyer takes the same view, explaining the fact that 'On Woman' predates Yeats's marriage by more than three years by noting that Yeats was attending seances with George in the period when this poem was written. (BG 188) However, Jeffares, presumably based on conversations with Mrs. Yeats, says definitively that the poem 'was not written to Mrs. Yeats.' (NC 152) Perhaps Yeats, who wrote to Gregory in October 1917 that 'I have always believed that the chief happiness & favour of my life has been the nobility of three or four woman friends,'[14] had more than one woman in mind. That Iseult was one of them seems apparent from the steady progress of Yeats's relationship with her in terms of both aspects of the poem's praise of woman.

Yeats's desire to fashion Iseult into her mother's successor is explicit in 'To a Young Girl' (*VP* 336), written in May 1915. It opens with a salutation Yeats reserved for his most intimate addressees, and then finds in Iseult the same excitement he had celebrated in her mother in 'A Memory of Youth':

> My dear, my dear, I know
> More than another
> What makes your heart beat so;
> Not even your own mother
> Can know it as I know,
> Who broke my heart for her
> When the wild thought,
> That she denies

> And has forgot,
> Set all her blood astir
> And glittered in her eyes.

The prospect of repeating his pursuit of the unattainable Maud Gonne with her daughter was well calculated to arouse in Yeats the feeling that Freud describes as 'the uncanny,' an emotion stirred by a 'factor of involuntary repetition which surrounds what would otherwise be innocent enough with an uncanny atmosphere, and forces upon us the idea of something fateful and inescapable....'[15] The profound unease in Yeats's psyche as to the role being played by Iseult is reflected in 'Presences' (*VP* 358), written in November 1915, at the beginning of the period Bloom characterizes as the most significant in Yeats's imaginative life. (*WSC MM* 205) The poem tells a fascinating tale of an experience 'so strange that it seemed/As if the hair stood up on my head.' The triggering event was a dream in which three women who knew more than a little about his pursuit of the Muse – indeed, they had read all he had rhymed of 'that monstrous thing/Returned and yet unrequited love' – '[c]limbed up my creaking stair' and hovered about the poet's room '[i]n rustle of lace or silken stuff' until he heard their hearts beating. Yeats's characterization of the core concept of courtly love – 'Returned and yet unrequited love' – as monstrous was carefully considered. He called it 'curst' or 'cursed' through several drafts, before settling on 'monstrous.' (*WSC MM* 204–9) The creaking stair that announces the arrival of the nocturnal Presences, forerunners of the Furies who will climb the stairs to Dorothy Wellesley's bedroom in 'To Dorothy Wellesley' (*VP* 579), is reminiscent of the 'heavy tread' of the nighttime visitor heard by the child in E. T. A. Hoffmann's story, 'The Sand-Man,' that Freud regarded as a classic example of the uncanny. (*The Uncanny* at 227) The three Presences are indistinguishable from one another until the last three lines of the poem. For example, the poet hears their hearts beating, but they all seem to beat alike, and there is no difference from one to another in their rustling lace or silken stuff. Even at the end of the poem, the differentiation amongst the three Presences is described in terms of generic categories of feminine presence, rather than qualities specific to a particular individual:

> One is a harlot, and one a child
> That never looked upon man with desire,
> And one, it may be, a queen.

The generic nature of the Presences suggests that, like the Presences in 'Among School Children' (*VP* 443), they are Platonic forms, albeit forms that bear biographical traces of Yeats's Muses incarnate. The presence of 'a queen' in the trio of inspiring Presences is no surprise. Queen, lady, priestess, goddess are traditional guises of the Muse. The 'child' reference bespeaks Yeats's continuing effort to characterize Iseult as younger, and less of a sexual presence, than she was. The 'harlot' Presence is, at least initially, surprising, and perhaps it is surprise that has led to suggestions that the word refers to a particular individual, rather than a generic aspect of the Muse. Jeffares suggested that the word referred to Mabel Dickinson. (*NC* 159) Although the Dickinson pregnancy scare (see Chapter 3) still rankled,[16] there is no reason to single out Dickinson as the unique face behind the word 'harlot' in 'Presences.'

Another possible candidate for the role of harlot is Alick Schepeler, long-time mistress of Augustus John and the model for his *La Seraphita*. Yeats was sufficiently involved with Schepeler in the period leading up to the composition of 'Presences' that he wrote her in September 1915 of a dream in which 'I was paying devoted but anxious & rather distant attention to an entire stranger – my dread being that she might be on the edge of that infirmity we spoke of & my fear, which you attributed to the vanity of man.' (*CL InteLex* 2763) Schepeler attended a number of Yeats's Mondays in his rooms in Woburn Buildings in the period before and after the composition of 'Presences,' and, as Foster suggests, may be the 'lady in the white bath-robe' sitting in the 'great chair/ [b]etween the two indolent candles' in Pound's 'Albâtre.' (*Life 2*, 30) John's biographer, Michael Holroyd, concludes that Schepeler's 'mind was a polished vacuum where the imagination of the artist was free to roam unimpeded,' a quality that seemed to elicit visual art from John.[17] She did not, however, provide the exchange of ideas that Yeats required in his Muses, and is not identifiable in his poetry. There is no reason to think that 'Presences' refers to her as a harlot.

The term 'harlot' in 'Presences' is better understood as a generic quality of the Muse. This usage accords with the traditional belief, noted by Bloom without particular reference to Yeats, that 'the Muse is mother and harlot at once' because she presides at the birth of a poem but 'has whored with many before.'[18] Bloom suggests that the fusion of mother and harlot in the 'wholeness of the poet's imagination' is an instance of Freud's remark that 'a pressing desire in the unconscious for some irreplaceable thing often resolves itself into an endless series in actuality,' a pattern, notes Bloom, 'particularly prevalent in the love life of most poets....' (*Id.*)

As noted in Chapter 1, the idea of the Muse as the eternal harlot Helen or Ennoia was familiar to Yeats from G. R. S. Mead's book on Simon Magus, which contained the early Church Father Irenaeus's account of how Simon identified a prostitute named Helena as 'the first conception (or Thought)..., the Mother of All....' (*Simon Magus* 8–9) This eternal feminine figure, according to Tertullianus, quoted in *Simon Magus*, 'transmigrate[s] from body to body, in the extreme of dishonor... ticketed for hire.' (*Id.* at 11) Moreover, Yeats knew from Flaubert's *The Temptation of Saint Antony* that this Ennoia figure had many names, including Helen of Troy, but 'really is the Moon.'[19] Warwick Gould and Deirdre Toomey, in their exhaustively annotated edition of Yeats's *Mythologies,* point out that the idea of the eternal harlot, as recounted by Flaubert and Mead, lies behind Yeats's story *The Adoration of The Magi*, in which the voice of a harlot is the source of the wisdom that would 'so transform the world that another Leda would open her knees to the swan, another Achilles beleaguer Troy.'[20] In his 1909 diary, Yeats explored the idea of Simon Magus and Helena in a way that anticipates the notion he would later develop in an essay dedicated to Iseult that a poet finds his Muse in his anti-self. In his diary, he posits that there 'is an astrological sense in which a man's wife or sweetheart is always an Eve made from a rib of his body' and that 'a man may find the evil of his horoscope in a woman, and in rescuing her from her own self may conquer his own evil, as with Simon Magus who married a harlot.' (*Au* 480–1)

Yeats applied these ideas to the concept of the Muse in the preface to *A Vision*, saying that 'Muses resemble women who creep out at night and give themselves to unknown sailors and return to talk of Chinese porcelain –... virginity renews itself like the moon....' (*AVB* 24) He put the notion of the Muse as harlot more simply in The Death of Cuchulain, where the tale he tells is one 'the harlot/Sang to the beggarman.' (*VPl* 1063) In short, the notion of the Muse as harlot – unreliable and prone to shift her favor to a rival – was part of the fabric of Yeats's thought. As he recognized the emergence of the Muse in a young woman who regarded him as something of a father figure, there must have been enormous pressure to separate her childhood from her Musedom. Thus, 'Presences' bifurcates Iseult into two categories: one a harlot, and one a child who never looked upon man with desire. The harlot attribution recognizes that Iseult is becoming a Muse, but the child attribution tries to deny it. The compartmentalization was so powerful that, years later, when Yeats enjoined poets to 'Call the Muses Home' in 'Those Images,' the harlot and the child would still be two separate elements of the five that 'make the Muses sing':

> Seek those images
> That constitute the wild,
> The lion and the virgin,
> The harlot and the child.
>
> Find in middle air
> An eagle on the wing,
> Recognize the five
> That make the Muses sing.   (*VP* 600)

Iseult shares three of the attributes of the five that 'make the Muses sing': she is child, emerging harlot-like Muse and, so Yeats insists, virgin. Her mother, at one time or another, had manifested traits of all five and contemporaneously displayed aspects of four. As Muse, she is a harlot. In 'Presences' itself, Yeats remembers 'What eagle look still shows' in her once-virginal presence, and in 'Against Unworthy Praise,' she is '[h]alf lion, half child' (*VP* 260).

Jeffares glossed 'Those Images' with the final passage of Yeats's 'An Introduction for My Plays,' in which he tells of an Indian tale in which certain men asked 'the greatest of sages' to identify his 'Masters,' and he replied: 'The wind and the harlot, the virgin and the child, the lion and the eagle.' (*E&I* 530) 'Presences' eliminates the wind from the sage's Masters, locates his 'five that make the Muses sing' in middle air, and limits itself to the five attributes manifested in the combination of Maud and Iseult Gonne. The conjunction of harlot and child remained at the core of Yeats's notion of the Muse. In 'Long-legged Fly,' written within a year of 'Those Images,' Helen, inspirer of both love and war, and linked with the harlot Helena by Simon Magus and Flaubert, is 'part woman, three parts a child.' (*VP* 617) Iseult-like, she dances in her moment of creativity while, '*Like a long-legged fly upon the stream/Her mind moves upon silence.*' (*Id.*) The notion behind 'Presences' of the conjunction of child and harlot in the Muse, although surprising at first glance, is a recurrent one in Yeats's thought.

Of course, the author of 'Presences' was well aware that the twenty-one-year-old Iseult was no childish stranger to looking upon man with desire. 'To a Young Girl,' written just a few months earlier, implies precisely the opposite, and Yeats's letter of the previous autumn to Tagore described Iseult as 'the start of a beautiful woman.' 'Presences' nonetheless insists on creating the category of an innocent child with whom Yeats could have a relationship consistent with the fact that, as he said in a letter to Gregory, 'Iseult has always been something like a daughter to me....'[21]

While emerging as Muse, Iseult continued to pursue her *serieuse* intellectual interests and simultaneously tried to find her way in the world. By the spring of 1916, she had written, at least in her mother's view, 'some really remarkable things,' including essays on d'Annunzio and Huysmans.[22] Yet she was no dilettante. She spent substantial time in 1914 and 1915 nursing wounded soldiers (IG 229) and took a job at an aviation association, a dull one, but, as she wryly observed, 'still earning ones life is a new impression though rather a minor one.'[23]

The year 1916 brought a deepening of Yeats's relationship with Iseult. They saw a good deal of each other when she visited London in May. (IG 230) On 21 May, Yeats advised Maud Gonne that Iseult was going to bring him to Colleville. 'She is quite a commanding person now,' he wrote, 'no longer a fanciful child.'[24] By 25 May, Yeats was reporting to Gregory that Iseult was 'making a little stir' and 'would be a reigning beauty in no time' if she lived in London.[25] The trip to Colleville was timely because John MacBride's execution by the British for his role in the Easter 1916 uprising reopened the question of Yeats's relationship to Maud Gonne. Yeats spent the summer of 1916 at Colleville with both Gonnes, where, among other things, he began writing 'Easter 1916,' which celebrates MacBride even though 'He had done most bitter wrong/To some who are near my heart.' (*VP* 393) 'Easter 1916' also articulates a thought about Maud Gonne that had previously been confined to prose, as, for example, in the passage from 'J.M. Synge and the Ireland of His Time' that Yeats wrote at Colleville in the summer of 1910. Then, he spoke of 'the morbid persistence of minds unsettled by some fixed idea... They no longer love, for only life is loved, and at last a generation is like an hysterical woman who will make unmeasured accusations and believe impossible things, because of some logical deduction from a solitary thought which has turned a portion of her mind to stone.' (*E&I* 313–14) 'Easter 1916' put it more simply: 'Too long a sacrifice/Can make a stone of the heart.' (*VP* 394) Although the poem is speaking generally of the 1916 rebels, Gonne, who shared their mindset, would not have missed the poem's implicit criticism of herself. Her response was unsurprising. 'No I don't like your poem,' she wrote upon reading the final version, 'it isn't worthy of you & above all it isn't worthy of the subject....'[26] Gonne insisted that 'sacrifice has never yet turned a heart to stone....' (*Id.*)

Yeats's conduct shows that he had concluded that his own long sacrifice as courtly lover needed a definitive conclusion. As he reported matter of factly to Gregory from Colleville in the summer of 1916, he 'asked Maud to marry me, a few days ago. She said that it would be bad for her work & mine, & that she was too old for me.'[27] Yeats seems not to have disputed either proposition. Instead, his letter moves quickly to Gonne's daughter: 'I am very much taken up with Iseult, not in the way of love or desire, but her joyous childhood absorbs my thought, & I hardly know what I feel.' Tellingly, he concludes, 'It makes Madame Gonne seem older than she is.'

Yeats and Iseult spent many hours walking and swimming at Colleville in the summer of 1916. Yeats's letter the following spring to the dying Florence Farr remarks, in a concluding comment, that his companion of the previous summer was 'now a tall beauty, very mystical & subtle.'[28] His letter to Gregory of 18 July 1916 shows him struggling to define Iseult. He has been looking over 'a kind of diary' she keeps in which she writes her prayer for 'quiet and seclusion, the company of one or two dear friends, a wild and beautiful bit of earth to live in I ask for no more.'[29] Her conversations with Yeats are serious. She has told him that she left the Catholic Church because, 'loving nature as I do, loving each thing for itself & not for its creator,' she found it impossible. Obviously, she is an adult. Yet, Yeats insists, 'she is in many things a willful child,' a comment explained, at least in part, by her insistence on smoking. Yeats goes on to report that she repented and handed over her cigarettes, which showed, he believed, 'that she considers me an elderly family friend, a position which I do not care to risk.' He tells Gregory that 'she has probably genius, at any rate, I have not met anybody of her age that has so delicate a gift,' but '[u]nhappily she has no confidence in herself.'

Not having heard from Gregory, Yeats writes again, testing the water further: 'I think by your silence that you may blame me for staying on here – & I know that my last letter was not quite candid – there are things it is easier to say.'[30] Iseult, he says, 'is really a child & when she trusts trusts comple[te]ly.' He relates that Iseult told him that when she was in Dublin four years ago she wished to marry him and this thought lasted two years and then she made up her mind that she was not in love and perhaps would fall in love with someone of her own age. 'I need hardly say that I told her that she might marry me if she would & that there were exceptional cases where even 30 years difference would not prevent happiness.' Her response was 'Ah if you were only a young boy,' and Yeats 'left it there & am now established not as husband not as father....' Iseult wrote to her cousin Thora Pilcher that Yeats 'lost no appetite' over her refusal (IGL 56), an insouciance probably explained by Yeats's failure to regard the refusal as definitive. His letter of 18 August to Gregory ruefully sums up the situation: 'as father, but as father only I have been a great success.'[31]

This bleak state of affairs is captured in the ironically titled 'Men Improve with the Years' (*VP* 329), written in July 1916. (*WSC MM* 65) The poet is 'Delighted to be but wise' with the wisdom that attends pursuit of a Muse, but finds himself to be a 'weather-worn, marble triton/Among the streams' inhabited by a much younger nymph:

> I am worn out with dreams;
> A weather-worn, marble triton
> Among the streams;
> And all day long I look
> Upon this lady's beauty
> As though I had found in a book
> A pictured beauty,
> Pleased to have filled the eyes
> Or the discerning ears,
> Delighted to be but wise,
> For men improve with the years;
> And yet, and yet,
> Is this my dream, or the truth?
> O would that we had met
> When I had my burning youth!
> But I grow old among dreams,
> A weather-worn, marble triton
> Among the streams.

The poet's wish that 'we had met/When I had my burning youth' seems a direct rejoinder to Iseult's response ('Ah if you were only a young boy') to his proposal.

Yeats's exasperation is apparent in his short letter to W.T. Horton of 8 September 1916: 'No Iseult is not my daughter & alas she knows our ages very well.'[32] In 'Lines written in Dejection' (*VP* 343), composed a few weeks later (*WSC MM* 125), Yeats sees the impasse with Iseult as blocking his access to the wisdom of the White Goddess, the 'heroic mother moon' who has vanished, leaving the poet to lament:

> When have I last looked on
> The round green eyes and the long wavering bodies
> Of the dark leopards of the moon?

Yeats's age was no obstacle, however, to his long-standing intellectual collaboration with Iseult, which found expression in the summer of 1916 in a joint project designed to replace the idea of an edition of Iseult's compositions, which she had rejected on the ground that admitting 'spectators into the soul' destroyed sincerity.[33] The new project involved a possible book by Iseult, and a lecture by Yeats at the Abbey, on the French poets... Peguy, Claudel, and Jammes.[34] Iseult's book never materialized, but their conversations are memorialized in the Epilogue to *Per Amica Silentia Lunae*, where Yeats, addressing Iseult in print, recounts how 'you read to me for the first time from Jammes a dialogue between a poet and a bird, that made us cry, and a whole volume of Peguy's *Mystere de la Charité de Jeanne d' Arc.*' (*Myth* 368)[35] Yeats's Epilogue notes how things have changed since he was Iseult's age and first read Mallarmé and Verlaine because, in the poets he and Iseult read, 'It was no longer the soul, self-moving and self-teaching – the magical soul – but Mother France and Mother Church.' Seemingly carried away by a sense of solidarity with Iseult, Yeats concludes the Epilogue by suggesting that he detects a similar pattern in his own thought: 'Have not my thoughts run through a like round, though I have not found my tradition in the Catholic Church, which was not the Church of my childhood, but where the tradition is, as I believe, more universal and ancient?' (*Myth* 368–9)

Iseult would have none of it. The fineness and independence of her mind are apparent in her letter commenting on a draft of the Epilogue, the last part of which, she says 'puzzled me extremely':

> For nowhere before in your work or in your thoughts
> as I know them have I discerned a sense of collectivity
> as in Peguy; I thought, on the contrary, that your mind
> moved more on the lines of the individual evolution, not
> quite as the 'soul self-moving and self teaching' of
> Villiers de Lisle Adam, but as the soul moving among,
> and sharing its gifts with the very few and the best like
> Huysmans or Pater.[36]

The outspoken Iseult must have held her own when their summertime conversation touched, as *Per Amica Silentia Lunae* suggests, on Dante – conversations that likely had resort to Iseult's Doré edition, of which she said Yeats was extremely fond. (Man and Poet 202[37]) Even allowing Yeats a poetic license, Iseult's knowledge of Dante was sufficient to engender his later description of her as 'A girl that knew all Dante once' in 'Why Should Not Old Men be Mad?' (*VP* 625) Iseult's comment on the Epilogue is of a piece with the tone and content of all of her letters to Yeats. They show a genuine intimacy, colored by her recognition of Yeats's status as mentor, but laced with her wit and sense of self. For example, Iseult's letter of 9 November 1916 reflects her understanding that she is Yeats's 'pupil,' but adds '(and your teacher??).'[38] The give and take apparent in the letters bears out the comment of Ezra Pound, who later became Iseult's lover (IG 242)[39] and memorialized her as one of his '*familiares*' in Canto CIV, that 'No one else so appreciated the spectacle of Unc Wm/as we two from the Non-prix Nobel angles.'[40] Although Yeats's letters to Iseult of this period have not survived, we know from her letters that he commented on her writing, and did so frankly. Iseult's letter of 29 March 1917 tells Yeats '[w]hat you said on those little fragments I send you, has been very useful to me....'[41] Apparently referring to his comments, she observes 'that a second rate archaïsme is a pretentious and suburban vice in style,' which 'I will try in future to avoid....' (*Id.*) In July 1917, she thanks Yeats 'for those criticisms you have made on my scribblings,' adding '[y]es they *are* bad.'[42] Iseult's letters also reflect her periodic bouts of 'great gloom'[43] and her sense of Yeats as 'one of the very few whose thought brings me a life giving power....' (*Id.*)

The range of Iseult's conversations with Yeats in the summer of 1916, and her sense of the finer points of Musedom are apparent in her letters to him in the following autumn and winter. For example, her letters show that she is reading his favorites, including Pater, Landor, Donne, Keats, and Shelley.[44] Their minds seem so intertwined that her commentary could sometimes be mistaken for that of her mentor. For example, '[o]nly the fool or the saint,' she wrote, 'can stand serene amid the discordance of modern civilization, for the first is part of it and the other stands above; but for the artist it seems to me it is more difficult....'[45] Striking another Yeatsian note, she observes that ''tis only in the country that things are pure and simple, for there they exist in their natural essence....' (*Id.*) Muse-like, she adds, with an enticing blend of absence and potential presence, 'it will be lovely to go and see you' at his tower in the Irish countryside. (*Id.*)

Her letters show a highly developed sense of the role of absence or unattainability in the construction of a Muse. In her 9 November 1916 letter, she chides Yeats that he 'cannot think' that absence will cause her to forget him: 'You know as well and better than I do that absence means nothing or rather means a very great deal.'[46] 'Tis in the presence of companionship,' she explains, 'that we take the rough block of appearance and melt it into the hot wax of thoughts and emotions and give it plastic life,' but it is absence that leads to enduring art. '[T]is absence,' she writes, 'that selects and purifie's and finally fixes and polishes the wax into imperishable shapes. Thus it is that now you are nearer to me than when we were together, for, from all our common memory I have kept but the best and I can shut myself up in a small but very dainty treasure room and play with my gold like a miser.' Iseult's letter encapsulates Yeats's own process of constructing herself and her mother into Muses, and anticipates the idea that animates Proust's great novel of memory. Proust most clearly articulates the idea in a passage in *Contre Sainte-Beuve* that was eventually rewritten into the climatic scene of *À La Recherche du Temps Perdu* in which the narrator relates his thoughts as he paused on the slightly uneven pavement of the baptistery of San Marco in Venice:

> I felt an invading happiness, I knew that I was going to be enriched by that purely personal thing, a past impression, a fragment of life in unsullied preservation (something we can only know in preservation, for while we live in it, it is not present in the memory, since other sensations accompany and smother it) which asked of it that it might be set free, that it might come and augment my stores of life and poetry.[47]

Iseult's letters also show her awareness that Muses are fashioned of illusions. Harking back to Yeats's work on his *Memoirs* the previous summer – which Yeats had told John Quinn left Iseult 'certainly interested & impressed'[48] – Iseult observes that '[w]hile you were writing your biography I was merely interested in those evocations of the past, but little did I think of the agony of it and of the courage it needs to settle memories into a definite order. You did it to give them a lasting life in the soul, but did you not at the same time,' she wonders – no doubt with reference to his account of meeting her mother and his relationship with her – 'have to give the last death stroke to many old pathetic illusions?'[49]

Iseult's letter of 2 October 1916, shows that she and Yeats had discussed his theory of the daimon, and suggests that she saw Yeats as her anti-self or daimon: 'I had many thoughts for you at Colleville during those days I seemed to get a kind of insight into your soul and seeing to all your needs, and the kind of mental answers I got were full of good cheer and boyancy yet somewhat stern as the voice of a daimon always is.'[50] The idea of an anti-self or mask had long been congenial to Yeats. For example, in the spring of 1914, he had written in a notebook that he had 'schemed out a poem, praying that somewhere upon some seashore or upon some mountain I should meet face to face with the divine image of myself. I tried to understand what it would be if the heart of that image lived completely within my heart, and the poetry full of instinct full of tenderness for all life it would enable me to write.'[51] He was thus disposed to be attentive when, at one of the many seances he attended, a spirit who identified himself as Leo Africanus, told him, through the automatic handwriting of the medium, that '[h]e was drawn to me because in life he had been all undoubting impulse... [and] I was doubting, conscientious and timid.'[52] Leo went on to say that he and Yeats were 'contrary' and that 'by association with me would be made not one but two perfected natures.' (*Id.*)

Yeats accepted Leo's invitation to write him a letter giving all his doubts about spiritual things 'and then to write a reply as if from him to me.' (*Id.*) Leo's message, as drafted for him by Yeats, knew its man: 'You are sympathetic,' Leo told Yeats, 'you meet many people, you discuss much, you must meet all their doubts as they arise, & so cannot break away into a life of your own as did Swedenborg, Boehme & Blake.' (*Id.* at 28)

Yeats never published his dialogue with Leo Africanus, but its thinking informs the fascinating 1917 essay on poetic creativity, *Per Amica Silentia Lunae*, that he dedicated to Iseult Gonne and described as recounting 'all that I had said or would have said' in 'those conversations' in Calvados during the summer of 1916. The book contains two essays and one poem, all of which address, in one way or another, the question that Yeats says '[a] poet, when he is growing old, will ask himself,' namely how can he keep his creativity alive. (*Myth* 342) This question is first explored in the poem, 'Ego Dominus Tuus' (*VP* 367), with which the volume opens. The poem's title – the message ('I am your master') of Love to Dante in *La Vita Nuova* – signals that Dante, who is described in the poem as '[t]he chief imagination of Christendom,' will play a central role in Yeats's theories of creativity. The form of the poem – a conversation between two aspects of the poet, named '*Hic*' (the *one*) and '*Ille*' (the other) – reflects the division in Yeats's mind as to how to answer the book's central question. *Ille* suggests an approach similar to that Yeats recorded in his notebook in the spring of 1914:

> By the help of an image
> I call to my own opposite, summon all
> That I have handled least, least looked upon.

To which *Hic* replies: 'And I would find myself and not an image.' *Hic* claims that Dante so utterly found himself that his hollow face is 'More plain to the mind's eye than any face/But that of Christ.' *Ille's* response implicitly argues that Dante's identity was derived from his pursuit of the unattainable Beatrice:

> And did he find himself
> Or was the hunger that had made it hollow
> A hunger for the apple on the bough
> Most out of reach?

Ille goes on to say that Dante succeeded as a poet because 'He set his chisel to the hardest stone,' and, driven out of Florence,

> To climb that stair and eat that bitter bread,
> He found the unpersuadable justice, he found
> The most exalted lady loved by a man.

Ille then concludes the poem with an echo of the spring 1914 passage in Yeats's notebook in which he writes of gaining access to creative inspiration by giving expression to his anti-self:

> I call to the mysterious one who yet
> Shall walk the wet sands by the edge of the stream
> And look most like me, being indeed my double,
> And prove of all imaginable things
> The most unlike, being my anti-self,
> And, standing by these characters, disclose
> All that I seek; and whisper it as though
> He were afraid the birds, who cry aloud
> Their momentary cries before it is dawn,
> Would carry it away to blasphemous men.

In the first of the two essays that follow the poem, Yeats asserts that he searches for creativity by 'invit[ing] a marmorean Muse' (*Myth* 325), thus evoking the idea of Dante setting his chisel to the hardest stone, and perhaps remembering his own image worshipping a marble statue in Olivia Shakespear's vision. In short, he seeks creativity by pursuing the unattainable or, at least, 'the apple on the bough/Most out of reach.'

Yeats's essay, which Bloom calls 'a kind of love letter and preparatory leave-taking' of Iseult (Bloom 198), contrasts his relationship to his 'marmorean Muse' with the way in which, after 'meeting men who are strange to me, and sometimes *even* after talking to women, I go over all I have said in gloom and disappointment' because of a tendency to overstate 'everything from a desire to vex or startle, from hostility that is but fear....' (*Myth* 325) (emphasis added) The situation is quite different when he searches for inspiration. Then, he says, echoing Iseult's letter of November 1916 in which she shuts herself up in a dainty treasure room to play with the gold of her memory, 'I shut my door and light the candle, [and] invite a marmorean Muse, an art where no thought or emotion has come to mind because another man has thought or felt something different, for now there must be no reaction, action only, and the world must move my heart but to the heart's discovery of itself....' (*Id.* 325)

Yeats conceptualizes this hunger for a marmorean Muse in terms of his theory of the anti-self – which he now calls the Daimon. He struggles to 'divine an analogy that evades the intellect' between Daimon and sweetheart. (*Id.* 336) The Petrarchan enmity implicit in the poet-Muse relationship is mirrored in the fact that the poet's Daimon is his opposite, and thus 'it may be,' adds Yeats, quoting Blake, '"sexual love", which is "founded upon spiritual hate" is an image of the warfare between man and Daimon; and I even wonder if there may not be some secret communion, some whispering in the dark between Daimon and sweetheart.' The Daimon, he suggests, 'would ever set us to the hardest work among those not impossible,' but pursuit of the all but impossible is fruitful for the poet because '[t]he poet finds and makes his mask in disappointment,' a corollary of the fact that '[t]he desire that is satisfied is not a great desire....' (*Id.* 336–7) Unsatisfied passion leads directly to poetry:

But the passions, when we know that they cannot find fulfillment, become vision; and a vision, whether we wake or sleep, prolongs its power by rhythm and pattern, the wheel where the world is butterfly.

(*Id.* 341) Desire for his Muse is a necessary precursor to the influx of inspiration from the great memory – the Anima Mundi of the second of *Per Amica*'s essays – but the desire must lead to weariness rather than satisfaction: 'we who are poets and artists...must go from desire to weariness and so to desire again, and live but for the moment when vision comes to our weariness like terrible lightning....' (*Id.* 340) Whereas Yeats had rationalized Maud Gonne's unattainability as necessary to her role as an iconic figure of Parnell-like solitude and a partner in an exemplary philosophical marriage, the essay that arose out of his conversations with Iseult speaks in terms of desire for the sake of unsatisfied desire – something akin to what Tony Tanner calls 'the indefinable and unconfinable pleasure of absence, a pleasure which is indistinguishable from pleasure deferred, or that deferral which is pleasure.'[53] With a hint of proto-Derrida in this enthronement of deferral at the heart of the writing process,[54] Yeats casts Iseult as a marmoream Muse who stimulates a desire that exists to be deferred.

In the course of concluding that desire and its deferral are essential components of inspiration, Yeats dismisses two celebrated Freudian theories as inadequate to explain his own creative process. Although he does not specifically refer to Freud's theory that creative literary works are sublimations of unsatisfied desires,[55] he instances John Synge as someone who found 'the fulfillment of his own life' in his dramatic creations, which he characterizes as the kind of literary work that is 'a compensation for some accident of health or circumstance' in the author's life. (*Myth* 327–8) He rejects any such model for his own work, citing the half-remembered sentence 'A hollow image of fulfilled desire' as descriptive of literature produced by wish fulfillment. (*Id.* 329) Seeking something more, Yeats looks to Dante, who wrote out of unfulfilled desire and found his inspiration both in longing for the absent Beatrice and in the 'struggle in his own heart with his unjust anger [at being driven out of Florence] and his lust....' (*Id.* 329–30) In other words, Dante needed to retain, even cultivate, his desire for Beatrice, rather than create literary works in which it was sublimated and fulfilled.

Yeats also concludes that the Freudian theory 'that certain dreams of the night...are the day's unfulfilled desire...' is inadequate to explain the workings of his marmorean Muse. (*Id.* 341)[56] He argues that the Freudians 'have only studied the breaking into dream of elements that have remained unsatisfied without purifying discouragement.' (*Id.*) The meaning of the 'purifying discouragement' that distinguishes Yeats's unsatisfied desires from those discussed by Freud is illuminated by the idea in Iseult Gonne's November 1916 letter that it is absence 'that selects and purifie's' experience. In other words, the poet's choice to defer the pleasure of attaining his Muse in favor of worship from afar purifies the experience and eliminates a sense of discouragement. This interpretation is reinforced by the echoes of Iseult's letter in Yeats's draft of his essay. Just as Iseult found that memory was a realm in which she could purify her experience as she fashioned it into imperishable shapes,

Yeats's draft asserts that the poetic faculty excludes – not, as in Freud's theory, a censored aspect of the dreams – but 'our ordinary life,' highlighting certain matters and omitting others, all the while 'mak[ing] all colours more fine and more intense.'[57]

Yeats's distinction of his theory from Freud's is also informed by an idea propounded to Yeats by his father in a letter of 2 February 1916, which is implicitly invoked in Yeats's observation in the draft of his essay that 'I did not get my thought from Freud but from my own observation, & letters from my father....' John Butler Yeats's letter posits that 'we are always dreaming' day and night, but 'we who are artists' have '*the cunning and the genius of poignant feeling*' to control the dreams of wakefulness and sleep 'so as to deprive them of their power to do mischief.'[58] The letters from both Iseult Gonne and John Butler Yeats elucidate the insistence of the published essay that the poet will assert control over his dreams and desires, hammering them into the stuff of poetry, but that, in order for the poet to act, he needs the bitterness of disappointment to engender poetic vision.

Against this background, Yeats poses the central question of his little book: 'A poet, when he is growing old, will ask himself if he cannot keep his mask and his vision without new bitterness, new disappointment.' (*Id.* 342) Taking Landor as his model, he suggests that there is no alternative to the 'bitter crust' of unrequited pursuit of the Muse.

Could he if he would, knowing how frail his vigour from youth up, copy Landor who lived loving and hating, ridiculous and unconquered, into extreme old age, all lost but the favour of his Muses?

> The Mother of the Muses, we are taught,
> Is Memory; she has left me; they remain,
> And shake my shoulder, urging me to sing.

This conclusion was fraught with peril for Yeats, both as man and poet, because it suggested that, in order to retain his access to poetic inspiration, he needed to relive his unsatisfied pursuit of Maud Gonne in what was promising to be a similarly unsatisfying pursuit of her daughter. Yeats intuited that doing so would require that he sacrifice himself to the White Goddess in return for her wisdom. Nonetheless, he is prepared, as he says, stealing a phrase from Virgil's account of the Greeks approaching Troy by the friendly quiet of the silent moon, to put himself to school 'where all things are seen: *A Tenedo tacitae per amica silentia lunae.*' (*Id.* 343)

Pursuit of Iseult was not without its attractions. In addition to stimulating unsatisfied desire, she also inspired by providing the atmosphere of supportive conversation between poet and irreverent pupil from which the essay emerged. This aspect of Iseult's Musedom is captured in 'Men Improve with the Years,' where Yeats says he is 'Pleased to have filled the eyes/Or the discerning ears,/Delighted to be but wise....' The poet's 'wisdom' has a double sense. He not only achieves the wisdom that attends pursuit of a Muse, but basks in the attributed wisdom implied by his Muse's 'discerning ears.' Iseult may thus be thought of as an instance of 'the pupil as Muse' phenomenon – a tradition at least as old as Plato's *Phaedrus* – in which the mentor finds inspiration in an erotic attachment to the pupil. Yeats expanded this tradition by locating his Muse-like pupil in the opposite sex and eliminating any age ceiling. Such a Muse could inspire by 'giv[ing] up all her mind,' as in 'On Woman,' to the exchanges between 'mind and delighted mind' celebrated in 'Friends.' This Muse attribute seems socially, rather than biologically, constructed because Iseult's mother, the quintessential Muse, would hardly fit the category of one who gave up all her mind to Yeatsian thinking. Iseult was a very different kind of Muse from her mother. Her mixture of great sexual attraction with the sympathetic yet irreverent attention of a pupil-teacher made her the Muse for which Yeats was longing in the prose draft of 'On Woman.'

Yeats's construct of Iseult as Muse is not vulnerable to criticism as either silent or stereotypical. Iseult's ideas find their way into *Per Amica Silentia Lunae* and, as discussed in the next chapter, her distinctively playful and questioning voice is clearly heard in 'Michael Robartes and the Dancer' (*VP* 385). She was a uniquely fascinating Muse. Nonetheless, her deeply-touching poem, 'The Shadow of Noon,' published in the *English Review* in April 1918, contends that being a Muse is but 'a strangely useless thing':

> I thought this book in my hand
> When walking by the water
> On the sun-delighted strand,
> This grey pictureless book,
> This book of weighty thought,
> This so elaborate book
> That some slow mind has wrought,
> A strangely useless thing.
>
> The hours of noon are done,
> My shadow is twice my length
> This violet afternoon

> As I in my indolence
> Tread on the delighted strand.
> And yet when all is said,
> The beauty of the place
> Seems like the words I read,
> A strangely useless thing.
>
> But even the sun-flecked blue
> And this elaborate book
> Have got a work to do:
> Not to be out of place,
> To be eager, solemn and gay,
> Solemn to run their race.
> I neither rule nor obey
> A strangely useless thing.[59]

Yeats disagreed. In fact, he seems to have admired her lyric sufficiently to borrow part of it. When he finally wrote a poem about Iseult that moved beyond exploration of his own emotions – the celebration of her beauty in the dramatic opening lyric of 'The Only Jealousy of Emer,' published in January 1919 (*OJE MM* xix) – his description of a woman's beauty as 'A strange, unserviceable thing' seems to reflect the influence of the refrain – 'A strangely useless thing' – of Iseult's poem.[60] The apparent borrowing from Iseult informs and animates Yeats's poem:

> A woman's beauty is like a white
> Frail bird, like a white sea-bird alone
> At daybreak after stormy night
> Between two furrows upon the ploughed land:
> A sudden storm, and it was thrown
> Between dark furrows upon the ploughed land.
> How many centuries spent
> The sedentary soul
> In toils of measurement
> Beyond eagle or mole,
> Beyond hearing or seeing,
> Or Archimedes' guess,
> To raise into being
> That loveliness?
>
> A strange, unserviceable thing,
> A fragile, exquisite, pale shell,
> That the vast troubled waters bring
> To the loud sands before day has broken.   (*VPl* 529–31)

The drafts of this lyric suggest that Yeats's psyche was so firmly imprinted with the image of Iseult's beauty that it continued to assert itself even after he thought he had completed the play. Although he had written Gregory on 14 January 1918 that he had finished his 'new Cuchulain play' (*CL InteLex* 3390), he wrote to Pound on 6 June 1918 that he could not send 'the "Only Jealousy" which will be the better of two more lyrics.' (*CL InteLex* 3447) The letter also says that he has 'in my head...a bundle of stories & dialogues concerning Michael Robartes.' A manuscript of such a dialogue includes language describing a woman's beauty as 'a frail exquisite shell.' (*YVP 4*, 128)[61] This language found its way into *The Only Jealousy of Emer* when the opening lyric was added to a revised draft of the play. (*OJE MM* xiii, 180–1) The revised draft also added language describing a woman's beauty as 'A fragile unserviceable thing,' which was then revised to 'A strange unserviceable thing,' a line that even more closely echoes Iseult's 'A strangely useless thing.' (*Id.*)

In addition to the compliment of imitation, Yeats showed his regard for Iseult's talent in his description of women of the lunar phase (fourteen), to which he and his wife's spirit communicators assigned Iseult:[62] '[w]hile seeming an image of softness and of quiet, she draws perpetually upon glass with a diamond.' (*AVB* 132) Yeats's note about 'The Only Jealousy of Emer' in *Four Plays for Dancers* adds another dimension to his understanding of Iseult's role as Muse by suggesting that her inspiring beauty was not simply a passive state, but the product of active virtue. Much of what will ultimately be published in *A Vision*, Yeats says, 'might be a commentary on Castiglione's saying that the physical beauty of woman is the spoil or monument of the victory of the soul, for physical beauty, only possible to subjective natures, is described as the result of emotional toil in past lives.'[63] The notion of Iseult's beauty as the product of emotional toil in prior incarnations is especially poignant in light of Yeats's knowledge that she was conceived in an effort to reincarnate her deceased brother – knowledge that reverberates beneath Yeats's question 'What wounds, what bloody press,/Dragged into being/ This loveliness?' (*VPl* 531)

It is easy to understand how, in the summer of 1917, Yeats was unable to escape his obsession for Iseult Gonne, even though pursuit of her lunar wisdom threatened destruction. He returned to Colleville to visit both Gonnes in August 1917. Letters to Gregory on 12 and 15 August reported that 'Iseult & I take long walks, & are as we were last year affectionate & intimate & she shows me many little signs of affection...', but he nonetheless concluded 'I dont think she will accept. She "has not the impulse".'[64]

Yeats's 8 September letter to Gregory from Paris, where he had accompanied the Gonnes *en route* to London, reflects that a law of diminishing returns was imposing itself on Yeats's pursuit of his Muse. Although, as he had said in the essay on creativity dedicated to Iseult, he needed some new bitterness and disappointment, he confessed to Gregory that he was 'just now too restless' to undertake the 'mass of work' he wanted 'to start on in Dublin and London if I can make some settlement in my life.'[65] He anticipates that '[a]s soon as I reach London I shall be in the midst of another crisis of my affairs, ... so you must not expect to get much good of me for a while.'

On 18 September, Yeats reported to Gregory from London that Iseult had cried on the journey from Paris '[b]ecause she was so ashamed "at being so selfish" in not wanting me to marry & so break her friendship with me. I need hardly say,' he added, 'she had said nothing to me of "not wanting".'[66] With more than a little understatement, he adds that 'as you can imagine life is a good deal at white heat.' He closes by noting that he 'would be glad of a letter of council.' However, his letter of the following day announces a startling decision. Borrowing a phrase from Florence Farr – who had told him three years earlier of her decision to be 'true of voice'[67] – he tells Gregory that 'I have decided to be what the Indian calls "true of voice".'[68] He will go to visit Mrs. Tucker and 'will ask her daughter to marry me.' (*Id.*) Mrs. Tucker's twenty-six-year-old daughter was George Hyde-Lees, whom Yeats had met through Olivia Shakespear in 1911, and with whom he might have discussed marriage in 1915 and in March 1917.[69] Apparently alluding to some such prior understanding, he adds, '[p]erhaps she is tired of the idea.' The awful tension in his mind is apparent in his idea of institutionalizing his ambivalence about Iseult by making clear to Mrs. Tucker 'that I will still be friend & guardian to Iseult.'

The decision to break with his obsessive pursuit of mother and daughter Gonne marks a fundamental change in Yeats's relationship to his Muse. He had long needed 'a hunger for the apple on the bough/Most out of reach' as a stimulus to creativity, but the prospect of a second generation of such pursuit was unnerving. He feared, as he said in a letter to Gregory, 'that I might become unhappy through a long vain courtship....'[70] In fact, after Yeats's death, Iseult told Ellmann she had considered 'keep[ing] Yeats about as her mother had done.' (M&M xi) On the other hand, as he recognized in the letter to Gregory, there was a risk that Iseult might accept. The letter to Gregory attributes that possibility to 'mere kindness and gratitude,' but Yeats knew that Iseult was dependent upon him to rescue her from what he described in a letter to Gregory as 'alarming moods – deep meloncholy & apathy,'[71] and he thus ran the risk that a successful courtship would plunge him into a whole new universe of responsibilities. Yeats seemed to be facing the specific 'uncanny effect' that Freud said often arises 'when the distinction between imagination and reality is effaced, as when something that we have hitherto regarded as imaginary appears before us in reality, or when a symbol takes over the full functions of the thing it symbolizes....' (*The Uncanny* at 244)

The strain was enormous. At times he 'thought I loved Iseult & would love to my lifes end....'[72] In a letter of 22 September, however, he told Gregory that 'I have not I think been in love with Iseult – I have been nearly mad with pity & it is difficult to distinguish between the two emotions perhaps.'[73] According to his 22 September letter, Iseult had told him that 'even if I loved you wildly (and I do not love) I would not marry you because it would distress Moura so deeply.' But the hesitation was not all on Iseult's side of the relationship. She told Ellmann that she had asked Yeats 'You wouldn't say you love me would you?' Being uncertain, Ellmann reports, 'he would not.' (M&M xi) Yeats had reached an impasse. He confessed to Gregory that be believed his 'mind was unhinged by strain,'[74] and that his decision to write to Mrs. Tucker was designed 'to end by a kind of suicide an emotional strain that had become unendurable....'[75] In sum, he needed to strike a death blow to his role as a courtly love poet. His poem 'The Living Beauty,' written in that fateful summer of 1917, recounts the life and death of his career as a pursuer of the marmorean Muse of unattainable beauty. (*WSC MM* 83) Recalling the passage in *Per Amica Silentia Lunae* where he invites 'a marmorean Muse,' the poem tells how he has pursued beauty 'cast out of a mould/In bronze, or that in dazzling marble appears,' but that he cannot pay the tribute of wild tears required by a living beauty:

> I bade, because the wick and oil are spent
> And frozen are the channels of the blood,
> My discontented heart to draw content
> From beauty that is cast out of a mould
> In bronze, or that in dazzling marble appears,
> Appears, but when we have gone is gone again,
> Being more indifferent to our solitude
> Than 'twere an apparition. O heart, we are old;
> The living beauty is for younger men:
> We cannot pay its tribute of wild tears.   (*VP* 333–4)

The pursuer of 'a marmorean Muse' was himself a 'marble triton' growing old among streams inhabited by a vibrant nymph.

'A Song' (*VP* 334), written in September 1917 (*WSC MM* 85), reflects the crisis in Yeats's career as a Muse poet. Perhaps harking back to 'Words,' he laments that, although he has 'many words,' he does not know 'What woman's satisfied,' and complains that his heart grows old. The poem's equation of the poet's words with a woman's satisfaction goes to the heart of the courtly lover's enterprise: his words are his sexual instrument. The centrality of Yeats's experiences as a lover to his poetic enterprise is apparent from the fact that his words fail because his heart rows old:

> I thought no more was needed
> Youth to prolong
> Than dumb-bell and foil
> To keep the body young.
> *O who could have foretold*
> *That the heart grows old?*
>
> Though I have many words,
> What woman's satisfied,
> I am no longer faint
> Because at her side?
> *O who could have foretold*
> *That the heart grows old?*
>
> I have not lost desire
> But the heart that I had;
> I thought 'twould burn my body
> Laid on the death-bed,
> *For who could have foretold*
> *That the heart grows old?* (*VP* 334)

The poet's 'post-suicide' prospects seemed bleak. In place of a Muse – that 'strange unserviceable thing' – he will, as he tells Gregory, 'be content if I find a friendly serviceable woman' who will suit his 'great longing for order, or routine....'[76] Perhaps, he tells Gregory, Iseult's view, conveyed through Maud, is correct: '"he is tired of Romance & the normal & ordinary is now to him the romantic".' (*Id.*) A comment in Yeats's letter of 13 October 1917 to Gregory suggests that Iseult knew her man: 'I am longing for all to be over', Yeats confided to Gregory, 'that a new life of work and common interest may give Georgie & myself one mind & drive away after a time these wild gust[s] of feeling.'

5. George and W.B. Yeats, 1920 (Bettmann/Corbis).

5
Out of a Medium's Mouth: George Hyde-Lees

Yeats's abrupt decision to seek refuge in marriage to George Hyde-Lees from the unbearable strain of pursuing the Muse embodied in Iseult Gonne posed a potentially lethal threat to his poetic enterprise. Because the essence of the courtly love poem was its praise of an unattainable woman, marriage and sexual satisfaction threatened to cut off the source of inspiration. Had he not just reaffirmed, in *Per Amica Silentia Lunae*, the necessity of some new Muse-engendered disappointment as a source of inspiration?

As so often before, Yeats found his way out of the inspirational impasse, but this time it took what he described in a letter to Gregory as 'something very like a miraculous intervention.' Just days after his marriage, Yeats found himself 'in great gloom,' feeling that he had 'betrayed three people' – no doubt having in mind Iseult and Maud Gonne, whom he had not married, and George, whom he had.[1] In this volatile mood, he dispatched a letter to Iseult, who, as he requested, burned it.[2] The talkative Yeats must have discussed the letter with George because his papers describe George's 'moment of greatest disquiet' as 'caused by me ... (through letter) & IG.' (*YVP 3*, 349) George told Richard Ellmann that she considered leaving her husband but, instead, sought to improve his mood by faking receipt of a consolatory message through automatic handwriting. (M&M xii-xiii) Suddenly, she maintained, a superior force took over, irresistibly guiding her hand to write words from beyond her mind. (*Id.*) Yeats's letter to Gregory describes his understanding of what happened: saying that 'she felt that something was to be written through her, George

> ... got a piece of paper, & talking to me all the while so that her thoughts would not effect what she wrote, wrote these words (which she did not understand) "with the bird" (Iseult) "all is well at heart. Your action was right for both but in London you mistook its meaning." (*Id.*)

Within half an hour of receiving this message, Yeats continued, my rheumatic pains & my neuralgia & my fatigue had gone and I was very happy. From being more miserable than I ever remember being since Maud Gonne's marriage I became extremely happy. That sense of happiness has lasted ever since. The misery produced two poems which I will send you presently to hide away for me – they are among the best I've done.

Seven years later, Yeats was ready to publish the two poems, which he merged into a single poem with two sections, 'Owen Aherne and his Dancers.' (*VP* 449) The first part tells how, 'when love had come unsought' during his walks with Iseult Gonne in Normandy, his heart could not bear the burden of fearing 'the hurt that she could give' and therefore went mad, causing him to run from his love's side:

> A strange thing surely that my Heart, when love had come unsought
> Upon the Norman upland or in that poplar shade,
> Should find no burden but itself and yet should be worn out.
> It could not bear that burden and therefore it went mad.
>   *   *
> It feared to give its love a hurt with all the tempest there;
> It feared the hurt that she could give and therefore it went mad.
>   *   *
> I ran, I ran, from my love's side because my Heart went mad.

In essence, the first section recounts what Yeats had told Gregory just prior to the marriage – that he could not stand the strain of repeating with Iseult his obsessive pursuit of her mother – and adds a note of self-blame for not having pursued Iseult more forcefully.

In the second section, the poet's heart borrows the automatic writing's use of the word 'bird,' and advises the poet to let 'the wild bird mate in the wild.' 'Now that your tongue cannot persuade the child till she mistake/ Her childish gratitude for love and match your fifty years,' the poet's heart bids him to 'let her choose a young man now. . . .' The most important part of the heart's message is its response to the poet's concern that his wife's 'heart would break to learn my thoughts are far away': '"Speak all your mind", my Heart sang out, "speak all your mind; who cares. . . ."'

Speak everything that was on his mind he did. Fascinated by the apparent receipt of messages from the spiritual world, Yeats pressed George into almost daily efforts to communicate his thoughts and questions to the variously named 'controls' whose messages came in the form of automatic writing. The information contained in the automatic writing must have seemed, at last, to validate Yeats's long-standing and 'unshakeable conviction...that the gates would open as they had opened for Blake, as they opened for Swedenborg, as they opened for Boehme...' to reveal the spiritual world at the heart of reality. (*Au* 254) He later wrote that the content of the 'disjointed sentences...was so exciting, sometimes so profound,' that he 'offered to spend what remained of life explaining and piecing together those scattered sentences.' The answer contained in George's automatic writing earmarked the influx from beyond Yeats's mind as the stuff of inspiration: '"No, we have come to give you metaphors for poetry".' (*AVB* 8) The sessions continued until March 1920, when the format switched to messages spoken by George during or just after sleep. The latter continued through the summer of 1922 and there were other sporadic communications thereafter. The messages are reflected in 3600 pages of automatic script and related documents.[3]

As startling as this experience may be to most readers, efforts to communicate with the spiritual world had long been central to Yeats's life. He had attended hundreds of seances over a period of many years, observed many experiments in automatic writing (*MYV 2*, xii), and attempted something similar with Leo Africanus. Moreover, he made extensive efforts in the spring and summer of 1913 to validate automatic writing generated by a young woman named Elizabeth Radcliffe, and wrote a manuscript supporting its authenticity.[4] Significantly, he was assisted in his efforts to validate Radcliffe's automatic writing by George Hyde-Lees, whom he had met, probably in 1911, through Olivia Shakespear, whose brother was married to George's mother. (*Life 1*, 437) As Olivia's daughter Dorothy wrote to her future husband, Ezra Pound, George was 'awfully intelligent' and '[a]larmingly intuitive' (EP-DS Letters 58), a perfect blending of faculties for joining Yeats in his long struggle to learn, as he asked at one of the early automatic writing sessions, 'What legitimate part has the supernatural in life?' (*YVP 1*, 99)

Yeats's early biographer Joseph Hone reported that George and Yeats met frequently during the five years following their acquaintance. (Hone 259) Like Yeats, George had been an art student who abandoned painting (*Life 2*, 95), but it is likely that their meetings centered around their shared interests in occult pursuits – a matter that, as Yeats later told George's mother, was 'a very flirtatious business.'[5] George's interests are reflected in her library, which reveals 'a wide interest in occult subjects, especially astrology which pre-dates her association with' Yeats. (*YL* xx) It is not surprising that, like Maud Gonne and Florence Farr before her, George became a member of the Golden Dawn, taking the Order name

'*Nemo Sciat*'(Let nobody know'). (*BG* 66) She was initiated in 1914 with Yeats as her sponsor. (*Life 2*, 106) There was much truth in Yeats's comment in a letter to John Quinn announcing his marriage that George was 'a deep student in all my subjects.'[6]

Given George's background, it is not surprising that Yeats sought her help in validating the Radcliffe automatic writing. He spent two long weekends as a guest of George and her mother in August 1913 during the midst of his work on the Radcliffe manuscript, following which George undertook research in support of the validity of the writing. (*Occult* at 140–1[7]) George's biographer, Ann Saddlemeyer, believes it is 'quite likely' that George read Yeats's manuscript. (*BG* 51) In sum, Yeats was inclined to be credulous of automatic writing, and George knew his credulity.

George's own automatic writing – often provided in response to highly leading questions posed by Yeats – covered a great variety of subjects, including Yeats's relationships with prior lovers, his cyclic theory of history, the psychological types assigned to the phases of the moon, the adventures of the soul after death, and a recurring inquiry into how the individual mind of the poet could access the storehouse of inspiration in the *Anima Mundi*.

The last subject was of profound interest to Yeats. In fact, the first recorded question of the automatic script picks up this question exactly where Yeats had left it at the end of *Per Amica Silentia Lunae*. In the pre-marriage essay, Yeats had recounted how he had 'always sought to bring my mind close to the ... general mind,' 'a vast luminous sea' of images that he characterized as 'a Great Memory passing on from generation to generation.' (*Myth* 343–6) Yeats's essay had identified his anti-self or *daimon* as the vehicle that could open the door to the riches of the Anima Mundi. In the first recorded questions of the automatic script, Yeats asked:

1. What is the relation between the Anima Mundi and the Antithetical Self?
2. What quality in the Anima Mundi compels that relationship?

The answer states that Anima Mundi

> ... is the purely instinctive & cosmic quality in man which seeks completion in its opposite which is sought by the subconscious self in anima mundi to use your own term while it is the conscious mind that makes the E[vil] P[ersona] in consciously seeking opposite & then emulating it.... (*YVP 1*, 65)

Under the tutelage of George's instructors, Yeats discovered the analogy that had eluded him in *Per Amica Silentia Lunae* between *daimon* and sweetheart. He was told that the 'moment of sexual union' is the locus of the 'supreme activity of the daimons,' (*YVP 2*, 507) the moment when he could receive some knowledge or power from beyond his mind. Yeats was thus likely to have been attentive to the instructors' insistence that the 'finish' or orgasm was essential because 'at End woman becomes male, male becomes female' – 'each receives masculinity or femininity from the other....' (*YVP 2*, 484) Thus instructed, Yeats summarized the *daimon*'s role as Muse in the first edition of *A Vision*. Asserting that a man's *daimon*, being of the opposite sex, 'may create a passion like that of sexual love,' he posited that the *daimon* 'is in possession of the entire dark of the mind,' but when, in the case of an 'antithetical' or subjective man like himself, 'the *Daimonic* mind is permitted to flow through the events of his life... and so to animate his *Creative Mind*,' the 'man becomes passionate and this passion makes the *Daimonic* thought luminous with its peculiar light – this is the object of the *Daimon* – and she so creates a very personal form of heroism or of poetry.' (*AVA* 27–8)

At bottom, Yeats was finding his Muse in his ability to interact with what he defined as his anti-self or *daimon* in a way that opened the door to the storehouse of creativity in a great memory, which he had long maintained 'is still the mother of the Muses, though men no longer believe in it.' (*E&I* 91) Although the *daimon* was sometimes referred to as 'another mind, or another part of our mind' (*AVA* 27), Yeats's ultimate sense that his *daimon* was part of his own psychic make-up is suggested by his assertion that '[t]he blessed spirits must be sought within the self which is common to all.' (*AVB* 22) In *The Trembling of the Veil* (1922), Yeats put it this way: '... revelation is from the self, but from that age-long memoried self that shapes the elaborate shell of the mollusc and the child in the womb, that teaches the birds to make their nest; and that genius is a crisis that joins that buried self for certain moments to our trivial daily mind.' (*Au* 272) With the help of George's communicators, Yeats had internalized the idea of the unattainable Muse in the notion of an antithetical feminine aspect of his own psyche, thus giving new life to the Greek idea of the Muse as a feminine voice speaking through a male poet.

The author of the messages that informed Yeats's definition of his *daimon* in terms of a sexual metaphor had a very clear answer to the question whether satisfaction of the poet's desire for his beloved would still the voice of inspiration. 'What is important,' George conveyed to her husband, in writing both automatic and, to protect the medium's eyes from its content, backwards, is 'that both the desire of the medium and her desire for your desire should be satisfied' because 'there cannot be intellectual *desire*... without *sexual & emotional* satisfaction' and 'without intellectual desire there is no force – *or* truth especially *truth* because truth is intensity.' (*YVP 2*, 487) In other words, whereas sexual fulfillment was inconsistent with the courtly lover's access to inspiration, it was the *sine qua non* of revelation from George's instructors.

The link between sexual satisfaction and mediumistic messages is hinted at in 'Solomon to Sheba' (*VP* 332), and driven home forcefully in 'Solomon and the Witch' (*VP* 387), both of which were written in March 1918.[8] The first of these poems presents a happy image of Solomonic Yeats kissing his Sheba as they talk '[a]ll day long,' going 'round and round/In the narrow theme of love,' presumably in conjunction with George's communicators. Yeats's satisfaction with the process is apparent in Solomon's assertion that:

> 'There's not a man or woman
> Born under the skies
> Dare match in learning with us two....'

In the latter poem, Sheba becomes a medium in the midst of intercourse with Solomon:

> 'Last night, where under the wild moon
> On grassy mattress I had laid me,
> Within my arms great Solomon,
> I suddenly cried out in a strange tongue
> Not his, not mine.'
>   Who understood
> Whatever has been said, sighed, sung,
> Howled, miau-d, barked, brayed, belled,
>   yelled, cried, crowed,
> Thereon replied: 'A cockerel
> Crew from a blossoming apple bough
> Three hundred years before the Fall,
> And never crew again till now,
> And would not now but that he thought,
> Chance being at one with Choice at last,
> All that the brigand apple brought
> And this foul world were dead at last....'

The gist of Sheba's message is that sexual union can restore the unity that existed before the Fall. The poem then plays upon the notion that lovers clasp each other in an effort to find eternity, with the interesting twist that the lovers in this poem find something different from what they expected in the bride-bed:

> 'He that crowed out eternity
> Thought to have crowed it in again.
> For though love has a spider's eye
> To find out some appropriate pain –
> Aye, though all passion's in the glance –
> For every nerve, and tests a lover
> With cruelties of Choice and Chance;
> And when at last that murder's over
> Maybe the bride-bed brings despair,
> For each an imagined image brings
> And finds a real image there;
> Yet the world ends when these two things,
> Though several, are a single light,
> When oil and wick are burned in one;
> Therefore a blessed moon last night
> Gave Sheba to her Solomon.'

Despite the lovers' consummation, and the receipt of a mediumistic message, eternity is not achieved. As Solomon reports, 'Yet the world stays.' Sheba's response anticipates the advice from George's instructors that Yeats should seek multiple orgasms to sustain his powers: 'it is like not taking enough exercise,' they warned, '& a long walk exhausts you.' (*YVP 2*, 349) In answer to Yeats's query whether 'you mean by only doing it once I will lose power of doing it twice,' George delivered an alarming message: 'Yes & then of doing it once.' (*Id.*) Sheba says it succinctly: 'O! Solomon! let us try again.' (*VP* 389)

The path to 'Solomon and the Witch' – where wife functions as Muse or *quasi*-Muse – was not an easy one, nor was the destination stable. The confusion in Yeats's mind as to his relationship with his Muse is reflected in the play, *The Only Jealousy of Emer*, on which he was working shortly after his marriage. On 3 November 1917, he wrote to Gregory that 'I have just begun a new Cuchulain play on the Noh model – I think it very dramatic & strange. It is "only Jealousy of Emer" story & much that I have felt lately seems coming in to it.'[9] Not only were Yeats's contemporaneous anxieties about his relationship to his Muse coming into his play, but, in a fascinating insight into his thinking, they were the subject of questions he posed during the automatic writing sessions with George.

The play centers around a choice that Cuchulain, Yeats's 'adopted alter ego,'[10] is required to make among three women who are readily identifiable as Muse, wife, and lover. As the play opens, Emer, Cuchulain's wife, is trying to recall the unconscious Cuchulain from apparent death, and seeks help from his mistress (Eithne Inguba) in the belief that Cuchulain's passion for Eithne might rouse him. Cuchulain, however, is in the otherworld, where he is fascinated by Fand, a woman of the Sidhe. Fand's identity as Muse is suggested by the facts that the Sidhe fish for men '[w]ith dreams upon the hook' (*VPl* 549), that she enthralls Cuchulain with a dance, and that she radiates the light of the moon: 'Who is it stands before me there,' Cuchulain asks,

> Shedding such light from limb and hair
> As when the moon, complete at last
> With every labouring crescent past,
> And lonely with extreme delight,
> Flings out upon the fifteenth night? (*VPl* 551)

Moreover, the automatic script confirms that Fand is of the Leanhaun Shee (*YVP 1*, 209), whom Yeats had identified in his collection of fairy and folk tales as the Gaelic Muse, noting that: '[t]he *Leanhaun Shee* (fairy mistress), seeks the love of mortals... The fairy lives on their life, and they waste away... She is the Gaelic muse, for she gives inspiration to those she persecutes....' (FFT 86) In other words, Fand is exactly the kind of indifferent Muse Yeats had pursued in Maud Gonne. Drafts of the play confirm Fand's status as a Platonic archetype of the Muse by referring to the theory in Plato's *Symposium* that humans were originally double persons of double sexuality 'like yolk &/white in the one egg' and that, after birth, 'always the half that has been born/seeks in many woman [sic] images of the half unborn....' (*OJE MM* 63) An earlier draft refers to the missing half as 'the true mistress', and declares that man, 'in all his loves/... can but find its image, or its symbol Spirit.' (*Id.* at 35)[11]

Cuchulain faces the choice whether to stay in the otherworld with Fand or to return to the world of the living, where both wife and mistress seek him. During the automatic writing, Yeats asked whether there was 'symbolism not apparent to me in my Cuchulain plays.' (*YVP 1*, 91) George's writing answered affirmatively: 'There is a symbolism of the growth of the soul – If you take certain symbols & use them on the medium prevision you may get information I can not give you.' (*Id.*) Convoluted messages from the script identify Emer as George and wife; Eithne as Iseult and passion; and Fand as Maud Gonne and love.[12] In a telling moment in the automatic writing sessions, Yeats asks 'who will C love?' 'I cannot tell you till you know yourself,' George wrote, 'and you do know I think perhaps unconsciously.' His next question – 'Emer?' – went unanswered. (*Id.* at 219)

In the play, Cuchulain dithers. About to embrace Fand in a symbolic kiss, he pauses at the memory of his wedding day with Emer, and is spared from having to make a definitive choice when Emer, learning that she can rescue Cuchulain by renouncing hope of happiness with him, does so, thus bringing him back to life. The ambiguity of the play's ending stands in sharp contrast to an earlier version in which Cuchulain's fate is not determined by Emer, but results from his deliberate choice to abandon Fand – something he is apparently unwilling to do in the final version of the play. (*OJE MM* 37) In sum, three months into his marriage, Yeats had written the core of a play whose Yeats-like hero has a lingering passion for a lover like Iseult Gonne and vacillates among her, a Muse in the image of Maud Gonne, and a selfless wife like George.

'The Double Vision of Michael Robartes' (*VP* 382), written between April and June 1918[13] shows how difficult it was for Yeats to eradicate his idea of Maud Gonne as the quintessential image of his Muse. The poem is constructed around two visions that appear to 'the mind's eye' as projections against the rock of Cashel, ancient site of the kings of Munster. The first vision is a puppet, with 'wire-jointed jaws and limbs of wood,' that has no will of its own but is '[o]bedient to some hidden magical breath.' In the second vision, 'a girl at play' dances with evident freedom between an all-knowing Sphinx and an all-loving Buddha.

The third section of the poem identifies the dancing girl as a woman the poet had previously glimpsed only in dreams that he could not remember, but which resulted in an influx 'into my meat' of

> A crazy juice that makes the pulses beat
> As though I had been undone
> By Homer's Paragon
>
> Who never gave the burning town a thought;
> To such a pitch of folly I am brought,
> Being caught between the pull
> Of the dark moon and the full,

> The commonness of thought and images
> That have the frenzy of our western seas.
> Thereon I made my moan,
> And after kissed a stone,
>
> And after that arranged it in a song
> Seeing that I, ignorant for so long,
> Had been rewarded thus
> In Cormac's ruined house.

The girl, who has 'outdanced thought', offers an escape from the determinism of the puppet in the first vision. Like Fand, she is an idealized or platonic image of the poet's Muse.[14] Once again, that image resembles Maud Gonne, successor to 'Homer's Paragon', Helen of Troy, but Yeats recognizes that he 'had been undone' by pursuit of Gonne who, as he said in, 'Subject for lyric,' was indifferent to his poems,[15] much as Helen 'never gave the burning town a thought.' He thus explains Gonne's functioning as Muse quite differently from the accounts of her role in his earlier verse. Whereas 'A Woman Homer Sung' (1910) tells how Gonne inspired him by bringing his thought '[t]o such a pitch' that his mind was open to a creative influx,[16] he now maintains that Gonne ultimately brought him to 'a pitch of folly' (VP 384), specifically, as he would later say in 'A Dialogue of Self and Soul' (VP 477) (1927),

> The folly that man does
> Or must suffer, if he woos
> A proud woman not kindred of his soul.

Moreover, the Muse of Michael Robartes' vision is more overtly sexual than the Muse of poems like 'The Arrow,' who penetrated the poet's consciousness with a 'wild thought' like an arrow.[17] Robartes' Muse stimulates the poet by means of 'a crazy juice that makes the pulses beat,' a notion perhaps influenced by Yeats's sexual experience, and frank conversation about sexual experience, with George. Even so, although Gonne the person no longer functions as Muse, her image, whether transmitted by a wild thought or a crazy juice, lingers in the poet's memory.

In 'Michael Robartes and the Dancer' (VP 385) (1918),[18] the dancer descends from the vision and has a conversation with the poet. This time, however, the dancer is not Maud Gonne, but her daughter, as is apparent in the poem's borrowing of the image of a beautiful woman's use of a 'mirror for a school' and the metaphor of the 'wages beauty gives' from the exhortation to Iseult not to be so free '[w]ith every Jack and Jill' in 'To a Young Beauty.' (*VP* 335)(1918)[19] Yeats's alter ego Robartes espouses the apparent meaning of the symbolic dancer in 'The Double Vision of Michael Robartes,' namely the advantages of 'outdanc-[ing] thought' and attaining the wisdom of the body:

> For what mere book can grant a knowledge
> With an impassioned gravity
> Appropriate to that beating breast,
> That vigorous thigh, that dreaming eye?
> And may the devil take the rest.

The dancer responds with the playfulness and independence of thought reflected in Iseult's Gonne's letters to Yeats:

> And must no beautiful woman be
> Learned like a man?

The two Robartes poems offer a revealing insight into Yeats's thinking about his Muse in the early stages of his marriage. His wife's automatic writing has rekindled his creativity, but his idea of the Muse is still animated by memories of Maud and Iseult Gonne. The process has been good for the poetry, producing a fascinating dialogue in which a strong feminine voice challenges male orthodoxy.

Two changes in Yeats's life played important roles in the re-ordering of his idea of the Muse as his marriage progressed. First, Yeats's satisfaction at establishing roots in his own home is apparent in 'Two Songs of a Fool' (*VP* 380), written in September 1918 as the Yeatses moved into the cottage adjoining the tower at Ballylee. (Kelly Chronology 200) The poem reflects its author's sense of self-possession as he at last becomes a landowner after years of wandering. He sees himself as protector of both George, the 'speckled cat', and Iseult, 'a tame hare.' As he resumes the role of Iseult's guardian and protector, her allure as nymphic Muse is eased back into the bottle. The taming of Iseult was nurtured in the automatic writing sessions, in which Yeats was encouraged to untie the 'knots' or 'complexes' associated with Iseult and to understand that both she and George needed his protection, one material and the other emotional. (*YVP 1*, 104–10)

'A Prayer for My Daughter' (*VP* 403) reflects the fundamental changes in Yeats's psyche attendant upon his becoming a father in February 1919. The poem implicitly asserts the poet's hope that his daughter will be more like George Yeats than Maud Gonne, a preference that follows from Yeats's shift away from the courtly love tradition's insistence on the incomparable beauty of the beloved. Gonne, victimized by 'intellectual hatred,' has regressed from being 'the loveliest woman born' to 'an old bellows full of angry wind.' Yeats concedes that his choice of Gonne as Muse had left his creativity 'dried up':

> My mind, because the minds that I have loved,
> The sort of beauty that I have approved,
> Prosper but little, has dried up of late,....

Yeats's concession that his own creativity has dried up because of his choice of Muse is tied to his recognition that he, too, is subject to the 'intellectual hatred' attributed to Gonne, even if only because, as he had told his journal in 1909, she taught him hate 'by kisses to a clown.' (*Mem* 145) On the other hand, he has been 'made wise' by a Muse who is 'not entirely beautiful':

> Hearts are not had as a gift but hearts are earned
> By those that are not entirely beautiful;
> Yet many, that have played the fool
> For beauty's very self, has charm made wise,
> And many a poor man that has roved,
> Loved and thought himself beloved,
> From a glad kindness cannot take his eyes.

This firm public rejection of Maud Gonne as Muse was fueled, at least in part, by automatic writing sessions in which George's communicators had no answer to Yeats's question 'why had I so wild a passion for MG?', but had a ready response to the question 'will MG attain a wisdom older than the serpent?' The response was definitive: 'She will attain to the wisdom of folly.' (*YVP 1*, 200, 233) Yeats's attitude was also affected by a severe quarrel with Gonne when she unexpectedly returned to Ireland in violation of a bar imposed by Britain because of her political activities. Fearing the effect of a likely police raid on his pregnant and influenza-stricken wife, Yeats denied Gonne admittance to the house she had loaned to him and George. (*Life 2*, 135) Gonne was not pleased.

Yeats's prayer for his daughter has been criticized for its wish that she 'think opinions are accursed' and its hope that she might 'live like some green laurel/Rooted in one dear perpetual place.' The best known example is that of Joyce Carol Oates, who has taken Yeats to task for wishing that his daughter become 'a vegetable, immobile, unthinking, placid, "hidden"...brainless and voiceless, *rooted*.'[20] In addition to ignoring the poem's use of simile, Oates does not consider that Yeats himself longed to flourish like a perpetually rooted tree and thought opinions were accursed for himself as well as for his daughter.

The vituperation directed toward Yeats's prayer that his daughter 'think opinions are accursed' may turn on a misunderstanding of the way in which he used the word opinion. His usage in *Memoirs* suggests that he accepted the distinction urged on him by his father between 'opinions' – defined as 'ideas to which men are attached polemically' and which 'are snatched up in the heat of controversy for the purpose of defence or offence' – and 'convictions,' which are 'ideas sought and maintained in the spirit of truth....'[21] Yeats was following this distinction years before his father's letter. He wrote in his journal in 1909 that '[o]pinion...is the enemy of the artist because it arms his uninspired moment against his inspiration.' (*Mem* 170)[22] Opinion too easily elides into fantasy and, as Yeats would say in 'Meditations in Time of Civil War,' the heart fed on fantasies grows 'brutal from the fare.' (*VP* 425) This is true for father and daughter alike. As Edna Longley put it, 'Yeats is not disputing women's right to think, but questioning the tyranny of dogma and resisting his own "temptations to controversy".'[23]

Similarly, rootedness had virtues for both father and daughter. 'A Prayer for my Daughter' was written as Yeats was about to move into his tower at Thoor Ballylee, an action he regarded as a 'rooting of mythology in the earth,' something that was essential to 'all my art theories.'[24] 'Rooting' had important connotations in Yeats's thinking about poetic inspiration. He pictured creativity, both for himself and his daughter, in terms of the self-delighting soul that, like the Plotinian universe, springs from its own principles, 'branching out like a tree from the root,' as Stephen MacKenna put it in the volume of Plotinus that Yeats read in 1918.[25] Thus, the attribute Oates seems to find most offensive – 'rooted' – has entirely positive, and gender-neutral, connotations for Yeats. Indeed, in 'The Municipal Gallery Revisited,' he lauds John Synge as 'that rooted man.' (*VP* 603) The rootedness of Synge and Gregory armed their creativity and civility against the straitjacket of opinion. (*Mem* 154,170) Rootedness can be desirable in a Muse as well as in a creative artist. Longley suggests that the daughter's 'desired qualities of *kindness* and *rootedness* conflate mother, daughter and Lady Gregory' into a 'trio of Muses' opposed to Maud and Iseult Gonne. (Political Identities 214) In terms of a Yeatsian definition of Muse that requires the erotic attraction that was absent in the case of Gregory, one might say that kindness and rootedness reflect the Gregory aspect of George Yeats, and that Yeats's praise of these qualities signals George's displacement of Maud and Iseult Gonne as Muse. Finally, Yeats's prayer for his daughter that 'In courtesy I'd have her chiefly learned' is not a call for diminished status, but a plea for the essential discipline that, like style in the arts, rids the soul of hate and replaces it with, as Yeats said in 'Poetry and Tradition,' 'the freedom of the well bred' – 'a continual deliberate self-delighting happiness.' (*E&I* 253) Courtesy in life and style in art are inextricably bound up in Yeats's notion of the courtly love poet. The qualities he wishes for his daughter are the same as he long sought for himself as a poet in the courtly love tradition. Even as he redefined his Muse to emphasize kindness and rootedness, he clung to the ameliorating courtesy of the courtly lover.

Two poems written in 1919 flow from Yeats's re-definition of his Muse and show him at pains to assure George that she should not be troubled by the fact that his image of the Muse nonetheless continues to be colored by past loves. In 'An Image from a Past Life' (*VP* 389), written in the summer of 1919 (*YL* 317), the poet tells his medium that, even when her mediumship elicits an image of one of his past lovers, she should have no fear:

> But why should you grow suddenly afraid
> And start – I at your shoulder –
> Imagining
> That any night could bring
> An image up, or anything
> Even to eyes that beauty had driven mad,
> But images to make me fonder?

So also, in 'Under Saturn' (*VP* 390), written in November 1919, the poet assures his wife and medium that lost love, while 'inseparable from my thought/Because I have no other youth,' will not prevent him from recognizing that she brought him two gifts he desperately needed when he sought refuge in her from his obsessive pursuit of Iseult Gonne – comfort and wisdom:

> Do not because this day I have grown saturnine
> Imagine that lost love, inseparable from my thought
> Because I have no other youth, can make me pine;
> For how should I forget the wisdom that you brought,
> The comfort that you made?

An earlier draft of this stanza is even more stark, speaking of 'the kindness that you have brought/Into my empty life....' (*MRD MM* 45) 'Under Saturn' is a reminder of the unusual path Yeats followed in finding his Muse through George. Having married her in search of 'order and routine' as a refuge from the passions traditionally associated with the courtly love poet, he nonetheless found not only comfort and kindness, but, as he says in 'Under Saturn', 'wisdom' – the traditional gift of the White Goddess.

These poems show Yeats experiencing what the philosophy being developed in the automatic writing sessions identifies as the fate of the *Daimonic* man of phase seventeen – the phase of Dante, Shelley and Yeats – who 'selects some object of desire..., some woman perhaps,' but when circumstance 'snatches away the object,' 'must substitute some new image of desire....' (*AVA* 76) Yeats's evolving recognition of the wisdom of his choice of George as the new image of desire is apparent in his explanation in 'Under Saturn' that lingering images of past loves are unavoidable and harmless *sequelae* of the only youth he had.

That forsaking obsessive pursuit of Maud and Iseult for marriage to George was the right move for Yeats's poetic enterprise is the clear message of 'The Gift of Harun Al-Rashid.' (*VP* 460) (1923) The poem is filled with praise for George. Unlike the courtly love poem, however, in which the beloved is praised for her beauty, George is praised primarily for her role as a medium who opened the door to communications from the spiritual world. The 'gift' of his bride, the poet asserts, 'gave what now/Can shake more blossom from autumnal chill/Than all my bursting springtime knew.' The poem, which appeared in the first edition of *A Vision* as part of an elaborate fictional explanation of the source of that amazing text, is also, as Warwick Gould points out, part of 'the penumbra of works [including *The Thousand And One Nights*] upon which [*A Vision*] acroamatically depends.'[26] The poem purports to recount events at the court of Harun Al-Rashid, a character in certain of Shahrazad's tales in *The Arabian Nights*. In the poem, a Yeats-like member of Al-Rashid's court named Kusta ben Luka tells how Al-Rashid offered him a bride from his harem. Kusta ben Luka replies with an answer that sounds a lot like the Yeats of the fall of 1917 who feared that obsessive pursuit of Iseult Gonne could result in his losing her to someone her own age. He is reluctant to marry because, he says, I

> [t]hink when I choose a bride I choose for ever;
> And if her eye should not grow bright for mine

> Or brighten only for some younger eye,
> My heart could never turn from daily ruin,
> Nor find a remedy.

Al-Rashid responds with a description of a prospective bride that effectively paints a portrait of George Hyde-Lees:

> 'But what if I
> Have lit upon a woman who so shares
> Your thirst for those old crabbed mysteries,
> So strains to look beyond our life, an eye
> That never knew that strain would scarce seem bright,
> And yet herself can seem youth's very fountain,
> Being all brimmed with life?'

George's deep learning in all of Yeats's subjects prepared her to play a central role in his search for inspiration. When the communicators spoke, Yeats was displaced from the role of the courtly poet in command of the situation and became the child to George's 'learned man', much as Kusta ben Luka's bride delivered 'Truths without father':

> A live-long hour
> She seemed the learned man and I the child;
> Truths without father came, truths that no book
> Of all the uncounted books that I have read,
> Nor thought out of her mind or mine begot,
> Self-born, high-born, and solitary truths....

Yeats had no hesitation in proclaiming – in answer to the question 'where got I that truth? – that the truth came 'Out of a medium's mouth.' (*VP* 439) Whereas Maud Gonne had claimed paternity of Yeats's poems, his poetry is now hitched to 'truths without father' discovered in a joint exploration of the spiritual world with his wife.

The poet of 'The Gift of Harun Al-Rashid' recognizes that his wife's love, and her confidence in his love, are essential to maintaining his link with the wisdom of spiritual revelation. As Kusta ben Luka puts it, the medium's 'voice has drawn/A quality of wisdom from her love's/ Particular quality.' All of the abstract doctrines of *A Vision* and the complicated diagrams it contains were dependent on the medium's love and were 'but a new expression of her body':

> The signs and shapes;
> All those abstractions that you fancied were
> From the great Treatise of Parmenides;

> All, all those gyres and cubes and midnight things
> Are but a new expression of her body
> Drunk with the bitter sweetness of her youth.
> And now my utmost mystery is out.
> A woman's beauty is a storm-tossed banner;
> Under it wisdom stands....

After a long detour through the courtly love poem, Yeats had returned to an understanding akin to that expressed in 'The Travail of Passion,' where he saw his sexual relationship with Olivia Shakespear as the door to the wisdom of the White Goddess. He now finds wisdom – referred to in the scripts as the 'Wisdom of Two' (*YVP 3*, 146) – beneath the 'storm-tossed banner' of George's beauty, a quality not recognized until the 188th line of the poem, where it is lauded less for itself than its role in the process of revealing a wisdom that, in a philosophy based on the phases of the moon, may fairly be regarded as a gift of the White Goddess.

George's wisdom finds its way into the poetry in various ways. Echoes of her frank conversation about sexual matters can be heard in the brash, feminine voices of 'Words for Music Perhaps.' (*VP* 507) George's influence can also be found in poems that, as Saddlemeyer puts it, 'arose out of the crucible of the script' (*BG* 200), such as 'The Phases of the Moon' (1918), which describes psychological types according to the phases of the moon. While this influence is important, the literal content of the script is not poetry. Johnson's observation on *Paradise Lost* – none would wish it longer[27] – could easily be applied to 'The Phases of the Moon.' 'The Second Coming' (*VP* 401) (1919) and 'Leda and the Swan' (*VP* 441) (1923) reflect both the influence of the automatic script and its limits. Both poems can be read as illustrations of *A Vision's* theory that time unfolds in a series of 2000 year cycles that are inaugurated by an influx of energy from outside history. Indeed, Yeats inserted 'Leda and the Swan' in the text of *A Vision* just prior to observing that 'I imagine the annunciation that founded Greece as made to Leda....' (*AVA* 181) According to the theory of *A Vision*, another influx from outside history occurred at the birth of Christ, and a third is presaged in 'The Second Coming,' in which a rough beast slouches towards Bethlehem to be born. Although these poems illustrate *A Vision's* theory of history, the influence of the automatic writing on their genesis should not be overstated. For one thing, Yeats had viewed history as a series of cycles long before the automatic writing that gave rise to *A Vision*. His early stories *Rosa Alchemica* and *The Adoration of the Magi*, for example, were based on his belief that '[o]ur civilization was about to reverse itself, or some new civilization about to be born from all that our age had rejected....'[28] Moreover, *Per Amica Silencia Lunae*, written before his marriage, asserted that moments of vision, 'whether in one man's life or in that of an age,' arrive in 'heaving circles' or 'winding arcs' that 'are mathematical, and that some in the world, or beyond the world, have foreknown the event and pricked upon the calendar the life-span of a Christ, a Buddha, a Napoleon: that every movement, in feeling or in thought, prepares in the dark by its own increasing clarity and confidence its own executioner.' (*Myth* 340)

Not only had Yeats articulated the core ideas of *A Vision* prior to George's elaboration of those ideas in the automatic script, but both 'Leda and the Swan' and 'The Second Coming' are products of profound imaginative achievement, rather than mere text for exposition. Yeats's note on 'Leda and the Swan' is instructive. He traces its origin to an effort to provide a poem to a political review that would express the need for 'some movement from above preceded by some violent annunciation.' (*VP* 828) 'My fancy', he wrote, 'began to play with Leda and the Swan for metaphor, and I began this poem; but as I wrote, bird and lady took such possession of the scene that all politics went out of it....' (*Id.*) Yeats's pinpointing of the moment when his fancy 'began to play' with Zeus's rape of Leda as a metaphor for the influx of divinity into history offers fascinating insight into the process by which the dry theories of *A Vision* were transmuted into gripping poetry. This revealing moment is an example of what T.R. Henn described as Yeats's 'curious clarity of vision which is not a clarity of detail, but rather of imaginative focus; a sense of the processional element in life and in history.'[29] Translating that clarity of vision into poetry also brought to bear both Yeats's ability to seize what Lessing, in the context of visual art, called the 'significant and fruitful' moment that 'gives free play to the imagination,'[30] and his genius for using poetic form to engage the reader in the significance and excitement of the moment.[31]

All of these elements come together in the arresting opening of 'Leda and the Swan':

> A sudden blow: the great wings beating still
> Above the staggering girl, her thighs caressed
> By the dark webs, her nape caught in his bill,
> He holds her helpless breast upon his breast.

The poem quickly moves across time and space to the events Yeats posits as consequences of the influx that founded Greece: the fall of Troy and the murder of Agamemnon:

> A shudder in the loins engenders there
> The broken wall, the burning roof and tower
> And Agamemnon dead.

The poem's closing question – 'Did she put on his knowledge with his power?' – is reminiscent of *Per Amica Silencia Lunae's* equation of moments of poetic vision with influxes of divinity into history. Indeed, it echoes the language Yeats used when he signaled his belief in inspiration by asking '[w]hen a man writes any work of genius, or invents some creative action, is it not because some knowledge or power has come into his mind from beyond his mind?' (*Au 272*)

Just as Yeats's fascination with the metaphor of 'Leda and the Swan' arose independently of the automatic writing, the 'rough beast' who 'slouches toward Bethlehem to be born' in 'The Second Coming' is a product of Yeats's imagination that preceded the automatic writing; it is traceable to his Golden Dawn experiments with symbols.[32] Like the Leda poem, 'The Second Coming' also begins with an arresting visual image that draws the reader into the imaginative life of the poem:

> Turning and turning in the widening gyre
> The falcon cannot hear the falconer;
> Things fall apart; the centre cannot hold;
> Meer anarchy is loosed upon the world,
> The blood-dimmed tide is loosed, and everywhere
> The ceremony of innocence is drowned....

'The Second Coming' also analogizes the new influx to the creative process, asserting that 'Surely some revelation is at hand.' And, like 'Leda and the Swan,' it ends with a question, wondering 'what rough beast, its hour come round at last,/Slouches towards Bethlehem to be born?'

In sum, both poems bear some relation to the script, but the script is not the source of their greatness, which arises out of the interplay between Yeats's imagination and his theory of history. The resulting poems reflect the prescience of Emerson's exhortation that the scholar of history is 'to esteem his own life the text, and books the commentary,' and that, '[t]hus compelled, the Muse of history will utter oracles, as never to those who do not respect themselves.'[33] Although there is no evidence that Yeats focused on this particular observation of Emerson, he was familiar with Emerson's work, and he knew, as he and Edwin Ellis wrote, that Blake wove 'historical incidents and names into mystical poetry... under the belief that he was following the highest example, and that "prophecy" was the right term for literature so conceived.' (*WWB 2* 152) The marriage of Yeats's imagination with his wife's oracular pronouncements produced a prophetic poetry.

The 'Double Vision of Michael Robartes' is another poem that at once echoes and transcends the automatic script.[34] Yeats conceded in a letter to Pound that the poem is 'too obscure,' but urged him to '[r]ead my symbol with patience – allowing your mind to go beyond the words to the symbol itself – for this symbol seems to me strange and beautiful. After all ones art is not the chief end of life but an accident in ones search for reality or rather perhaps ones method of search.'[35] As so often, Yeats's method of search is to seek inspiration and wisdom by writing a poem to or about a beautiful woman and finding his art as an accident of the search.

The automatic writing sessions became a necessary part of Yeats's search for reality, but caution should govern efforts to identify particular aspects of the writing as the source of poetic text. 'The Double Vision of Michael Robartes' is an interesting case study. The fact that the transcript of the automatic writing for 7 January 1919 contains a drawing of the rock of Cashel, where Michael Robartes experienced his visions, may have led both Ellmann and Jeffares to suppose that 'The Double Vision of Michael Robartes' was composed following the January 1919 automatic writing session.[36] However, subsequent scholarship has disclosed the existence of an April 1918 draft of the poem, and Yeats's letter to Pound referring to the poem in June 1918.[37] Moreover, George herself remembered that the poem was written at Glenmalure (*YL* 345), where the Yeatses stayed in March and April 1918. (Kelly Chronology 199) Thus, although the poem was intimately bound up with the automatic writing sessions, it appears that George's drawing was suggested by Yeats's poem rather than vice versa.

The drawing of Cashel has also been suggested as the source of two other poems. The drawing shows an eye, a hand, and a book, and George's handwriting refers to a butterfly and seems to draw an arrow toward the hand. Saddlemeyer points out that the automatic writing on 7 January 1919 specifically referenced the hand and eye and referred to a waterfall, a stag and a desire to grasp and a desire to see. She suggests that '[t]he scenarios provided on 7 January led to Willy's poem "Towards Break of Day"' (*VP* 398), which includes references to Yeats's dream of a waterfall that he longed to touch and his wife's dream of a stag. (*Id.*) Saddlemeyer also states that 'Another Song of a Fool' (*VP* 381) – which refers to a 'butterfly,/In the prison of my hands,' with 'learning in his eye' – was 'written in conjunction with' the 7 January 1919 automatic script and drawing. She thus concludes that 'Literally as well as symbolically, "George's ghosts" were providing metaphors for poetry.' (*BG* 199) However, according to George Yeats's recollection, 'Another Song of a Fool' was written in the summer of 1918 (*YL* 345) and 'Towards Break of Day' was written in December 1918 (*Id.* 317). Thus, the evidence suggests that, as in the case of 'The Double Vision of Michael Robartes,' the 7 January 1919 drawing and script were the product – rather than source – of the poems.

None of this diminishes George's contribution to Yeats's poetic enterprise. The principal significance of the automatic writing was not as the source of a particular word or image, but as the basis for Yeats's belief that direct communication from the spiritual world had confirmed the validity of his thinking about the relationship between the material and spiritual worlds and the nature of his creative process. In the introduction to *A Vision*, Yeats confesses that, prior to the experience on which the book was based, he 'knew no philosophy' because his father's 'convictions...had destroyed my confidence and driven me from speculation to the direct experience of the Mystics.' (*AVB* 12) Confirmation of his instincts by George's instructors, coupled with his own philosophical reading after the communications had ceased (*id.* at 12, 18–20), had given Yeats the sense of authority that underlies his poetry from the time he completed the first version of *A Vision* until his death.

Writing to Edmund Dulac in 1924, Yeats conceded that his book might mean nothing to others, but insisted that '[t]o me it means a last act of defence against the chaos of the world; & I hope to write for ten years out of my renewed security.'[38] Significantly, in the introduction to the first edition of *A Vision*, Yeats saw the importance of the experience that led to its writing as lying – not in the poems written during the automatic writing – but rather in the poems that it made possible: 'I am longing to put [*A Vision*] out of reach,' he wrote, 'that I may write the poetry it seems to have made possible.' (*AVA* xii) Implicit in Yeats's observation is a judgment likely to be shared by most students of his life, namely that the enormous expenditure of time and energy devoted to the automatic writing sessions could not be justified by the contemporaneously generated poetry. Fortunately, Yeats's hopes for the poetry that the automatic writing seemed to have made possible were fulfilled. By the time of the second version of 'A Vision' in 1937, Yeats was able to say '... I put *The Tower* and *The Winding Stair* into evidence to show that my poetry has gained in self-possession and power. I owe this change to an incredible experience' – namely George's automatic writing. (*AVB* 8)

Yeats's claim can be tested by measuring it against the 'evidence' of three of the iconic poems – 'The Tower,' 'Among School Children,' and 'Byzantium' – in the two volumes he cites. The evidence supports the claim. The poems reflect a 'self-possession and power' traceable to the automatic writing's confirmation of his belief in a spiritual world and his increased familiarity with a philosophical mode of thinking. Moreover, all three poems show Yeats employing the theory of creativity described in *A Vision*, in which he seeks inspiration by plumbing his own psyche until it opens the door to what he characterizes as a general mind. Thus, for example, in 'The Tower' (*VP* 409), standing 'upon the battlements,' he 'send[s] imagination forth' and calls up '[i]mages and memories.' Those images, 'in the Great Memory stored,' include his fictional character and doppelganger, Red Hanrahan, who, in Yeats's eponymous story, forsook a living woman to pursue a figure of the White Goddess, in whose awesome presence he was struck dumb. Yeats's poem follows his story by recounting how an ancient ruffian 'bewitched the cards' into a hare and a pack of hounds that led Hanrahan astray. However, now that Yeats has himself engaged in deep conversation with his wife's communicators, he professes an inability even to remember Hanrahan's destination:

> Hanrahan rose in frenzy there
> And followed up those baying creatures towards –
> O towards I have forgotten what – enough! (*VP* 412)

Yeats has no trouble remembering Hanrahan's 'horrible splendour of desire' that could open the pathway to the Muse, and thus enjoins Hanrahan to 'Bring up out of that deep considering mind' images for poetry. Consistent with Yeats's self-conception as a Muse poet, the recollected images have been 'lured by a softening eye,/ Or by a touch or a sight':

> Old lecher with a love on every wind,
> Bring up out of that deep considering mind
> All that you have discovered in the grave,

> For it is certain that you have
> Reckoned up every unforeknown, unseeing
> Plunge, lured by a softening eye,
> Or by a touch or a sigh,
> Into the labyrinth of another's being....

Unsurprisingly, the Yeats-Hanrahan foray into the collective mind has progressed through the labyrinth of a Muse's being, and brings the poet back to the still troublesome question whether his wife or the image of the courtly beloved is a more fruitful source of inspiration:

> Does the imagination dwell the most
> Upon a woman won or woman lost?

However, Yeats now locates this dilemma in the context of a philosophical meditation on the relation of life and death, and moves beyond his obsessions to constructing a 'Translunar Paradise,' which contains 'learned Italian things/And the proud stones of Greece,' but is fundamentally anchored, as appropriate for a Muse poet, in:

> Poet's imaginings
> And memories of love,
> Memories of the words of women....

In 'Among School Children' (*VP* 443), the poet again seeks inspiration in his own psyche, starting with a Muse-like image, in this case, Maud Gonne, who appears as a 'dream of a Ledaean body.' As he recalls Gonne's account of a childhood experience, his imagination calls up an image of Gonne's girlhood:

> And thereupon my heart is driven wild:
> She stands before me as a living child.

The confident and philosophically-tutored poet of 'Among School Children' moves from this image to the celebrated meditation on the relation of images to reality, dancer to dance. It is a short step from 'Among School Children' to 'Byzantium' (*VP* 497), where Yeats plunges deeply into the general mind and finds in the holy city of Byzantium an image for the process by which his imagination retrieves from the general mind 'Those images that yet/Fresh images beget....'

These examples support both Yeats's public claim as to the contribution of the automatic writing to his poetry and his private assertion in a letter to Olivia Shakespear that the 'great sense of abundance' driving his poetry was attributable to the fact that 'Georges ghosts have educated me.'[39]

George's contribution was essential. Was it the contribution of a Muse? The education imparted by George's ghosts was not the silent inward impulse the Muse traditionally provides to a particular poem, but oral or written information, usually more general than the Muse's poem-specific stimulus. In these respects, George functioned more in the mode of an oracle, like the Pythia at Delphi, than a Muse. Moreover, unlike the spontaneous influx of the Muse's inspiration, George's automatic writing responded to particular questions, much as the Pythias answered questions rather than instigating conversations.[40] The transcripts of the automatic script show that, although George's communicators would sometimes volunteer an opening statement, the sessions were dominated by Yeats's leading questions.[41] Also, just as the Pythias 'issued ambiguous oracles full of promises that the clients could create, yet believe that they had discovered,'[42] George's responses left great latitude for Yeats to believe that he was discovering his own creations.

Saddlemeyer makes the interesting suggestion that George was another of the Greeks' feminine inspirational voices – a Sibyl (*BG* 107–8) – but George differed from a Sibyl in two important ways. First, Sibyls normally 'spoke without being spoken to' and did not usually engage in dialogue (Road 113–15), while George was a classic Pythia who spoke in response to questions. Moreover, Sibyls 'spoke in their own person' (*Id.* at 113), whereas the Pythia spoke on behalf of Apollo. Although George's communicators often sounded a lot like George, the structure of the process was that George was conveying messages from others. The automatic script initially identified her as 'the medium' but, after the birth of the couple's first child, the communicators changed George's title to 'interpreter.' (*YVP 2*, 200) In either case, the messages were those of the 'unknown instructors.' Yeats himself so firmly clung to the idea of the unknown instructors that he wrote and published a quite extraordinary poem addressed directly to them. 'Gratitude to the Unknown Instructors,' published in 1932, expresses Yeats's thanks to the eponymous spirits for delivering on their undertaking to bring him metaphors for poetry: 'What they undertook to do/ They brought to pass.' (*VP* 505)

Was George also a Muse? It will be remembered that, as Yeats approached his marriage to George, prospects for the erotic attachment essential to Musedom were dubious. He was fleeing the emotional strain of his passion for Iseult Gonne in search of 'a friendly serviceable woman' who would suit his 'great longing for order, or routine....'[43] His several letters to his bride-to-be in the days leading up to their wedding reflect a valiant, but too-insistent, effort to introduce a note of *eros*. His letter of 4 October 1917 closes 'I kiss your hands,' but the romantic element of the preceding text is limited to the less than ardent observation that 'I grow more fond of you every time we meet....'[44] Three days later, he offers – not love – but 'gratitude & affection,' then closes with an ambiguous admonition not to think 'that because your body and your strong bones fill me with desire that I do not seek also the secret things of the soul.'[45] Still, the impetus to the erotic in these letters became a self-fulfilling prophecy: as the automatic writing went forward, Yeats concluded, as he said in the description of George's lunar phase (eighteen), '[p]erhaps now, and for the first time, the love of a living woman ("disillusionment" once accepted) . . . is an admitted aim.' (*AVA* 80) Under the unknown instructors' guidance, he immersed himself in the erotic element, merging the enabling sense of stability and order that he found in Gregory with the erotic attachment essential to a Muse.

George and her unknown instructors injected sufficient erotic fuel into the marriage that Yeats insisted on her status as Muse. She was the reason he could lay claim to the inspiration of a youthful Muse when, in 1924, he completed his essay about his receipt of the Nobel prize. Looking at his medal, which showed 'a young man listening to a Muse, who stands young and beautiful with a great lyre in her hand,' he thought: 'I was good-looking once like that young man, but my unpractised verse was full of infirmity, my Muse old as it were; and now I am old and rheumatic, and nothing to look at, but my Muse is young.' (*Au* 541) Moreover, in 'The Gift of Harun Al-Rashid,' he lauds George's surrogate as someone who could 'shake more blossom from autumnal chill/Than all my bursting springtime knew.'

Looking back from the vantage point of the introduction to the second version of *A Vision*, Yeats defined the incredible experience it recounts in terms that cast George as his Muse. Noting that '[s]ome will associate' automatic writing with 'popular spiritualism,' and will 'hate me for that association,' he insists that the experience was necessary to finding his Muse, noting that 'Muses resemble women who creep out at night and give themselves to unknown sailors . . . [and] sometimes form in those low haunts their most lasting attachments.' (*AVB* 24)

This was a Muse with a twist. Whereas the beloved of the courtly love poet was indifferent to his pursuit, George's sense of Yeats's love was essential to her functioning as medium. She had answered John Butler Yeats's prayer that '[i]f only the fates would send [Willie] a very affectionate wife who would insist on being visibly and audibly loved . . . she would be like Aaron's rod striking the rock in the desert.'[46] George's messages reminded Yeats that '[m]ediumship in this case arises because of certain sexual emotions – When those lack there is no mediumship.' (*YVP 2* 487) Moreover, while the courtly love poet pursues his Muse because of her beauty and overall distinction, Yeats pursued George precisely to stimulate her functioning as a medium. Thus, in 'The Gift of Harun Al-Rashid,' the poet worries that if his bride 'Dream that I love her only for the voice,' he might lose his own voice as poet:

> What if she lose her ignorance and so
> Dream that I love her only for the voice,
> That every gift and every word of praise
> Is but a payment for that midnight voice
> That is to age what milk is to a child?
> Were she to lose her love, because she had lost
> Her confidence in mine, or even lost
> Its first simplicity, love, voice and all,
> All my fine feathers would be plucked away
> And I left shivering.

Yeats's poem affirms George's status as Muse even as it recognizes her variation from the traditional model. Unlike the classic Muse, who is chosen by the poet without her consent, George was the originator of her role as the voice of inspiration and, as the poem recognizes, her continuing assent was necessary to the process.

With his unerring instinct for what was good for his poetry, and an eye as always on how posterity would regard him, Yeats, in those desperate days leading up to his marriage, had intuited how George would fit into his poetic enterprise. His letter to her of 7 October 1917 suggests that he had in mind his old fantasy of a union 'devoted to mystic truths,' like that of alchemists Nicholas and Pernella Flamel, as a means of finding a way to live in the national memory other than as chronicler of his barren pursuit of Maud Gonne: 'I will live for my work & your happiness & when we are dead our names shall be remembered – perhaps we shall become a part of the strange legendary life of this country.'[47] And so they were, each playing a part. Ellmann's twin observations in George's obituary in the 25 August 1968 *New York Times* sum it up: had Yeats died instead of marrying in 1917, 'he would have been known as an important minor poet'; his greatness stems from the 'great exfoliation of his talent' that followed his marriage and was a shared achievement with George.

6
In Search of the Muse: Memories of Love and Lyrics for Imaginary People

The corollary to Yeats's recognition that an erotic relationship with his wife was essential to her functioning as a medium was that, as Foster put it, 'with the disappearance of her role as spirit medium, the erotic dimension of their marriage...faded.' (*Life 2*, 351) By 1926, the marriage 'had subsided into quotidian domesticity.' *(Id.* 317)[1] Yeats's unease about the loss of his Muse is apparent in 'The Tower,' written in October 1925, where he laments that 'It seems that I must bid the Muse go pack,/Choose Plato and Plotinus for a friend....' (*VP* 409) However, a series of lyrics written in the spring and summer of 1926, 'A Man Young and Old' (*VP* 451), shows that Yeats followed a different course – one true to his fundamental predisposition toward finding the emotional content of his poems in his experiences as a lover. Knowing that the mother of the Muses is memory, he turned to memories of his past loves for inspiration. In the absence of a living Muse, the path followed in 'A Man Young and Old' was, as he said in the last of the series, 'natural to a man/That lives in memory....' (*VP* 459) By focusing on these 'memories of love,/Memories of the words of women,' Yeats re-kindled his imagination, and opened the door to the magnificent 'Sailing to Byzantium.'

Yeats's tendency to seek inspiration in his experiences as lover is apparent in his 25 May 1926 letter to Olivia Shakespear. 'We are at our Tower,' he writes, '& I am writing poetry as I always do here, & as always happens, no matter how I begin, it becomes love poetry before I am finished with it.' (*CL IntelLex* 4871) The first poems, he told Shakespear, expressed 'the wild regrets, for youth & love, of an old man,' and then elided into 'a series in which a woman speaks, first in youth, then in age.'[2] The second series was published in *The Winding Stair* as 'A Woman Young and Old.'

Six of the ten male lyrics arose out of memories of Maud Gonne. 'First Love' describes a priestess of the White Goddess – one 'nurtured like the sailing moon/In beauty's murderous brood' – who seemed to have a 'heart of flesh and blood' but actually had 'a heart of stone.' (*VP* 451) This slight poem closes the link left open in 'Easter 1916' where Gonne was not specifically identified with the proposition that 'Hearts with one purpose alone/Through summer and winter seem/Enchanted to a stone.' (*VP* 393) The remoteness of the White Goddess is again emphasized in 'Human Dignity' (*VP* 452), in which the object of the poet's love, like Gonne in 'Subject for a lyric,'[3] does not understand the poems written for her:

> Like the moon her kindness is,
> If kindness I may call
> What has no comprehension in't,
> But is the same for all
> As though my sorrow were a scene
> Upon a painted wall.

'His Memories' (*VP* 454) recounts – with the peacock-like boast later explained in 'His Wildness' (*VP* 458) – how the poet, at last, had become his Helen's lover:

> The first of all the tribe lay there
> And did such pleasure take –
> She who had brought great Hector down
> And put all Troy to wreck –
> That she cried into his ear,
> 'Strike me if I shriek.'

'The Friends of His Youth' (*VP* 455) pictures a poet whose voice has been destroyed, or at least has a 'crack in it.' The 'old Madge' who comes down the lane nursing a stone as if it were a child must be the stone-hearted Maud Gonne of 'Human Dignity' because nursing a stone echoes so clearly Yeats's comment, based on his experience with Gonne, that women 'give all to an opinion as if it were some terrible stone doll.' (*Au* 504) Poet and Muse have a happier experience in 'Summer and Spring' (*VP* 456), a poem that, like the contemporaneously written 'Among School Children,'[4] describes a moment of luminous sympathy with Gonne. In both poems, reminiscence about childhood evokes a sense that speaker and listener – like the original humans described in Plato's *Symposium* – were once a single being that was split at birth, leaving each hungering for reunion with the other. In 'Among School Children' (*VP* 443),

> ... it seemed that our two natures blent
> Into a sphere from youthful sympathy,
> Or else, to alter Plato's parable,
> Into the yolk and white of the one shell.

In 'Summer and Spring,' poet and Muse ' Knew that we'd halved a soul/ And fell the one in t'other's arms/That we might make it whole....' (*VP* 443) The latter poem adds the ironic note that the poet's other half had shared a similar experience with another lover.

Memories of Olivia Shakespear inspire three of the poems, one of which she shares with George Yeats. 'The Empty Cup' (*VP* 454) is the wistful poem that Yeats sent to Shakespear in draft form lamenting that he had '[h]ardly dared to wet his mouth' with the cup of Shakespear's beauty in his youth.[5] In the context of these 'wild regrets, for youth and love,' as Yeats called them in his letter to Shakespear, 'The Mermaid' (*VP* 452) appears to arise out of Yeats's memory of Shakespear's introducing him to sexual love, but his effectively drowning in the experience:

> A mermaid found a swimming lad,
> Picked him for her own,
> Pressed her body to his body,
> Laughed; and plunging down
> Forgot in cruel happiness
> That even lovers drown.

The inference that Shakespear is the mermaid is strengthened by Shakespear's similarity to Madge of 'The Secrets of the Old' (*VP* 457) who tells the poet 'old women's secrets' with the result that 'what had drowned a lover once/Sounds like an old song.'[6] The third person of the trio who know 'the secrets of the old' – called Margery in the poem – resembles George Yeats, both because of Yeats's pleasure in sharing gossipy stories with her[7] and because, just as George Yeats remained jealous of Olivia Shakespear,[8] 'Margery is stricken dumb/If thrown in Madge's way....'

'The Death of the Hare' (*VP* 453) is a fascinating expression of the Muse poet's recognition that the praise he uses to pursue his Muse threatens to destroy the qualities that inspire his pursuit:

> I have pointed out the yelling pack,
> The hare leap to the wood,
> And when I pass a compliment

> Rejoice as lover should
> At the drooping of an eye,
> At the mantling of the blood.
>
> Then suddenly my heart is wrung
> By her distracted air
> And I remember wildness lost
> And after, swept from there,
> Am set down standing in the wood
> At the death of the hare.

Yeats must have had in mind both Iseult Gonne and her mother. Iseult appears as a hare in 'Two Songs of a Fool' (*VP* 380) and her wildness is emphasized in 'Owen Aherne and his Dancers.' (*VP* 449) Nonetheless, Nicolas Grene points out that the poem echoes a passage in *Memoirs* in which, when Yeats thought Maud Gonne might accept his love, he paused at the thought that he would destroy the very thing he pursued:

> I had even as I watched her a sense of cruelty, as though I were a hunter taking captive some beautiful wild creature.... I noticed that one evening when I paid her some compliment her face was deeply tinted. (*Mem* 49–50)[9]

Yeats no doubt had this feeling about both mother and daughter Gonne. He said that the poem could be read to mean 'that the lover may, while loving, feel sympathy for his beloved's dread of captivity',[10] but that explanation, while useful, does not explain the poet's desolation at the hare's death. Although he had captured neither of the Gonnes, something in them had died. By January 1926, when the poem was written, Maud Gonne was long settled into a single life and Iseult's marriage to Francis Stuart was deeply troubled. She had been ill in 1925, and her daughter had died in infancy in 1921, prompting a chilling comment by Yeats to Gregory that '[p]erhaps it is well that a race of tragic women should die out.'[11] 'The Death of the Hare' is a lament for the apparent passing of the red-cheeked wildness of the Gonne line.

'His Wildness' (*VP* 458) closes this series by comparing the state of the poet's wildness to the 'wildness lost' of mother and daughter Gonne. His wildness survives, but is not promising. Various lovers – referred to generically as 'Peg and Meg' – except for Maud Gonne, who is clearly identified as 'Paris' love/That had so straight a back' – are 'gone away' and 'some that stay/Have changed their silk for sack.' Were the poet in their presence, he'd have nothing but 'a peacock cry',/For that is natural to a man/That lives in memory....' His poetic prospects are bleak:

> Being all alone I'd nurse a stone
> And sing it lullaby.

Without the inspiration of a Muse, Yeats is reduced to giving all to opinion – the enemy of inspiration – as if it were some stone doll – a depressing prospect for a would-be Muse poet. Thus, as he told Shakespear in a letter of 5 September 1926, he 'wrote a poem about Byzantium to recover my spirits.'[12] The drafts of 'Sailing to Byzantium' (*VP* 407) reveal that the background to the poem's abrupt beginning – 'That is no country for old men' – is the Muse poet's reverie, as reflected in 'A Man Young and Old', over past and lost love. The initial draft refers to 'those/Loves' that the poet has 'had in play' and those '[t]hat my soul loved', noting that '[f]or many loves have I taken off my clothes... but now I will off my body/& show I live on love' – something no one here has ever done, an enterprise that holds out the prospect that 'we shall be enfolded in our arms/& how should we ever grow weary.' (*Tower MM* 3) Further drafts speak of '[f]lying from nature/Towards Byzantium, (*id.* 15), the chief attraction of which is that it is a place of 'ageless beauty... [w]here nothing changes....' (*Id.* 17) There, '[t]he sensual stream being passed,' the poet shall 'take/ No shifting form of Natures fashioning/But such a form as Grecian/ goldsmiths make.' (*Id.* 25) In sum, the poem that, as Foster aptly puts it, represents Yeats's work 'at its most complex, hieratic, and eerily suggestive' (*Life 2*, 325), arose out of the ageing Muse poet's meditation on his bleak prospects as he and his loves grew old, and the resultant search for a love that would survive in a realm of ageless beauty beyond the sensual stream. The poem's origins are not obvious in the final text, but they lurk beneath the taut reference to how, being '[c]aught in that sensual music all neglect/Monuments of unageing intellect.' The poem's origins also animate the ageing man's depiction as '[a] tattered coat upon a stick, unless/Soul clap its hands and sing'; the lament for a heart 'sick with desire/And fastened to a dying animal'; and the poet's prayer that the sages of the holy city of the imagination become 'the singing-masters of my soul.'

Memories of past Muses helped to stoke the bitterness that, as Yeats had said in *Per Amica Silentia Lunae*, was a prerequisite to his creativity, but the bitterness functioned differently in this period of phantom Muses than it had when Yeats was developing the theories of *Per Amica* in supportive conversations with his pupil – Muse, Iseult Gonne. Then, creativity arose only 'the moment I cease to hate' (*Myth* 365), and the bitterness was resolved in the process of creating the poem. The bitterness behind *The Tower*, however, survived into the text of the poetry. Still, it had its uses. Writing to Olivia Shakespear in 1928, Yeats observed that '[r]e-reading THE TOWER I was astonished at its bitterness,' but insisted that the 'bitter-ness gave the book its power and it is the best book I have written.'[13]

One of the fruits of the bitterness engendered by meditation on lost Muses was the notion of the timeless Muse of the sages in the holy city of the imagination. Although this notion is readily apparent in the final text, the original draft's search for an eternal relationship with the poet's earthly beloved is not. This idea, however, was very much alive in the poet's mind. One of the lyrics that Yeats sent to Shakespear on 2 July 1926 uses the image of the soul taking its body off, which later appears in the first draft of 'Sailing to Byzantium,' as a basis for constructing a vision of an eternal sexual relation of soul to soul.[14] The woman old of 'A Last Confession' (*VP* 538) puts it this way:

> I gave what other women gave
> That stepped out of their clothes,
> But when this soul, its body off,
> Naked to naked goes,
> He it has found shall find therein
> What none other knows,
>
> And give his own and take his own
> And rule in his own right;
> And though it loved in misery
> Close and cling so tight,
> There's not a bird of day that dare
> Extinguish that delight.

Moreover, Yeats's letter of 27 October 1927 to Shakespear suggests that he thought the idea of his beloved becoming paradise itself was implicit in 'Sailing to Byzantium.' The letter tells how, just after he had completed that poem with its appeal, as he put it, 'to the saints "in the holy fire",' he asked a medium to give him 'a book test,' and was told to look for page 48 or 84 of the third book from the right on the bottom shelf of his study. The book turned out to be Blake's illustrations to Dante, plate 84 being 'Dante entering the Holy Fire' and plate 48 being 'The Serpent attacking Vanni Fucci,' which, as he learned by consulting Dante, was followed by Fucci's being burnt to ashes and then recreated from the ashes. After first making a pungent comment on the nature of inspiration – 'Certainly we suck always at the eternal dugs' – Yeats summarized this experience in terms of the way in which his poem of the artifice of eternity arose out of his reverie over his lost and ageing Muses: 'How well too it puts my own mood between spiritual excitement, & the sexual torture and the knowledge that they are some how inseparable!' Yeats goes on to illustrate this conclusion in terms of Dante and Beatrice in a way that exactly parallels the way in which his meditation on his earthly Muses led him into the artifice of eternity: 'It is the eyes of the Eart[h]ly Beatrice . . . that make[s] Dante risk the fire "like a child that is offered an apple".' Driving the point home, Yeats cites the fact that '[y]esterday as if my soul already foresaw todays discovery,' he had rewritten a poem of his youth, naming it 'The Countess Cathleen in Paradise,' in which 'the dancer Cathleen has become heaven itself.' (*CL InteLex* 5040)

The notion of a relationship with a living Muse that transcends the ageing process found more graphic expression as Yeats took further steps toward, as Samuel Hynes put it, 'becom[ing] his own Muse, by the extraordinary act of assuming a woman's private sexual identity as a poetic persona.'[15] This approach to re-energizing his poetic imagination, which began in the lyrics of 'A Woman Young and Old,' burst into full vigor in the Crazy Jane poems, certain of which were written following a lung hemorrhage in the fall of 1927, and others of which were written following a serious bout of Malta fever in late 1929 and early 1930. These illnesses could not but have exacerbated the anxiety reflected in 'A Man Young and Old' as to the future prospects of an ageing Muse-poet. Nonetheless, in an astonishing feat of *jujitsu*, Yeats managed to turn the tables so that, as he told Olivia Shakespear of the Crazy Jane poems, '[s]exual abstinence fed their fire–I was ill & yet full of desire. They some-times came out of the greatest mental excitement I am capable of.'[16]

Contemporaneously with writing certain of the Crazy Jane poems, Yeats was reading von Hügel's *The Mystical Element of Religion as Studied in St. Catherine of Geona and her Friends*, which argued for the essential goodness of the body and its ultimate reunion with the soul after death.[17] Von Hügel's insistence on the survival of the body – exemplified by a saint's body 'undecayed in tomb,/Bathed in miraculous oil,' as Yeats put it in Vacillation (*VP* 499) – spoke directly to Yeats's concern about his Muses who have 'gone away, and some that stay' having 'changed their silk for sack.' Instructed by von Hügel, Crazy Jane insists on various forms of post-death love involving both body and soul. She maintains that '*All things remain in God*', that 'Love is all/ Unsatisfied/That cannot take the whole/Body and soul', and that 'All could be known or shown/If Time were but gone.'[18]

Two poems written about the same time as the last of the Crazy Jane lyrics reflect Yeats's extraordinary assertion that his poetic imagination can restore and preserve his youthful Muses – 'summon back/All their wholesome strength' and 'Straighten aged knees.' The drafts of the poem from which these quotations are taken, 'The Results of Thought' (*VP* 504), show that the poem arose out of Yeats's meditation on what he perceived as the 'folly' of friends that led to 'wrecked lives,' and his own ability, after long years of thought, to summon them back 'from insanity.' (*WFM MM* 296–305) Although the earliest draft seems to focus on Maud Gonne – a 'woman dearer than ones self' (*id.* 297), the final poem refers to a broader group of 'the best-endowed, the elect,' and specifies 'Acquaintance; companion;/One dear brilliant woman,' who might fairly be taken to be respectively Constance Markiewicz – pictured as '[c]onspiring among the ignorant' in 'In Memory of Eva Gore-Booth and Con Markiewicz' (*VP* 475) – Maud Gonne, and Iseult Gonne – 'a girl that knew all Dante once.' The extraordinary thing about the poem is its author's conviction that he can 'shift Time's filthy load' and restore his Muses to their pristine purity:

> Acquaintance; companion
> One dear brilliant woman;
> The best-endowed, the elect,
> All by their youth undone,
> All, all, by that inhuman
> Bitter glory wrecked.
>
> But I have straightened out
> Ruin, wreck and wrack;
> I toiled long years and at length
> Came to so deep a thought
> I can summon back
> All their wholesome strength.
>
> What images are these
> That turn dull-eyed away,
> Or shift Time's filthy load,
> Hesitate or stay?
> What heads shake or nod?

The second poem, 'Quarrel in Old Age' (*VP* 503), focuses on Maud Gonne, and insists that she will continue to live in a realm where '[a]ll lives that has lived':

> Where had her sweetness gone?
> What fanatics invent
> In this blind bitter town,
> Fantasy or incident
> Not worth thinking of,
> Put her in rage.
> I had forgiven enough
> That had forgiven old age.
>
> All lives that has lived;
> So much is certain;
> Old sages were not deceived:
> Somewhere beyond the curtain
> Of distorting days
> Lives that lonely thing
> That shone before these eyes
> Targeted, trod like Spring.

The drafts of the poem make clear that Yeats is pursuing the idea that his Muse can transcend time. As one of the drafts puts it: 'Nothing can fade or die/That much is certain/Unless the sages lie....' (*WFM MM* 291). The Maud Gonne who 'shone before these eyes' and 'trod like Spring' will live '[s]omewhere beyond the curtain,' protected – as Yeats told a correspondent he meant by 'Targeted'[19] – from the onslaught of 'distorting days.'

The aura of omnipotence surrounding these lyrics of the summer and autumn of 1931 was punctured by the death of Augusta Gregory in May 1932. Writing in 1934, Yeats spoke of a barren 'imaginative life' following Gregory's death, and wondered if 'the subconscious drama that was my imaginative life end[ed] with' her death, but concluded that 'it was more likely that I had grown too old for poetry.'[20] Interestingly, although the loss of inspiration was real, the omnipotence of late 1931 was sufficiently potent that, only a month after Gregory's death, Yeats insisted on his own ability not only to recreate and renew his Muses but, as he claimed in 'Stream and Sun at Glendalough' (*VP* 506–7), to renew *himself*:

> Through intricate motions ran
> Stream and gliding sun
> And all my heart seemed gay:
> Some stupid thing that I had done
> Made my attention stray.
>
> Repentance keeps my heart impure;
> But what am I that dare
> Fancy that I can

> Better conduct myself or have more
> Sense than a common man?
>
> What motion of the sun or stream
> Or eyelid shot the gleam
> That pierced my body through?
> What made me live like these that seem
> Self-born, born anew?

Nonetheless, Yeats encountered a barren period. To overcome it, much as he had found inspiration by writing in the imaginary voice of Crazy Jane, he wrote 'the prose dialogue of *The King of the Great Clock Tower* that I might be forced to make lyrics for its imaginary people.' (*VP* 855–6) He elaborated on this explanation in a letter to Olivia Shakespear, saying he wrote the play 'that I might write lyrics out of dramatic ex-perience, all my personal experience having in some strange way come to an end.'[21] Significantly, the theme of the play Yeats wrote in search of inspiration was, as Helen Vendler has convincingly shown, the poet's relationship with his Muse as figured by a beautiful and remote woman.[22] However, Yeats could fuel his poetic engine on these old memories and imaginary people for only so long. More drastic measures would be required.

6. Margot Ruddock from *Ah, Sweet Dancer.*

7

A Foolish, Passionate Man: Margot Ruddock and Ethel Mannin

In April 1934, Yeats confided 'that for about three years... he had lost all inspiration and had been unable to write anything new.'[1] The recipient of this confidence was Dr. Norman Haire, a London surgeon and author of a book about the rejuvenation operation pioneered by Eugen Steinach in Vienna in 1918, where its recipients had included Sigmund Freud. The operation was no more than a vasectomy, but was widely believed to improve erotic performance and vitalize the entire body. Associating his loss of inspiration with an inability to have erections, (Second Puberty 7–8), Yeats evidently concluded that renewal of inspiration required a new encounter with the Muse – 'that dream of Eros which inspires art' (Croce 168) – and hoped that the Steinach operation would restore both sexual potency and inspiration.

Today there is a considerable, but not undisputed, body of learning that the Steinach operation had no physical effect on sexual performance.[2] Nonetheless, it had a sufficient contemporary reputation that Frank O'Connor feared that Yeats's undergoing the operation would be 'like putting a Cadillac engine in a Ford car.' (Second Puberty 8) Although Dr. Haire told Ellmann that the operation did not cure Yeats's impotence (*id.* at 8), Yeats boasted to Shakespear in a letter of 1 June 1934 that 'I am still marvelously strong... in some ways better than I was at Woburn Buildings,' where he and Shakespear had had the 'many days of happiness' celebrated in *Memoirs*. (*CL InteLex* 6051) The boast is ambiguous, and does not outweigh Dr. Haire's informed report that Yeats's impotence was not cured. It seems indisputable, however, that the aftermath of the operation witnessed an increase in Yeats's sexual desire, paving the way to a new burst of poetry – and conduct – in which sexual desire is valued for its own sake. Yeats described this process as 'the strange second puberty the operation has given me, the ferment that has come upon my imagination,' adding that '[i]f I write more poetry, it will be unlike anything I have done.'³ Later, he linked restored inspiration directly to rekindled desire, asserting that the operation revived both 'my creative power' and 'also sexual desire....'⁴

Within four months of the Steinach operation, Yeats had again succeeded in jump-starting his imagination with yet another imaginary voice, this time that of the outspoken hermit Ribh, the principal voice of 'Supernatural Songs.' Ribh shares Yeats's interest in bodily life after death, and reads by the light given off by the post-death intercourse of Baile and Aillinn, lovers who were '[t]ransfigured to pure substance' with the result that

> when such bodies join
> There is no touching here, nor touching there,
> Nor straining joy, but whole is joined to whole;
> For the intercourse of angels is a light
> Where for its moment both seem lost, consumed.⁵

The centerpiece of 'Supernatural Songs' is 'He and She' (*VP* 559), which, Yeats told Shakespear, was 'of course my central myth.'⁶ It involves the moon and a woman:

> As the moon sidles up
> Must she sidle up,
> As trips the scared moon
> Away must she trip:
> 'His light had struck me blind
> Dared I stop.'
> She sings as the moon sings:
> 'I am I, am I;
> The greater grows my light
> The further that I fly.'
> All creation shivers
> With that sweet cry.

The reader may be forgiven for puzzling over the meaning of Yeats's reference to his 'central myth,' or, at least, at his offhanded 'of course.' Yeats's comment would have been clearer to Shakespear, who knew that Yeats believed his inspiration was associated with the goddess of the moon, and thus would have recognized the 'she' of the poem, who waxes and wanes with the moon, as the poet's Muse – a meaning even more apparent in the initial draft of the poem which begins 'In love she was like the moon....' (*PF MM* 191) Muse-like, she is at once sexually enticing and remote: her creative song has the shiver of sexual ecstasy, but the more distant she is from the poet, the greater her light. The 'Supernatural Songs' explore Muse-related ideas, but show no trace of the inspiration of a living Muse. In fact, 'Ribh considers Christian Love insufficient' (*VP* 558), written in the summer of 1934 (*PF MM* xxiii), attributes to hatred the function of clearing Yeats's psyche and readying it for inspiration that had hitherto been performed by his Muse. Ribh asks 'Why should I seek for love or study it?/It is of God and passes human wit. . . .' Rather, Ribh studies 'hatred with great diligence,/For that's a passion in my own control,/A sort of besom that can clear the soul/Of everything that is not mind or sense.' The author of these lines was clearly ready for a new encounter with a live Muse. He later told Edith Shackleton Heald that 'George ceased to have an interest in sex,'[7] and, as Ellmann summed it up, George 'countenanced more than she discountenanced' her husband's late relationships with other women. (M&M xxv) An implicit prayer for a new Muse underlies the lyric with which Yeats closed the preface to *The King of the Great Clock Tower* and published as 'A Prayer for Old Age' (*VP* 553). He realizes that he may look foolish pursuing a living Muse at age sixty-nine, but is more than willing to 'seem/For the song's sake a fool':

> God guard me from those thoughts men think
> In the mind alone;
> He that sings a lasting song
> Thinks in a marrow-bone;
>
> From all that makes a wise old man
> That can be praised of all;
> O what am I that I should not seem
> For the song's sake a fool?
>
> I pray – for fashion's word is out
> And prayer comes round again –
> That I may seem, though I die old,
> A foolish, passionate man.

He still adheres to the 'First Principles' of 1912: 'Not to find one's art by the analysis of language or amid the circumstances of dreams but to live a passionate life, and to express the emotions that find one thus in simple rhythmical language.'[8]

As fate would have it, within six months of the Steinach operation Yeats received a letter from a twenty-seven-year-old actress and poet, Margot Ruddock, seeking his help with her poetry and in developing a poets' theater in London. Ruddock had lived her young life intensely. Married while still in her teens, to Jack Collis, a Cambridge friend of her brother, she had a son, Michael, who remained in Collis' custody when they divorced.[9] She then married actor Raymond Lovell while they were both playing at Bradford, and gave birth to a daughter, Simone, about six months before meeting Yeats. (*Id.*)[10] Nonetheless, Yeats sensed in her letters that she was ready to assume the role of Muse. Here was an opportunity to drink of those cups that had been left untasted with Olivia Shakespear. 'Do not think,' he wrote, 'that I await our meeting with indifference.'[11] The meeting did not disappoint. Describing Ruddock in his introduction to a book of her poems, Yeats employed the adjective he had used to characterize Shakespear in *Memoirs*, calling Ruddock a woman 'of distinguished beauty.' Ruddock, however, was fated to wear the mantle of Florence Farr. In words that could have had Farr as their subject, Yeats opined that Ruddock 'might be a great actress, for she possessed a quality rare upon the stage or, if found there, left unemployed – intellectual passion.'[12] Indeed, the image of Farr hovers over Yeats's early correspondence with Ruddock, as he tells her that he may 'put a book into your hand & ask you to read out some poems,' and suggests that, 'as you are a trained actress, a lovely sense of rhythm will make you a noble speaker of verse – a singer & sayer.'[13] While stopping short of threatening to bring Farr's psaltery to London, he will 'probably bring over a zither that we use at the Abbey with Dulacs music' in the hope that 'you would think out the singing or speaking of (say) half a dozen of my poems.'[14]

Frederick Ashton, to whom Yeats brought Ruddock after hearing her recite, bore out Yeats's instinct as to her potential as an actress. He told Roger McHugh that he felt that she had 'definite potential as an actress but had obviously never fallen into the right hands.' Much struck by Ruddock's beauty, he found her very intense, a seeming 'lost soul.' (LMR 10 n. 2) Yeats, Ashton recalled, 'was obviously very taken with her.' (*Id.*) A first-hand account of Yeats's emotions is preserved in the unpublished poem, 'Margot,' that he sent to Ruddock in November 1934. The poem grounds Ruddock in the context of the regret over '[l]ost opportunities to love' that had been on Yeats's mind at least since the writing of 'The Empty Cup':

> All famine struck sat I, and then
> Those generous eyes on mine were cast,
> Sat like other aged men

> Dumfoundered, gazing on a past
> That appeared constructed of
> Lost opportunities to love.

The hope of sexual renewal attendant upon the Steinach operation is reflected in the third stanza, which prays that

> The Age of Miracles renew,
> Let me be loved as though still young
> Or let me fancy that it's true[.]   (*CL InteLex* 6136)

The accompanying letter suggests that one hoped-for miracle did not occur. It expresses Yeats's 'utter black gloom' that 'perhaps after all... this nervous inhibition has not left me,' and tells how he 'pictured Margot unsatisfied and lost.' Linking inspiration to sexuality, he wonders: 'How could I finish the poem? How could I finish anything?'

The poem itself is unsatisfying – perhaps suggesting that an unattainable Muse was more of a stimulant to creativity than failed sexual relations with the attainable Margot. In fact, something of a reverse inspirational process seems to have been at work. In a 29 October 1935 letter to Ruddock, for example, Yeats borrowed from 'Upon a House shaken by the Land Agitation' (1910) (*VP* 264) to praise the 'precision and passion' of Ruddock's acting. (*CL InteLex* 6425)

At this stage, Ruddock was more Siren than Muse. According to Homer, the Sirens' song is thrilling, but those who listen to it will be transfixed, 'lolling there in their meadow, round them heaps of corpses,/rotting away, rags of skin shriveling on their bones....'[15] Although the Sirens trace their lineage to one or more of the Muses,[16] their appeal, unlike the Muses, is, as Jean-Pierre Vernant puts it, 'unequivocally in the realm of sexual attraction or erotic appeal,' as evidenced by 'their cries, [t]heir flowering meadow (*leimōn*, meadow, is one of the words used to designate female genitalia), [and] their charm (*thelxis*).'[17] Vernant explains that '[t]he Sirens are the opposite of the Muses' because their song leads to disabling death:

> The Sirens are the opposite of the Muses. Their song has the same charm as that of the daughters of Memory; they too bestow a knowledge that cannot be forgotten. But whoever succumbs to the attraction of their beauty, the seduction of their voices, the temptation of the knowledge they hold in their custody, does not enter that region to live forever in the splendor of eternal renown. Instead, he reaches a shore whitened with bones and the debris of rotting human flesh.   (*Id.* at 105)

Ruddock's erotic song was not particularly inspiring, but neither was it disabling. It was more of a call to a longing that could not be satisfied, akin to Plutarch's view of the Sirens' song as engendering in the soul a longing to break the tie with the body that cannot be satisfied.[18]

Neither inspired nor disabled, Yeats set about addressing the question posed in the second stanza of 'Margot':

> O how can I that interest hold?
> What offer to attentive eyes?   (*CL InteLex* 6136)

A letter of 11 October 1934 suggests one answer. Yeats tells Ruddock that he is 're-writing *The King of the Great Clock Tower* giving the Queen a speaking part that you may act it....' (*CL InteLex* 6110) The revised play, titled *A Full Moon in March*, eliminates the King from the trio of King, Queen and poet. Yeats explained in the preface that there had been 'a character too many' in the first play, and that, 'reduced to the essentials, to Queen and Stroller, the fable should have greater intensity.'[19] The stark essence of the fable enacts the core Muse principles: the Queen-Muse is remote and demanding, but, like the Ennoia or Wisdom figure, needs 'desecration' through union with the human poet to complete herself, while the poet must sacrifice himself to his Muse to achieve inspiration. This quintessential Muse play was not only written with Ruddock in mind, but, in lines that Yeats told Ruddock were 'partly addressed to you,' suggests that the poet is an old man:

> Should old Pythagoras fall in love
> Little may he boast thereof
> (What cares love for this and that?)
> Days go by in foolishness
> But O how great the sweetness is,
> (Crown of gold or dung of swine.)
>   (*CL InteLex* 6124; *Cf. VPl* 979)

At the outset of the short play, the Queen confirms the understanding of the Swineheard (who replaces the Stoller of the prior play) that '[h]e that best sings his passion' for the Queen shall take her for a wife and acquire her kingdom in the bargain. With echoes of the ageing Yeats who feared he had not satisfied Margo, the Swineheard seeks and obtains assurance that the bargain will hold even 'if some blind aged cripple sing/Better than wholesome men.' (*VPl* 981) Even though the Queen reminds the Swineheard that 'they that call me cruel speak the truth', the Swineheard vows to 'embrace body and cruelty.' (*Id.* 982–83)

One of the Attendants poses a question about the Queen that goes to the heart of Musedom: 'What can she lack whose emblem is the moon?' The answer – 'desecration and the lover's night' (*VPl* 989) – is a reminder that the Wisdom principle must become incarnate in human form, like Simon's Helena, in order to bring her wisdom fully into the world through the words of her inspired poet. Thus, when the Queen asks what she will gain if she proclaims the Swineheard's song the best, the Swineheard offers a song:

> A song – the night of love,
> An ignorant forest and the dung of swine.   (*VPl* 983)

The compressed action of the play quickly reveals the Queen holding the severed head of the Swineheard, her hands covered in red. The stage directions tell that she dances with the head 'to drum-taps, which grow quicker and quicker' and, as they 'approach their climax, she presses her lips to the lips of the head' while her 'body shivers to the very rapid drum-taps.' (*Id.* 989)

Although Margot had been no more than Siren when Yeats first addressed a poem to her, the play he wrote for her captures the essence of Musedom. The fact that Yeats had Florence Farr in mind when he wrote *The King of the Great Clock Tower* (see Chapter 2) suggests that his re-writing the play for Ruddock was another way of re-writing his life, with Ruddock in the role of Farr, whose play, *The Shrine of the Golden Hawk*, also featured an ecstatic dance by a priestess of the White Goddess.

Yeats's efforts to hold Ruddock's interest also led to his commenting on, and editing, drafts of her poems. His comments reflect his long-standing belief that poetry requires both inspiration and '*techne*' or craft. 'You always have passion,' he told Ruddock, 'that is to say the substance of all art/, but you want a greater technical precissino, a greater mastery of deliberately chosen detail.'[20] Yeats's attraction-holding efforts extended to including seven of Ruddock's poems in his *Oxford Book* of *Modern Verse*. 'I take thee, Life' (*OBMV* 418) is representative of the selections:

> I take thee, Life,
> Because I need,
> A wanton love
> My flesh to feed.
>
> But still my soul
> Insatiate
> Cries out, cries out
> For its true mate.

This poem is consistent with Yeats's description of Ruddock in his introduction as a 'religious' poet. (*id.* xli) Others, such as, 'Autumn, crystal Eye' (*OBMV* 419) are not readily identifiable as 'religious':

> Autumn, crystal eye
> Look on me,
> Passion chilled am I
> Like to thee,
>
> Seeking sterner truth,
> Even now
> Longing for the white
> Frozen bough.

All of the Ruddock selections were characterized in Yeats's introduction as 'little poems, which remind me of Emily Bronte....' – an affinity suggested to Yeats by Dorothy Wellesley.[21] Ruddock continued to send Yeats her work after he made the selections for the Oxford anthology, but his estimation of Ruddock's newer verse was even less enthusiastic than the tepid praise in the anthology. Recuperating in Majorca from an illness and working with Shri Purohit Swami on an English version of the *Upanishads*, Yeats advised Ruddock to 'Leave off verse for a time' because it seemed she did not work at her technique, and '[w]hen your technic is sloppy your matter grows second-hand – there is no difficulty to force you down under the surface – difficulty is our plough.'[22] This advice seems to have reached Ruddock at a time when the emotional instability suggested in her letters was on the verge of deteriorating into a mental breakdown. Not having heard any response to the many poems she had sent Yeats, Ruddock presented herself in Majorca and, according to the account she later published under the title 'Almost I Tasted Ecstasy' in *The Lemon Tree*, 'told Yeats that if I could not write a poem that would live I must die.'[23]

As Yeats recalled in a letter to Dorothy Wellesley, he 'was amazed by the tragic magnificence of some fragment & said so.'[24] He later described this material by saying '[h]ere in broken sentences, in ejaculations, in fragments of all kinds was a power of expression of spiritual suffering unique in her generation.' (Lemon Tree xi) An excerpt from Yeats's catalogue of examples includes the fragment that gave rise to the title of Ruddock's account of her adventures in Majorca and Barcelona:

'O Song, song harshened, I have leashed you to harshness.' ... 'I will shut out all but myself and grind, grind myself down to the bone.' ... 'Follow, follow lest that which you love vanishes, Let it go, let it go.' ... 'Shape me to Eternal Damnation to rid me of the phlegm that spits itself from unbearable cold.' ...

'Bleed on, bleed on, soul, because I shall not cease to knife you until you are white and dry.'... 'Almost I tasted ecstasy and then came the Blare, and drowned perfection in perfection.'

Ruddock had a different view of her meeting with Yeats. As she saw it, Yeats questioned the punctuation of one of her poems, and she thought '"there should be a comma after fulfillment", and that it meant I must die.' (Ecstasy, *LMR* 93) She approached the ocean, but 'could not go into the sea because there was so much in life I loved, then I was so happy at not having to die I danced.' (*Id.*) The next day, as Yeats recounted to Wellesley, 'she went to Barcelona & there went mad, climbing out of a window, falling through a barbers roof, breaking a kneecap, hiding in a ship's hold, singing her own poems most of the time.' In this extreme state, Ruddock seemed to sense the age-old equation between Muse and harlot, imagining that a voice (which could have been that of Simon's Helena) told her to 'Make yourself a prostitute for me as I did for you.' In search of lodging, she declared that 'I am a prostitute, and outcast from all Nations, I wander without hope of death.' (*Ecstasy, LMR* 94–5) Her essay closes with one of the poems she sang in Barcelona, a song of the 'Sea-starved, hungry sea':

> Sea-starved, hungry sea,
> In a stretched hand humility,
> Lapped there in a dream stand
> Shut eyes to the sea and sand
> Knowing that the sea is there
> Drink deep... O weeping cry...
> O my love leaned a little from me.   (*Ecstasy, LMR* 97)

Yeats did not hesitate to use these terrible events as part of the passionate life in which he would find the emotion necessary to inspiration. One of the resulting poems, 'Sweet Dancer' (1937), adds a poignant refrain to its narrative:

> The girl goes dancing there
> On the leaf-sown, new-mown, smooth
> Grass plot of the garden;
> Escaped from her bitter youth,
> Escaped out of her crowd,
> Or out of her black cloud.
> *Ah, dancer, ah, sweet dancer!*
>
> If strange men come from the house
> To lead her away do not say

> That she is happy being crazy;
> Lead them gently astray;
> Let her finish her dance,
> Let her finish her dance.
> *Ah, dancer, ah, sweet dancer!* (*VP* 568)

'A Crazed Girl' (1936) moves beyond description to reimagine the experience in light of Yeats's long fascination with the dance as an image – one that, as Frank Kermode put it, 'contain[ed] life in death, death in life, movement and stillness, action and contemplation, body and soul.'[25] The Margot of 'A Crazed Girl' bears traces of Iseult Gonne dancing on the Normandy shore, and sings her own song to the sea-starved, hungry sea. She is more Muse than Siren:

> That crazed girl improvising her music,
> Her poetry, dancing upon the shore,
> Her soul in division from itself
> Climbing, falling she knew not where,
> Hiding amid the cargo of a steamship,
> Her knee-cap broken, that girl I declare
> A beautiful lofty thing, or a thing
> Heroically lost, heroically found.
>
> No matter what disaster occurred
> She stood in desperate music wound,
> Wound, wound, and she made in her triumph
> Where the bales and the baskets lay
> No common intelligible sound
> But sang, 'O sea-starved, hungry sea.' (*VP* 578)

This moving merger of Ruddock's and Yeats's lyric impulses suggests that both poets found inspiration in Ruddock's state of ecstasy. At the end of his introduction to *The Lemon Tree*, Yeats recognized the transient nature of ecstasy, observing that '[t]he mystic who has found or approached ecstasy, whether in the midst of order or disorder, must return into the life of the world to test or employ knowingly or unknowingly his new knowledge.' (*Lemon Tree* xiv) He concluded by positing that Ruddock might return to the theatre 'and forget amid the excitement of the Boards that more perilous excitement.' (*Id.*) In fact, Ruddock appeared to recover almost immediately, and worked with Yeats in three of his 1937 BBC broadcasts, reading and sometimes singing his poems. (*LMR* 117)

Tragically, not long after the last of the broadcasts, her condition deteriorated and she was committed to an asylum, where she died in

1951 at the age of forty-four. George Barnes, who had produced the BBC programs, recalled how greatly Yeats valued her 'ability to pass naturally from speech to song' (*LMR* 118), an ability that could not have failed to put Yeats in mind of Florence Farr. More fundamentally, Ruddock had reinvigorated Yeats's notion of the Muse and inspired his dramatic embodiment of the Muse concept in *A Full Moon in March*. Ruddock's Siren-like Muse evoked desire rather than love. In an interesting letter of 11 August 1935, Yeats agrees with Ruddock that he also hates the word love and says that he has 'I think avoided it.' With an implicit nod to George's loyalty and devotion to a common interest in Yeats's work – his Ithaca – Yeats separates love from sexual pleasure:

[Love] is a name for the ephemeral charm of desire – desire for its own sake I do not think that is because I have grown old, that I value something more like friendship because founded on common interest, and think sexual pleasure an accessory, a needful one where it is possible. Paris and Helen were Romantic Lovers and both were probably fools; Odysseus returning to Penelope through ten years' heroic toil (though frequently unfaithful on the way), Penelope's patient waiting, was the classical ideal of man's and woman's wisdom. Both had Ithaca to think of. (*CL InteLex* 6316)

For the Yeats of 1935, he and Maud Gonne, like Paris and Helen, 'were probably fools.' What he needs now is George to help him focus on the Ithaca of his collected works, and Margot to stimulate the sexual desire essential to creation of still more poetry. She was thus both Siren and Muse. Moreover, her own poetry was in some ways an inspiration to Yeats. She showed him both the rewards and perils of mystic ecstasy, and her poem, 'The Apple' (*Lemon Tree* 17) may have pointed him toward that relentless paring away of the nonessential that dominated his last years:

>O apple life
>That swingeth where
>My hand can pluck
>Thee, poison fruit.
>
>I'll peel thee down
>Unto the core
>Imperishable,
>Absolute.

Ruddock retained her own distinct place in Yeats's pantheon. Near the close of his life, in 'The Man and the Echo' (1938), having asked the famous question whether his play *Cathleen ni Houlihan* had 'sent out/ Certain men the English shot,' Yeats wondered:

7. Ethel Mannin (Mansell/Time & Life Pictures/Getty Images).

Did words of mine put too great strain
On that woman's reeling brain? (*VP* 632)

Shortly after he had first met Margot Ruddock, Yeats sailed close to another potential Siren, Ethel Mannin. Their encounter was no accident. Norman Haire not only performed the Steinach operation on Yeats, but introduced him to Mannin for the purpose of testing its efficacy, encouraging her to dress seductively for the occasion.[26] Mannin was a prolific thirty-four-year-old author whose exuberant *Confessions and Impressions* lauded Haire as 'all contraception and rejuvenation and sex reform.'[27] Her own membership in the World League for Sexual Reform, her affair with Bertrand Russell, and the confessedly 'Hedonistic attitude toward life' trumpeted in *Confessions and Impressions* brought Mannin to Yeats with a decidedly racy reputation.[28] Beneath the reputation was an amazing story of achievement. As told in *Confessions and Impressions*, Mannin was born at Clapham, went to a board-school, and at fifteen got a job as a shorthand typist at Charles Higham's advertising organization. She had been attracted to writing from an early age, discovered poetry at school, and was writing advertisements and running two magazines at age sixteen. The next year, she 'was publishing my own stories, articles, verses, in a monthly magazine which Higham bought and left me to produce.' (Confessions 55) She married and gave birth to a daughter at nineteen, and managed to write four books in the ensuing five years. (*Id.* 64–8) She never slackened her pace, producing over a hundred books before her death in 1984. Her books were enormously popular, widely reviewed and judiciously praised. For example, L.T. Hartley found the satire of her third novel, *Sounding Brass*, sharper than that of Aldous Huxley in *Antic Hay*.[29] In sum, the woman Haire chose to test the efficacy of his operation was beautiful, passionate and accomplished.

Mannin wrote that Edmund Dulac 'and probably other people' considered her friendship with Yeats 'a little odd in view of the wide disparity in our ideas, Yeats with his innate mysticism and I with my inveterate materialism....' (Privileged Spectator 80–1) But Yeats was ready to bridge the gap. As Mannin pointed out, 'Yeats full of burgundy and racy reminiscence was Yeats released from the Celtic Twilight and treading the antic hay with abundant zest.' (*Id.*)

Almost immediately after meeting Mannin, Yeats wrote a two-line letter to Olivia Shakespear, at once revealing and mystifying: 'Are you back? Wonderful things have happened. This is Bagdad. This is not

London.'[30] As Foster recounts,[31] on 27 December 1934, the same day as this letter, Yeats drafted a 'theme for a poem' which progresses from the verses already sent to Ruddock, but seems to have been inspired by Mannin, to whom Yeats wrote on 30 December 1934, confiding: 'You are right, the knowledge that I am not unfit for love has brought me sanity & peace. Yet that is not altogether why I came from you with the fealing that I have been blessed.'[32] The experience was clearly worth repeating: Yeats wrote Mannin a week later suggesting, with implicit, if ironic, homage to Dante's term for the pleasure conferred by his beloved's greeting,[33] that 'we make Friday night "a beatitude".'[34] While the hauntingly beautiful poem suggests that its author was 'not unfit' for love, he seems not entirely fit either: he suffered anxiety, his breath failed, his heart ached, and he took a 'winding pathway' to 'Love's levelling bed':

> Port[r]ayed before his Eyes,
> Implacably lipped,
> It seemed that she moved;
> It seemed that he clasped her knees
> What man so worshipped
> When Artemis roved?
>
> He sat worn out & she
> Kneeling seemed to him
> Pitiably frail;
> Loves anxiety
> Made his eyes dim
> Made his breath fail
>
> Then suffered he heart ache;
> Driven by Love's dread
> Alternate will
> A winding pathway took,
> In Love's levelling bed
> All gyres lie still.[35]

The poem portrays Mannin as initially something of a marmorean Muse – she is 'implacably lipped' – but ultimately 'she moved' and found her way to 'Love's levelling bed.' Her status as Muse is signified by her association with Artemis, the Hellenic equivalent of Diana, who displaced Selene as the goddess of the moon. The Mannin-inspired Artemis thus succeeds the Selene invoked by Farr on that long ago night in 1890 when Yeats watched her performance in Bedford Park. Any doubt that Yeats saw Mannin as a figure of the moon goddess is removed by his letter of 15 November 1936, in which he tells her 'Mother Goddess, I put your hand to my lips.'[36]

Yeats's relationship with the White Goddess, however, had changed markedly since he pursued her in the form of Olivia Shakespear and Florence Farr. In *Per Amica Silentia Lunae*, written after his summer conversations with Iseult Gonne and just prior to his marriage, he had concluded that his Muse, his creative element, hovered somewhere in his own psyche, linking his mind to the general mind. As of the time of *Per Amica*, the notion that his daimon was his own feminine aspect was cloaked in the allusive notion that there was some whispering in the dark between Daimon and sweetheart. (*Myth* 336) After his long experience with George's communicators, Yeats more concretely expressed his theory in the 1925 edition of *A Vision*, where he asserted that the mind is composed of masculine and feminine halves, with the 'dark' or non-rational half – the source of creativity – being the opposite sex of the 'light' or rational side. (*AVA* 27) The masculine and feminine elements 'face each other in a perpetual conflict or embrace.' (*Id.*)

Thus schooled by his own speculations in *Per Amica Silentia Lunae* and his intensive interrogation of, and suggestion to, George's ghosts, Yeats was prepared to recognize that Mannin was at once his moon goddess – his Artemis – and a projection of an aspect of his own psyche. Accordingly, in a letter to her of 4 March 1935, he told her '[y]ou are doubly a woman, first because of yourself & secondly because of the muses whereas I am but once a woman.'[37] Yeats's letter assumes that Mannin's Muse is female – rather than a masculine anti-self – an erroneous assumption, unless Yeats was anticipating Gary Snyder's assertion that, in the Muse tradition, '[i]t is likely that men become creative when they touch the woman in themselves, and women become creative when they touch the woman in the man in themselves.'[38] In any event, the letter to Mannin contains a fascinating insight into Yeats's thinking about his relationship with his Muse.

Yeats's real life experimentation with these ideas took a startling turn when, in June 1935, he met Dorothy Wellesley, one of the poets whose work he had been reading in preparation for editing the proposed Oxford anthology of modern verse. Yeats's relationship with Mannin continued until his death, but by the time he met Wellesley, Mannin had met her future husband, and Yeats's quest for beatitude propelled him along multiple parallel paths.

8. Dorothy Wellesley and Yeats at Penns in the Rocks, *c.* 1936 (Robert W. Woodruff Library, Emory University).

8
Fury: Dorothy Wellesley

Yeats met Dorothy Wellesley in June 1935 as a result of an effort to 'be reborn in imagination.'[1] As he explained to her by letter, he had undertaken the task of making selections for the *Oxford Book of Modern Verse* for just that purpose, but had not foreseen 'that the work would bring me your friendship....' (*Id.*) Wellesley was a wealthy forty-five-year-old poet who lived on a Sussex estate, Penns in the Rocks, with her lover, Hilda Matheson (a BBC producer), and her two children by Lord Gerald Wellesley, from whom she was separated. Born Dorothy Ashton, her father died when she was five, and her mother married the tenth Earl of Scarborough five years later.[2] She was brought up between Lumley Castle and Scarborough's estate, Sandbeck. Her education consisted of early morning visits to the library at Sandbeck, and a series of governesses. Although life at Sandbeck revolved around hunting, rowing, fishing and tennis, Dorothy began writing poetry at an early age. (FT 61)

Country house life remained very much to her taste, and when her one-time lover, Vita Sackville-West, found Penns in the Rocks – perhaps in reciprocation for Dorothy's having found Sissinghurst for Vita – she felt that the house had been there waiting for her. (FT 158–9) In her biography of Sackville-West, Victoria Glendinning concludes that it is impossible to know what part Vita's influence and attraction played in the breakup of the Wellesleys' marriage, but it is clear that the worse things became for the Wellesleys, the more Dorothy 'clung to Vita.'[3] The intimacy between the two was sufficient to provoke Virginia Woolf's challenge to Vita that if 'Dotty's yours, I'm not,' and engender her belief that Vita 'left Dotty originally, I think, mostly on my account.'[4]

Yeats was attracted to Wellesley's poetry, especially 'Matrix,' which he characterized as 'the most moving philosophic poem of our time, and the most moving precisely because its wisdom bulked animal below the waist.'[5] 'Matrix' struck a chord with his own contemporaneous lyric impulse; he had been writing, as he told Olivia Shakespear, 'a lot of poetry of a passionate metaph[ys]ical sort.'[6] This combination of passion and metaphysics was a logical development for a poet who had long sought inspiration in his experiences as a lover, and had become increasingly philosophical following his involvement in his wife's automatic writing and the reading he undertook in its wake. Approaching age seventy, his search for a Muse was complicated by the fact that he was in the midst of a 'strange second puberty' in which he was filled with desire but unable to have erections. For someone who had located his creativity in what he regarded as the feminine part of his psyche, a lesbian poet like Wellesley presented an opportunity to explore the relationship between masculine and feminine in the work of the Muse. When Wellesley sent him a book of poems by Vita Sackville-West, he replied by praising the masculinity of Wellesley's own verse, noting that Sackville-West's poetry 'has not your masculine rythme,' and commenting on Wellesley's ability to 'play with the real world' not only 'as a child, as a young girl' plays, but also 'as a young man plays.'[7] The masculinity of Wellesley's poetry would become a recurring Yeatsian theme as he found new fodder for exploring the idea of the Muse in the contrast between her masculine rhythm and his notion that his own Muse was associated with the 'woman in me.' The exploration was conducted during frequent visits to Penns in the Rocks, the exchange of draft poems, and a prolific correspondence.

On the heels of his first visit to Penns in the Rocks, on which he was accompanied by Vita Sackville-West, Yeats proposed a second, asking by letter of 17 June 1935, '[m]ay I come to you then in the second part of August and for a few days....' (*CL InteLex* 6257) Thus began a pattern that would last until Yeats's death in which he spent substantial periods of time staying with Wellesley or her Musean successor, Edith Shackleton Heald. Wellesley's relationship with Matheson probably had the effect of confining the Yeats-Wellesley exploration of the androgynous Muse to the purely theoretical. Nonetheless, Yeats's letters to Wellesley were often flirtatious. For example, he confided on 25 June 1936 that he thought 'much of the most beautiful of Chinese lanthorns, your face. I found some Irish story once of men who threshed by the light of a lock of hair, but that was a more mundane light.' (*CL InteLex* 6594) The next month he wrote telling her of a dream in which 'Dorothy came to my room in middle of night' in 'a great country house.' He '[h]ad D in my arms carried her to my bed. Woke up – alas. Rest of night tried vainly to sleep, less for the sake of sleep than to find D.'[8] A bed with D seems to have been confined to the world of dream, and his letters are dotted with the 'O my dear' refrain that became his shorthand for a vague and unsatisfiable desire.

Again and again, Yeats's thoughts about Wellesley turned to her masculinity, initially in terms of her poetry, but then, increasingly, of Wellesley herself. For example, he extolled her 'powerful onrushing masculine rhythm' in the introduction he wrote for a selection of her poetry, and lauded her 'masculine rhythm' in his introduction to the *Oxford Book of Modern Verse*.[9] He did not hesitate to inform her that her horoscope suggested 'combative energy, masculinity.'[10] By the next year, his commentary on her masculinity had moved into more intimate contexts. In October 1936, he told her that 'I will never while I live forget your movement across the room just before I left, the movement made to draw attention to the boy in yourself' – an occasion that led him to believe that 'at last an intimate understanding is possible.'[11] He returned to the same idea the following month, writing 'My dear, my dear – when you crossed the room with that boyish movement, it was no man who looked at you, it was the woman in me. It seems I can make a woman express herself as never before. I have looked out of her eyes. I have shared her desire.'[12] Eventually, he merged poetry and person, commenting that '[w]hat makes your work so good is the masculine element amid so much feminine charm – your lines have the magnificent swing of your boyish body. I wish I could be a girl of nineteen for certain hours that I might feel it even more acutely.'[13]

Yeats was identifying the locus of creativity, for both himself and Wellesley, in the tension between the masculine and the feminine elements of their personalities. This is likely what he had in mind when he wrote to her that 'You must feel plunged as I do into the madness of vision, into a sense of the relation between separated things that you cannot explain, & that deeply disturbs emotion. Perhaps it makes every poets life poignant....'[14] Yeats detected this tension beneath the surface of Wellesley's 'Matrix', and saw it as the source of the visionary, oracular character of the poem that attracted him, even as others felt it a distraction from what might have been a poetry of precise description of natural beauty.[15] Yeats praised the poem because it went beyond descriptions of nature, believing that, as he said in his introduction to the *Oxford Book of Modern Verse*, for Wellesley, 'nature is a womb, a darkness; its surface is sleep, upon sleep we walk, into sleep drive the plow, and there lie the happy, the wise, the unconceived....'[16]

A few passages from 'Matrix' illustrate its attractions for Yeats and its limitations in the eyes of others. One passage of question and answer explains the poem's title:

> What this pain then, of men?
> This: the mind is a womb.
> A matrix, a matrix the mind,
> Of the whole of mankind.[17]

One can understand Yeats's fondness for ideas that parallel his theories in *A Vision*, such as the suggestion that love leads to an endless cycle of birth and death:

> Man chooses love for his guide.
> Love will not take him there
> Be she never so fair.
> This pleasure is torment for Man,
> Who all peace fully knew.
> What is this pleasure?
> Reversal: the birth pangs again,
> Is this not dying too?   (*Id.* 225)

Nor is it surprising that Yeats was drawn to the related notion that 'the womb and the grave are one' and thus:

> ...when love is greatly found,
> It outcries, as men cry
> When in pain to be laid on the ground;
> As men in pain moan for the grave;
> Hear: how in love the lips moan,
> For Man must pursue
> Love the lamp back to darkness again;
> Is not this death too?   (*Id.* 226–7)

'Matrix' convinced Yeats that Wellesley, along with the poet and music critic W.J. Turner, was one of the 'few of us [who] have in the very core of our being the certainty that man's soul is active.'[18] Wellesley would thus be a logical participant in Yeats's poetic projects, including what he told her would be 'another attempt to unite literature & music', a plan to have the Cuala Press publish 'a series of hand painted broadsides' containing poems by living poets and traditional ballads together with music and a picture for each.[19] It is likely that this idea led to Yeats's exploration of the masculine and feminine elements of his and Wellesley's contrapuntal Muses in a joint project in which they would share with each other a 'ballad of lovers, the lady & the servant.'[20] The ballads involve a lady who separates her love from her body, sending her maid to satisfy her lover's desires while impersonating the lady under cover of darkness. As appears from his letter of 9 July 1936 (*CL InteLex* 6609), Yeats was unable to restrain himself from attempting to revise Wellesley's poem, even as he worked on his own, which was eventually entitled 'The Three Bushes' (*VP* 569). Yeats's ballad featured a variation on the traditional device of picturing two bushes intertwining over the graves of two lovers. His penchant for splitting love into its carnal and spiritual aspects is reflected in the poem's post-death merger of three, rather than the traditional two, bushes. In the Yeatsian afterlife, the woman's body and soul retain their separate identities even as they intertwine with the male lover.

He also wrote a series of subsidiary lyrics in the voices of the lady, the lover and the chambermaid. Echoing themes from the Crazy Jane poems, the lady in Yeats's ballads tries to separate her soul's love from a carnality that is '[n]o better than a beast/Upon all fours.'[21] The songs attributed to the chambermaid by the unerect Yeats emphasize that pleasure has left the lover '[l]imp as a worm,'[22] an image on which Yeats insisted, despite Wellesley's objection that 'like all women I dislike worms....'[23]

The most interesting outgrowth of the exchange with Wellesley is 'The Lover's Song' (*VP* 574), of which T. R. Henn said 'I do not know of any short poem in which the workmanship is more perfect; with the virtue concentrated (as so often in Yeats's technique) on the single word *sighs* in the third line, with its depth and resonance.'(Lonely Tower 332) The poem is only six lines:

> Bird sighs for the air,
> Thought for I know not where,
> For the womb the seed sighs.
> Now sinks the same rest
> On mind, on nest,
> On straining thighs.

Yeats had sent Wellesley a draft of this poem as an explanation of his comment that the photograph on his wall of Moreau's *Les Licornes* conveyed a sense of 'mystery that touches the genitals, a blurred touch through a curtain.' His poem, Yeats told Wellesley, was '*Matrix* again but air not earth.'[24] Indeed, there is a distinct similarity between the themes of 'Matrix' and the suggestion in Yeats's more economical poem that the sexual drive is a drive toward oblivion. Yeats was not only rewriting Wellesley's ballad and incorporating its ideas into his own, but was, as it were, rewriting the long and complicated 'Matrix' into his own simple but profound lyric. What he had said to Wellesley of the merger of his feminine Muse with her masculine rhythm as he revised her ballad applied as well to his transposition and relocation of *Matrix*: 'Ah my dear', he wrote, 'how it added to my excitement when I re-made that poem of yours to know it was your poem. I re-made you and myself into a single being.'[25] In effect, he was reversing 'Plato's parable' by restoring the originary, double-sex humans posited in the *Symposium*.

The exploration of the creative potential of androgyny that made his interaction with Wellesley so exciting was highlighted, with characteristic Yeatsian misspelling, in a postscript to the letter in which he expressed the wish that he were 'a girl of nineteen.' His postscript asks 'Have you noticed that the Greek androginous statue is always the woman in man, never the man in woman? It was made for men who loved men first.'[26] His exploration of an androgynous Muse anticipated the suggestion advanced in Hélène Cixous's 'The Laugh of the Medusa' of an 'other bisexuality' characterized by 'each one's location in self (*repérage en soi*) of the presence... of both sexes, non-exclusion either of the difference or of one sex....'[27] In the context of writing, this approach is '[t]o admit that writing is precisely working (in) the in-between, inspecting the process of the same and of the other....' There can be little doubt that the Yeats who corresponded with Dorothy Wellesley had recognized that, as Cixous says, '[t]he dark continent is neither dark nor unexplorable.' (255) Clearly, he was not, as Cixous said of Freud and his followers, consumed 'by a fear of being a woman.' (254)

Yeats's tendency to mould himself and Wellesley into a single being reached its apex in 'To Dorothy Wellesley' (*VP* 579), in which he finds that their shared source of inspiration is not love for a Muse, but the angry emotions that were figured by the Greeks as Furies rather than Muses. As reflected in the bitterness that characterizes *The Tower* and the hatred of 'Ribh considers Christian Love insufficient,' Yeats was increasingly finding his inspiration through his propensity to anger and hatred. His study of psychological types in terms of phases of the moon grappled to explain how anger led to creativity by saying that 'antithetical men,' like himself and Dante, are 'violent in themselves because they hate all that impedes their personality.' (*AVB* 84–5) These denizens of phase seventeen are not unlike their neighbors at number sixteen who '[a]t one moment... are full of hate... and at the next produce the ... mythology of Blake, and discover symbolism to express the overflowing or bursting of the mind.' (*Id.* 138) Their hatred seems necessary to clear a passageway to the overflowing of the general mind and sweep away threatening ideas that impede the poet's personality. In the 'Letter to Ezra Pound' at the beginning of *A Vision*, Yeats links this idea with the Greek tradition of prophetic madness, suggesting that it was the rage of Oedipus that enabled him to know his own mind so thoroughly that 'Delphi, that rock at earth's navel', spoke through him. (*AVB* 28)

Fueled by these ideas, 'An Acre of Grass' (*VP* 575), written in November 1936, within months of 'To Dorothy Wellesley,' prays for 'an old man's frenzy' as the path to inspiration:

> Grant me an old man's frenzy.
> Myself must I remake
> Till I am Timon and Lear
> Or that William Blake
> Who beat upon the wall
> Till truth obeyed his call;
>
> A mind Michael Angelo knew
> That can pierce the clouds,
> Or inspired by frenzy
> Shake the dead in their shrouds;
> Forgotten else by mankind
> An old man's eagle mind.

Yeats's contemporaneous poetry reflects that, as he confided to Wellesley in a letter of 30 December 1936, he was seeking 'poetical emotion' in rage; his letter instances his rage over what he thought was the forgery of the Casement diaries and '[t]he present state of Europe' with Europe 'in the waning moon' and 'all those things that we love' waning with it. (*CL InteLex* 6764)

In 'To Dorothy Wellesley,' Yeats insists that it is Wellesley who finds her inspiration in the Furies. This electrifying poem contains an echo of 'Presences,' the 1915 poem in which the sleeping Yeats's 'hair stood up on my head' as the feminine Presences of harlot, child and queen 'climbed up my creaking stair.' (*VP* 358) Wellesley likely told Yeats that, as she later wrote, for the first several years of her residence at Penns, she felt a presence in her bedroom. (*FT* 161) Thus, in 'To Dorothy Wellesley', it is Wellesley, not Yeats, who waits in a bedroom 'Rammed full/Of that most sensuous silence of the night.' Yeats wonders:

> What climbs the stair?
> Nothing that common women ponder on
> If you are worth my hope! Neither Content
> Nor satisfied Conscience, but that great family
> Some ancient famous authors misrepresent,
> The Proud Furies, each with her torch on high.

Yeats's text, if difficult, is nonetheless detailed and specific. It suggests that Dorothy Wellesley knows the Furies in their true sense, and not as 'Some ancient famous authors misrepresent.' The most famous ancient misrepresentation was the work of Aeschylus, who transformed these primitive earth goddesses from the Erinyes, the angry ones who transmit a blood curse from generation to generation through the stained earth, to the Eumenides, the kindly ones who make the earth more fertile.[28] The true Furies who climb Wellesley's stair are angry, terror-inspiring spirits unleashed by violation of fundamental taboos (*id.*), and thus well-suited to preserve Wellesley from the 'Content' and 'satisfied Conscience' that 'common women' enjoy. Yeats presents the discontent and dissatisfaction sown by the Furies – the current drivers of his own enterprise – as desirable precursors of poetic achievement.

The close kinship between the Furies and Muses is illustrated by Erich Neumann's analysis of the archetype of the Feminine, in which he identifies the Muses and Furies as the positive and negative aspects of the archetype's transformative power.[29] Neumann suggests that at the 'extremes the opposites coincide or can at least shift into one another' and thus negative elements, such as those represented by the Furies, can 'be the forerunners of inspiration and vision. . . .' (Great Mother at 76) Yeats must have had Lionel Johnson's 'The Dark Angel' in mind when he identified Wellesley's Muses as Furies. In that poem, which Yeats quoted in 'The Tragic Generation' (*Au* 314) and included in his *Oxford Book of Modern Verse*, Johnson complains to the Dark Angel that

> Through thee, the gracious Muses turn
> To Furies, O mine Enemy!
> And all the things of beauty burn
> With flames of evil ecstasy.   (*OBMV* 105)

Although Sackville-West wrote that Wellesley was 'a natural rebel,' of 'fiery spirit' and given to 'temper, pride, and competitiveness' (*DNB* 1041), those emotions are not apparent on the face of her poetry. Moreover, writing after Yeats's death, Wellesley made a point of noting that the 'presence' in her bedroom was gentle rather than terrifying (FT 161), and that while she had 'always been in touch with the unseen world,' she had left such communication 'with my Muse to deal with' and '[o]nly when she visits me will I allow myself to be possessed by unseen forces.'[30] Wellesley is implicitly insisting that Yeats himself, the pursuer of a furious Muse, is the true subject of 'To Dorothy Wellesley.' Indeed, it is implicit in the poem that the Furies who pursue Wellesley are familiar presences in Yeats's room. As he told Wellesley in a letter containing a revised draft, the poem reflects a conflict that 'is deep in my subconsciousness, perhaps in every-bodies.'[31] The conflict is expressed, he says, in '[t]he moon, the moonless night, the dark velvet, the sensual silence, the silent room & the violent bright Furies' – all of which should give the impression of 'holding down violence or madness – "down Hysterica passio".' Although Yeats insists that '[a]ll depends on the completeness of the holding down, on the stirring of the beast underneath,' his contemporaneous writing, both prose and poetry, allows the beast to roam the surface, with little effort to confine it.

The role of the Furies as bearers of a blood curse passed on from generation to generation, like the inexorable impulse that tore apart the house of Atreus, is apparent in the poems immediately following 'To Dorothy Wellesley.' 'The Curse of Cromwell' (*VP* 580) tells how a curse is beaten into clay and destroys 'neighbourly content from generation to generation. 'The Ghost of Roger Casement' (*VP* 583) presents an angry spirit who cannot be contained in the tomb. Parnell still rankles the mind in 'Come Gather Round me, Parnellites' (*VP* 586). As Yeats told Wellesley, he hoped that these rage-inspired political ballads showed that he had 'recovered a power of moving the common man I had in my youth' and that the 'poems I am writing now will go into the general memory.'[32]

Yeats had long relied on an element of bitterness as an impetus to creativity. However, the enraged poet of the 1930s is writing in a different tradition from the younger courtly love poet for whom the Muse who inhabited Maud and Iseult Gonne engendered the requisite bitterness by spurning his amorous pursuit. Yeats's poetic model now focusses more on the creative potential of Dante's anger at being driven out of Florence (*Myth* 329–30) than on his longing for Beatrice. Yeats is too instinctively a love poet to abandon the amorous altogether, but he now emulates the Dante who, as Yeats quoted Boccacio, 'found room among his virtues for lechery' (*Myth* 330) rather than the chaste pursuer of Beatrice. Yeats highlights these two aspects of Dantean inspiration in a letter to

Wellesley of 28 November 1936, in which he confesses that his poems 'came out of rage or lust'[33] – a theme repeated in a quatrain he sent Wellesley in draft[34] and later published as 'The Spur' (*VP* 591):

> You think it horrible that lust and rage
> Should dance attention upon my old age;
> They were not such a plague when I was young;
> What else have I to spur me into song?

The word lust signals a break from the traditional notion of the courtly lover, whose love, if illicit, is nonetheless pure. While lust is synonymous with desire, it implies transgression, excess, and lack of control – notes sounded in 'To Dorothy Wellesley's repudiation of 'Content' and 'satisfied Conscience' in favor of the Furies unleashed by the violation of taboos. The married male poet's sexual attraction to a female poet who was sexually committed to another woman tapped sources of creativity outside the courtly tradition that required a new vocabulary. Although Yeats later conceded that we must love and not hate, he still insisted on the inspirational value of Swiftian indignation, which he described as 'a kind of joy.'[35] The joy of indignation, however, is a far cry from the overflowing self-delight of the poet who was not plagued by lust and rage 'when I was young.' The young courtly love poet's adherence to the Dantean praise tradition brought him what he described in 'Poetry And Tradition' as the 'shaping' power of 'courtesy and self-possession,' rooted in 'a continual deliberate self-delighting happiness,' that kept him from being 'swept away' by emotion. (*E&I* 253) The younger Yeats had recognized in his journal that a 'kind of Jacobin rage' threatened his writing, but ultimately 'helped me, for the knowledge of it has forced me to make my writing sweet-tempered and, I think, gracious.' (*Mem* 157) The richly creative emotions he had associated with the three women praised in 'Friends' – sweetness, delight, joy and ecstasy – had led to beautiful poems in the White Goddess and courtly love traditions, but were marginalized when rage predominated in his last decade.

The lustful and enraged author of 'The Spur' is manifesting what Theodor Adorno called 'late style.'[36] Adorno suggests that the artist's power of subjectivity shows itself in late works in the form of 'the irascible gesture with which it takes leave of the works themselves,' leaving only fragments of the works, and communicating

> itself, like a cipher, only thorough the blank spaces from which it has disengaged itself. Touched by death, the hand of the master sets free the masses of

material that he used to form; its tears and fissures witnesses to the finite powerlessness of the I confronted with Being are its final work. (EM 566)

Work inspired by the furious Muse threatens to break itself into no more than the tears and fissures that were once the motive power behind carefully constructed poetry. Poems like 'The Spur,' the political ballads, and 'The Black Tower' reflect what Edward Said, in his 'On Late Style,' called the 'self-imposed exile' of lateness, a drive that 'abjures mere bourgeois aging and that insists on the increasing sense of apartness and exile and anachronism, which late style expresses and, more important, uses to formally sustain itself.'[37] Yeats described his sense of the impetus to this late style in a 21 January 1937 letter to Wellesley in which he spoke of his 'utter solitude,' but claimed to have emerged 'out of that darkness... more man of genius, more gay, more miserable,' writing 'poem after poem,' all of them 'as a modern Indian poet has said, "no longer the singer but the song".' (*CL InteLex* 6785)

In March 1937, he managed to reassert his earlier persona as a courtly poet by addressing a lyric to a seemingly available Muse, Lady Elizabeth Pelham. The poem arose out of his effort to convince Pelham to accompany him to India. Pelham's letter declining the invitation is background to 'The Wild Old Wicked Man' (*VP* 587) Pelham begins by expressing her fear 'a second time to give you pain,' but feels the need to 'speak for fear that either you or I should again be led away by imagination from the right and the true path.'[38] A serious devotee of Indian mysticism, she tells Yeats that 'I have found it necessary for some years now because of the life I am attempting to lead, to quite reject personal friendships, especially those relationships of a more serious or of a more emotional variety – anything in fact that is likely to touch the imagination in any way....' (*Id.*) This gentle declination was followed by a kindly expression of willingness to always be available '[i]f you ever feel the necessity to talk over some point with a fellow student....' (*Id.*) Yeats's poem begins by taking note of both Pelham's kind words and her commitment to her Indian teacher, then returns to the recurring theme of the role of words in the intertwined lives of the poet-lover. In 'Words,' the words of his poems were the fruits of his Muse's unattainability. In 'A Song,' he had 'many words,' but wondered 'What woman's satisfied....' Now, he urges on Pelham his superiority to a man her own age because of his prowess with words as poet:

> 'Kind are all your words, my dear,
> Do not the rest withhold.
> Who can know the year, my dear,

> When an old man's blood grows cold?
> I have what no young man can have
> Because he loves too much.
> Words I have that can pierce the heart,
> But what can he do but touch?'

The response echoes Pelham's letter:

> Then said she to that wild old man,
> His stout stick under his hand,
> 'Love to give or to withhold
> Is not at my command.
> I gave it all to an older man:
> That old man in the skies.

The next stanza – read in light of Yeats's contemporaneous reminder, in letters to both Laura Riding and Dorothy Wellesley, that the 'Muses were women who liked the embrace of gay warty lads'[39] – suggests that the old man rebuffed by Pelham will nonetheless find his Muse:

> 'Go your ways, O go your ways,
> I choose another mark,
> Girls down on the seashore
> Who understand the dark;
> Bawdy talk for the fishermen;
> A dance for the fisher-lads;
> When dark hangs upon the water
> They turn down their beds.
> *Daybreak and a candle-end.*

The poem ends with lines that concede the validity of Pelham's spiritual quest, but insist that Yeats will remain a Muse poet to the end, seeking relief from suffering, not in the divine, but in the oblivion of love:

> 'That some stream of lightning
> From the old man in the skies
> Can burn out that suffering
> No right-taught man denies.
> But a coarse old man am I,
> I choose the second-best,
> I forget it all awhile
> Upon a woman's breast.'
> *Daybreak and a candle-end.*

Pelham's declination left Yeats bereft of a Muse. Wellesley had joined him on an astonishing exploration of the wellsprings of his creativity, but was herself more Fury than Muse, even as her Penns in the Rocks provided the 'intellect & sanity' that he had '[h]itherto... never found... any where but at Coole.'[40] His loquacity about his thinking in his letters to Wellesley suggests that there was bountiful conversation at Penns in the Rocks, and bears out Kathleen Raine's observation that Wellesley gave him 'the food his genius needed at the time of life when the friends of youth are becoming few.'[41]

Still, Wellesley's relationship with Matheson made her unavailable as Muse, and Yeats lacked the erotic attraction to a plausibly available, if presently unattainable, Muse that had so long been a part of his access to inspiration. Ethel Mannin might have supplied the missing erotic element but, as noted, she had met her future husband. Yeats's letters to her, while retaining a mischievous tone, reflect less frequent meetings, dampened ardour, and declining intimacy. Although he sometimes sent Mannin the same drafts of poetry he sent to Wellesley, they were unaccompanied by the commentary characteristic of his letters to Wellesley. For example, although he sent Mannin the draft of 'The Lover's Song' that he sent Wellesley, Wellesley's version was accompanied by an elaborate explanation of the Moreau painting in terms of the 'blurred touch through a curtain' metaphor, but Mannin was simply informed that she was receiving 'a scrap of a verse that came into my head.'[42]

Edmund Dulac and Helen Beauclerc were apparently attempting to supply the missing eros when they introduced Yeats to Edith Shackleton Heald in April 1937. The result would be a new chapter in Yeats's relationship with the Muse.

9. Edith Shackleton Heald and Yeats at Chantry House in 1937 or 1938 (The Huntingdon Library).

9
Golden Codger and Siren: Yeats and Edith Shackleton Heald

When Yeats met Heald, she seemed, as Foster points out, 'an unlikely successor to Ruddock and Mannin,' being fifty-three years old and 'neither stylish nor obviously attractive.' (*Life 2*, 583) On the other hand, like Mannin, she was an accomplished and intriguing journalist. Yeats claimed she was the best paid woman journalist of her time[1] and Arnold Bennett called her 'the most brilliant reviewer' in London.[2] Moreover, as one of her former colleagues said in her obituary in the 10 November 1976 *Times*, she spent 'her quick and noble mind generously.'[3] If she was an unlikely successor to Ruddock and Mannin, she perhaps stood midway between those decidedly heterosexual Sirens and the lesbian Wellesley in one respect: of ambiguous sexuality, she lived for many years following Yeats's death with the lesbian painter, Hannah Gluckstein.[4]

Although Heald's Lancastrian father abandoned the family in her youth, he left behind three extraordinarily talented children, including Nora Heald, who edited *The Queen* and later, *The Lady*, and Ivan Heald, who was Fleet Street's most acclaimed humorous writer before joining the Royal Flying Corp and meeting his death in World War I. At Ivan's suggestion, Edith entered journalism, establishing herself as a pioneering feminist voice. Her journalism of the decade before she met Yeats, for which she used her mother's name, Shackleton, reflects a supple mind, a playful imagination, and a familiarity with themes of Yeatsian interest. For example, her column of 5 July 1925 anticipates the theory Yeats would later explore in 'The Statues' (*VP* 610) that art and literature shape societal ideas of beauty and sexual attractiveness. Heald attributes the notion that 'the girl of the Period' has no grace or charm to the 'neglect or degradation of the girl in art,' asserting that 'poetry, painting and the theater mould life rather reflect it.' Heald argues that young women of an earlier era were moulded, for example, by Meredith's 'Love in the Valley,' which gave young women an image of themselves as tall lilies:

> When from bed she rises clothed from neck to ankle
> In her long white nightgown sweet as boughs of May,
> Beautiful she looks, like a tall garden Lilly,
> Pure from the night and splendid for the day.

In contrast, Heald suggests that the 'Girl of the Period probably appears at her window in striped pyjamas and drops down into the garden to smoke a cigarette or feed her ferret before dressing....' The Girl of the Period was no less neglected by painters. Instead of the 'anemic yearning of Burne Jones' maidens', the Girls of the Period have no pictures from which to 'get their ideals' or 'furnish their dreams.'[5]

Another column shows Heald vigorously deconstructing the myth of '[t]he adored one' in the course of commenting on a twenty-four-year-old woman's testimony, in a breach of promise action, that '[i]t was my young life I wasted with him.' Heald argued that the 'artificial melancholy' reflected in the young woman's testimony was the result of a Victorian mindset in which society was 'so happy and prosperous and felt so near the millennium that melancholy had to be cultivated as a genteel accomplishment, as in Rossetti's "The Lady's Lament"':

> Never happy anymore.
> Aye turn the saying o'er and o'er,
> It says but what it said before,
> And heart and life are just as sore.

Heald went on to argue that '[w]ith their growing independence of habit and thought, women realize that to be insulted by the passing of love is to deny that it has any quality of magic or passion.' Rather, '[t]he adored one' – a 'woman who has been passionately loved' – knows 'that in fact she was never the most beautiful woman in the world, nor fairer than the evening star, nor more lovely than the summer's day, but that something which neither of them understood compelled her lover to say – and perhaps believe – that she was. If this spell passes and he ceases to say or believe this enchanting nonsense, why should she be ashamed or insulted?' Her pride 'need not be damaged by the passing of something over which she had no control....'[6]

Heald had fun with a published quote from Yeats's diary in an October 1926 piece about the then new prospect of suits by a wife against another woman for alienation of her husband's affection. Heald's article began with Yeats's observation that '[m]y father says "A man does not love a woman because he thinks her clever or because he admires her, but because he likes the way she has of scratching her head".' Heald said this 'sound reflection has been running in my mind' since she read of the prospect of suits by wives for alienation of their husbands' affection.

Finding the prospect of such cases 'staggering,' she imagines a tribunal that will be

something like a burlesque of one of the Provençal Courts of Love. How is any woman going to assess the fascination of another and point to the particular charm which broke up her own dominance over her husband?

How is the fascinator ever to plead guilty to specific lures when, if she is honest, she cannot say if the defaulting husband loved her for her voice or her eyelashes, her wit, her piety, or merely for the way in which she scratched her head?

She wittily turns the tables, arguing

[i]f wives are actually going to sink to the ignominy of prosecuting other women for being more attractive than themselves, it ought to be made possible for other women to prosecute wives for allowing their husbands' affections to run so to waste that they become a public nuisance.[7]

Heald herself became that other woman shortly after her introduction to Yeats in April 1937. For the rest of his life, he would make frequent visits to the home she shared with her sister at Chantry House in the small Sussex village of Steyning, and share winter accommodation with her in the south of France. Yeats's letters to her are intimate and intensely erotic, filled with expressions of desire, but also with a longing for peace, stillness and sleep.

His arresting first letter of 4 May 1937 forwards the text of one of his lectures, telling her she need not read it: 'It is a tribute – that is all.' (*CL InteLex* 6923) Soon, he is anxious to 'again ask you for a friendship from which I hope so much,' telling her that you 'seem to me to have that kind of understanding or sympathy, which is peace.'[8] After a visit to Steyning in June – described to George as a visit to 'two elderly women' in 'a charming old house with an emmense garden in the middle of an old country town – house, furniture, pictures, garden all perfectly appropriate'[9] – Yeats tells Heald that 'I am happy & at peace – my only dread that I may not please you.' A tantalizing postscript observes that 'Sunday when we came together was my birth-day.'[10] A week later, Heald is the recipient of her first 'oh my dear,' along with the news that 'what is left me in life is yours.'[11] By 4 September he 'long[s] to be with you,' and a week later is 'longing for you in body & soul,' and, after another 'Oh my dear,' discloses – without apparent awareness of the ironic reprise of one of his addressee's *Sunday Express* columns, a desire 'to say all those foolish things which are sometimes read out in breach of promise cases.'[12] Anticipating their joint journey to the south of France, Yeats's letter of 7 November 1937 longs 'for the quiet of Monte Carlo & your quiet-bright still air (metaphorical and real)', before closing with an 'oh my dear.' (*CL InteLex* 7112)

After their visit to France, where she was replaced by George in February, he wonders if she knows 'how much you have given me' and asks 'no more of life except to see more of you.'[13] The effect of that encomium might have been undercut by Yeats's 15 March explanation that 'O my dear I want your arms to make me sleep....'[14] Sleep or no sleep, Yeats's next letter was signed 'your lover & your friend.'[15]

Throughout this period, and extending until his death, Yeats spent substantial periods of time with Heald, and found in her presence the quiet and peace in which he wrote an astonishing number of poems of the first rank and prepared himself and his body of poetry for his death. Yet none of the poems had Heald as addressee or subject. The Muse question is further clouded by a lack of clarity as to how the ardent desire of Yeats's letters was expressed during his frequent visits. The student of Musedom can only speculate on the basis of such hints as a letter in which Yeats 'begin[s] to touch you gently timidly at the top of your head & then' decides 'it is best to close,'[16] and a photograph of Heald sunbathing bare-breasted in the Chantry House garden under, as Foster says, Yeats's 'rapturous gaze.'[17] Although Heald provided Yeats with the sense of desire that, like the sense of order and serenity derived from Coole and Penns in the Rocks, was a necessary condition to his creativity, the absence of poetry to or about herself suggests she was more Siren than Muse.

Yeats's letters to Heald eschew the term lust that had been featured in his exchanges with Wellesley, but also avoid the term love, which he had denigrated in his 1935 letter to Margot Ruddock as 'a name for the ephemeral charm of desire – desire for its own sake.'[18] Yeats's assertion contradicts his own recognition elsewhere that love implies desire for another. Even as late as the second edition of *A Vision*, Yeats's alter ego Michael Robartes distinguishes between love and desire in the context of his assertion that 'Love contains all Kant's antinomies... Thesis, there is no beginning; antithesis, there is a beginning; or, as I prefer: thesis, there is an end; antithesis, there is no end. Exhausted by the cry that it can never end, my love ends; without that cry it were not love but desire, desire does not end.' (*AVB* 40) In other words, desire perpetuates itself by not seeking union with the other. The sense of Yeats's letters to Heald is that he is seeking neither an iconic mystical relationship, as with Maud Gonne, nor a mutually supportive two-way teacher/pupil relationship, as with Iseult Gonne, but is courting sexual desire solely as an end in itself, or perhaps as a necessary condition to poetry. Rather than seeking inspiration from deferral of desire for the other or the bitterness of loss, he moves directly from desire to poetry without pausing to seek union with, or even to praise, the other. The desire expressed in Yeats's letters to Heald seems too insistent, too constructed, too much, as he had said in his letter to Ruddock, 'desire for its own sake' or, as he hesitated to say to either Ruddock or Heald, desire for the sake of poetry. The cold logic of this approach lies beneath Yeats's thesis for a radio debate with Edmund Dulac in June 1937 that 'all the arts are an expression of desire.'[19]

The resultant poetry suggests that a generalized desire – what 'The Spur' calls lust – was a less effective Muse than a courtier's love for a particular woman. In 'News for the Delphic Oracle' (*VP* 611), written in August 1938,[20] Yeats looks back at unsatisfying lust-inspired adventures, and reports on the largely ineffectual results of pursuing lust as a spur to song. Ironically turning the tables on the oracle, who normally brought news from the company of the immortals to suppliant questioners, Yeats brings news *for* the Delphic Oracle. Knowing from his extensive reading of Henry More that souls in the afterlife engaged 'not only in rational discourses,' but pursued 'Musical and Amorous propension,'[21] Yeats presents the immortals as a group of languid 'golden codgers':

> There all the golden codgers lay,
> There the silver dew,
> And the great water sighed for love
> And the wind sighed too.
> Man-picker Niamh leant and sighed
> By Oisin on the grass;
> There sighed amid his choir of love
> Tall Pythagoras.
> Plotinus came and looked about,
> The salt flakes on his breast,
> And having stretched and yawned awhile
> Lay sighing like the rest.

The 'Tall Pythagoras' who sighs 'amid his choir of love' can be none other than Yeats, who so identified himself in the lines from *The King of the Great Clock Tower* 'partially addressed' to Margot Ruddock. Pythagoras and the other golden codgers seem to be in a state of depressed languor befitting someone who, like the unboastful Pythagoras of Yeats's lines to Margot, has not found sexual satisfaction. As Daniel Albright's learned analysis puts it, 'the codgers are in a state of postcoital depression associated with no act of coitus, a perpetually fulfilled condition which is the ironic reversal of the Keatsian condition where the lovers never, never kiss, though winning near the goal.'[22] When desire is an end in itself, the poet, unlike the Keatsian lover who never kisses, though winning near the goal, is in a state of perpetual fulfillment. The sexuality inaccessible to Yeats is relegated to a mere frenzy in the realm where Pan's 'Intolerable music falls':

> Foul goat-head, brutal arm appear,
> Belly, shoulder, bum,
> Flash fishlike; nymphs and satyrs
> Copulate in the foam.

Contemporaneously with writing 'News for the Delphic Oracle,'[23] Yeats attempted a poem praising 'the women that I picked,' a late reworking of the theme of 'Friends,' but this time his Muses fail to inspire a successful celebration of themselves. The poem, 'Hound Voice' (*VP* 621), grows out of a meditation on Dorothy Wellesley, who must be the woman who lived '[s]o many years companioned by a hound' – her great dane Brutus, mentioned in 'To Dorothy Wellesley,' who died in 1937.[24] The poem expands its scope to laud all the poet's lovers as having ' hound voices.' They spoke 'sweet and low,' knew '[w]hat hour of terror comes to test the soul,' and understood '[t]hose images that waken in the blood.' Instead of pursuing the shared understanding of those images, however, the poem degenerates into a celebration of the blood and wounds that will attend a renewed hunt. Neither Sirens nor Furies were bringing Yeats sufficient inspiration.

In fact, as discussed in Chapter 7, the Sirens are the opposite of Muses, and their song is ultimately, as Plutarch said, a call to the soul to break its tie with the body.[25] That is why the intense eroticism of Yeats's letters to Heald is accompanied by expressions of longing for peace, quiet, and sleep. Even her talk is praised for its 'quiet.'[26] That peace, quiet, and sleep are metaphors for death – that *Eros* and *Thanatos* have merged – is apparent from Yeats's letter of 20 October 1938 to Ethel Mannin, in which his oft-quoted belief that reality consists of 'two states of consciousness, beings or persons which die each other's life, live each other's death' is proclaimed to be 'true of life & death themselves.' (*CL InteLex* 7315) In his relationship with Heald, Yeats's death had begun to live his life. Indeed, he had written to Wellesley, that 'I thought my problem was to face death with gaety now I have learned that it is to face life.'[27] Achieving the equanimity to cast a cold eye on both life and death was a remarkable achievement, but, for a Muse poet, who found his inspiration in the turbulent emotions engendered by passionate relationships with women, it was, quite literally, a dead end. Thus, Yeats wisely crumpled, rather than published, the draft quatrain he dictated to Heald in May 1938 that asks 'What is explanation of it all? / What does it look like to a learned man?'[28] Although Ellmann suggests that the dark answer – a view in which '[f]rom nowhere unto nowhere nothings run' – is Yeats's (Second Puberty 26), it seems more likely that the answer is that of one of the three learned men with whom Yeats had dined the previous evening in All Souls College, Oxford. (*Life 2,* 621). The important point is that, after Yeats dictated the quatrain, man and poet went their separate ways. Man dictated the quatrain, the poet chose to discard, rather than publish, it. The poet knew he needed to search elsewhere for inspiration. Thus, in the poem he intended to be the penultimate of *Last Poems*,[29] 'The Circus Animals' Desertion' (*VP* 629), he tells of searching in vain for a theme until he concluded, like a true Muse poet, that he 'must be satisfied with my heart':

> I sought a theme and sought for it in vain,
> I sought it daily for six weeks or so.
> Maybe at last, being but a broken man,
> I must be satisfied with my heart, although
> Winter and summer till old age began
> My circus animals were all on show,
> Those stilted boys, that burnished chariot,
> Lion and woman and the Lord knows what.

Famously, satisfaction with his heart required that:

> I must lie down where all the ladders start,
> In the foul rag-and-bone shop of the heart.

In the poem intended as the last of his published poems,[30] 'Politics' (*VP* 631), Yeats made clear that a return to the 'foul rag and bone shop of the heart' would lead him to holding a beautiful woman in his arms. The message of 'Politics' can be traced to its origin in 'Those Images' (*VP* 600), in which Yeats shunned politics and the rage it generated for a return to 'the five/That make the Muses sing,' the hallmarks, as discussed in Chapter 4, of those unforgettable Muses, Maud and Iseult Gonne:

> What if I bade you leave
> The cavern of the mind?
> There's better exercise
> In the sunlight and wind.
>
> I never bade you go
> To Moscow or to Rome.
> Renounce that drudgery,
> Call the Muses home.
>
> Seek those images
> That constitute the wild,
> The lion and the virgin,
> The harlot and the child.
>
> Find in middle air
> An eagle on the wing,
> Recognize the five
> That make the Muses sing.

Yeats sent a draft of this poem to Wellesley in August 1937, telling her that it said the same thing as Blake's observation that 'Kings & parliaments seem to me something other than human life' and Hugo's belief that 'they are not worth one blade of grass that God gives for the nest of the linnet.'[31] A similar idea animates 'Politics.' Preceded by a quote from Thomas Mann – 'In our time the destiny of man presents its meaning in political terms' – Yeats insisted:

> How can I, that girl standing there,
> My attention fix
> On Roman or on Russian
> Or on Spanish politics?
> Yet here's a travelled man that knows
> What he talks about,
> And there's a politician
> That has both read and thought,
> And maybe what they say is true
> Of war and war's alarms,
> But O that I were young again
> And held her in my arms!   (*VP* 631)

Turning his back on the siren song of lust and rage, Yeats would return to the courtly and wisdom traditions, but, having no Muse incarnate ready to hand, fashioned 'Politics', as he told Wellesley, from 'a moment of meditation' rather than 'a real incident.'[32] Still, the poem reflects Yeats's impulse to conclude his career as lover, but this time as a pursuer of an attainable Muse. The old man who had left the cup half tasted in his youth has revised his theory of the Muse. Although his early career had been built on the unattainability of his beloved, he now embraces the view of the lady in 'The Three Bushes':

> Said lady once to lover,
> 'None can rely upon
> A love that lacks its proper food;
> And if your love were gone
> How could you sing those songs of love?
> I should be blamed, young man.' (*VP* 569)

Finale

After a lifetime of seeking inspiration from women, Yeats's last years brought him the happy state he had wished John Synge might have enjoyed: 'that communion with idle, charming and cultivated women which Balzac in one of his dedications calls "the chief consolation of genius".' (*Au* 509) His selfless wife, whose oracular intervention had shown him the way out of the dead end of the courtly love tradition, now contributed to his consolation by managing his relations with his publishers, organizing travel arrangements for his visits with Dorothy Wellesley at Penns in the Rocks and Edith Shackleton Heald at Chantry House, alternating with Heald as her husband's companion in the south of France in his last two winters, and even watching over his needs from afar, writing, for example, to remind Heald to be sure that her wandering husband took his 'digitalis mixture.' 'He needs so much intellectual stimulus that you and others can give,' George explained, 'but he unfortunately needs that heart stimulus.'[1] Heald's own efforts to stimulate Yeats's heart were passed over in silence.

These same years were enriched by 'memories of love/Memories of the words of women,' memories of his Muses. Although he wrote that, to preserve Florence Farr's psaltery, he did 'not hang it up on the wall to revive old memories' (*VPl* 1009), her memory lingered anyway. In the same passage, his Notes to the 1934 Cuala edition of *The King of The Great Clock Tower*, he recalled that '[t]hirty years ago I persuaded Florence Farr, beautiful woman, incomparable elocutionist, to rediscover with the help of Arnold Dolmetsch, what seemed the ancient art of singing or speaking poetry to notes....' (*VPl* 1008) His 18 September 1937 letter to Farr's niece, Dorothy Paget Rhodes, contains his last words on Farr: 'she has I think a place in history as well as in the memory of friends & those who in their youth heard her recite.'[2] Her recitations had inspired him with a vivid demonstration of how moving the chanted word could be, her Demeter-like beauty had lured him from preoccupation with platonic images of Beauty to experience of a real woman as equal, her candor and wit had enabled him to be his very self, and her shared interest in his occult pursuits had led him to sources of inspiration that reached him even from beyond the grave.

Iseult Gonne was in his memory as well. Not long after writing to Farr's niece, he wrote Maud Gonne about a recent visit with Iseult: 'I thought Iseult looked very charming the other day,' he reported, adding 'I have a portrait you made of her years ago on a little easel on my study table.'[3] Iseult's image in his study was a reminder of those conversations of two decades earlier that led to his revealing essay on the role of desire, and the deferral of desire, in the creation of his poetry.

Iseult's mother was never far from his mind. He wrote his last poem about Maud Gonne, 'A Bronze Head' (*VP* 618), in February 1938, after seeing her image as rendered in Lawrence Campbell's bust in the Dublin Municipal Gallery. She seems 'withered and mummy-dead' in the bust, but Yeats remembers 'her form all full/As though with magnanimity of light,/Yet a most gentle woman.' He then recalls the 'vision of terror' that threatened her all her life, and from which he had tried to warn her in the early poem 'The Two Trees' (*VP* 134). The core of 'A Bronze Head' memorializes Gonne's role as Muse, with Yeats recapitulating how concentration on her had enabled him to bring his consciousness to that Wordsworthian state of 'wise passivity' in which it was ready to receive inspiration:

> Propinquity had brought
> Imagination to that pitch where it casts out
> All that is not itself....

In that state of heightened receptivity, he had perceived the supernatural presence of the Muse:

> Or else I thought her supernatural;
> As though a sterner eye looked through her eye....[4]

Her Musedom had fulfilled the promise of the early days when he saw her as the icon around which to mould a proud, solitary and stern national consciousness. Now, his work was nearly finished, and Gonne was preparing to summarize her own life in an autobiography. On 16 July 1938, Yeats wrote to give her permission to 'say what you like about me' in her autobiography. Even at the last, Yeats was more poet than lover, adding 'you can of course quote those poems of mine but if you do not want my curse do not misprint them.'[5] Poet and Muse met for the last time on 26 August 1938 at Yeats's home outside

Dublin. Ethel Mannin, who had become friendly with Gonne, was present as well. (Kelly Chronology 310) Gonne recalled that as they parted, Yeats said '"Maud we should have gone on with our Castle of the Heroes, we might still do it"'.[6]

A little more than a month later, on 8 October 1938, Yeats wrote to Dorothy Wellesley that he had received the 'tragic news' that Olivia Shakespear ' has died suddenly.' His letter to Wellesley brings vividly to life the image of the distinguished beauty and delighted mind that opened the door to poetry evoking the beauty that had long faded from the world:

> For more than forty years she has been the centre of my life in London and during all that time we have never had a quarrel, sadness sometimes but never a difference. When I first met her she was in her late twenties but in looks a lovely young girl. When she died she was a lovely old woman.... She was not more lovely than distinguished – no matter what happened she never lost her solitude.... For the moment I cannot bare the thought of London. I will find her memory everywhere.[7]

Ironically, Shakespear had found in life the solitude that Yeats had created in poetry with images of Gonne.

Yeats did not need to bear much of London without Shakespear. After sporadic visits there in November 1938, he and George set out for France. By December, they were staying in the Hôtel Idéal Séjour on Cap Martin, and exchanging visits with Dorothy Wellesley and her lover Hilda Matheson, who were at Wellesley's nearby villa, La Bastide. Edith Shackleton Heald was expected to arrive at the end of January to take over as companion from George. By New Year's Day 1939, he had completed his last play, *The Death of Cuchulain*, in which the great Yeatsian surrogate is surrounded at his death by a group of women competing for his attention.[8] On 13 January, he completed what Seamus Heaney calls '[o]ne of the greatest ever death-bed utterances,'[9] 'Cuchulain Comforted.' (*VP* 634[10]) This account of Cuchulain's post-death comfort is Yeats's sole venture into *terza rima* – a choice clearly evoking Dante, exemplar of the poet inspired by 'the suffering of desire.' At the urging of 'certain Shrouds,' the dead Cuchulain threads a needle and begins to sew his own shroud, thus emulating the Yeats of 'Adam's Curse' by taking on the traditionally feminine task of stitching. Cuchulain was thus about to achieve the desideratum of 'Sailing to Byzantium,' an after-life of singing. The Shrouds begin to sing, but have 'nor human tunes nor words': 'They had changed their throats and had the throats of birds.' (*VP* 635)

On 21 January, Wellesley, Matheson and W. J. Turner visited the Yeatses at the Idéal Séjour. Wellesley told Rothenstein she 'had never seen [Yeats] in better health, wits, charm or vitality.'[11] By 26 January, however, Wellesley and Matheson found him greatly weakened, although he retained sufficient energy to alter the title of the poem containing his epitaph from 'His Convictions' to 'Under Ben Bulben.' (*Life 2*, 651) The next day, George, with a gracious nod to Wellesley's status as Muse, asked her to 'Come back and light the flame,' but Wellesley saw that the end was near and that Yeats knew it. (*LDW* 214) Heald arrived the next day and sat by his bedside. He died on Saturday 28 January 1939. Like Cuchulain, he was surrounded by women, a fitting finale for a poet for whom women had been the source of so much wisdom.

Individually and collectively, Yeats's Muses had taught him that a poet's relationship with a Muse is largely a question of belief. His Muses inspired him because he believed that passionate relationships with women would provide a necessary emotional impetus to poetry and open the door to knowledge and power from beyond his mind. Ultimately, the Muse notion was like the 'circuits of sun and moon' in the theories of history, biography and psychology advanced in *A Vision*. His famous answer to the question whether he believed 'in the actual existence' of those circuits applies equally to his belief in the idea of a Muse:

> ... To such a question I can but answer that if sometimes, overwhelmed by miracle as all men must be when in the midst of it, I have taken such periods literally, my sense has soon recovered; and now that the system stands out clearly in my imagination I regard them as stylistic arrangements of experience comparable to the cubes in the drawing of Wyndham Lewis and to the ovoids in the sculpture of Brancusi. They have helped me to hold in a single thought reality and justice. (*AVB* 25)

The Muse notion was Yeats's way of arranging his experience of women in terms of his desire to be a poet who spoke in the role of lover. Over a long and productive lifetime, his Muses taught him that, for a poet of genius, a Muse knows no limits of age or gender. Helping him hold in a single thought passion and poetry, his Muses were essential to his becoming the love poet he always wanted to be.

Endnotes

INTRODUCTION

1. See Preminger, Alex and Brogan, T.V.F., eds., *The New Princeton Encyclopedia of Poetry and Poetics* (Princeton: Princeton University Press, 1993) 802. The Muses can be identified in terms of arts relevant to the poet: Calliope (epic or heroic poetry); Clio (history, lyre-playing); Erato (love poetry, hymns lyre-playing); Euterpe (tragedy, flute-playing, lyric poetry); Melpomene (tragedy, lyre-playing); Polymnia or Polyhymnia (hymns, pantomime, religious dancing); Terpsichore (choral dancing and singing, flute-playing); Thalia (comedy); and Urania (astronomy, i.e. cosmological poetry). (*Id.*)
2. Plato, *Ion*, trans. Jowett.
3. Homer, *The Odyssey*, trans. by A.T. Murray, rev. by George E. Dimock (London: Harvard University Press, 1995).
4. Hesiod, *Theogony*, tr. Hugh G. Evelyn-White, in *Hesiod: The Homeric Hymns and Homerica* (London: Heineman, 1982) 79–80.
5. John M. Synge, *Poems and Translations* (Dundrum: Cuala Press, 1909) ('Synge') 45 (translating Petrarch's Sonnet 280).
6. Robert Graves, *The White Goddess*, 4th ed. (London: Faber & Faber, 1999) ('White Goddess') 6–10, 439, 480–1, 492, 501. According to Graves, the White Goddess was an inspirational force so potent that the nine Greek Muses were originally but one of her aspects. *Id.* 381–4.
7. William Wordsworth, 'Preface to Lyrical Ballads,' in Stephen Gill, ed., *William Wordsworth: The Major Works* (Oxford: Oxford University Press, 1984) ('Wordsworth') 611.
8. Unpublished notes for a London lecture on 'Contemporary Poetry,' quoted in Richard Ellmann, *Yeats: The Man and the Masks* (New York: Norton, 1979) ('M&M') 5.
9. Maud Gonne MacBride, *A Servant of the Queen*, 1938; rpt. (Gerrards Cross: Colin Smythe, 1994) ('SQ') 318–19. As discussed in Chapter 3, much of Yeats's writing about Gonne echoes Dante on Beatrice in Dante Alighieri, *La Vita Nuova*, trans. by Dante Gabriel Rossetti in *Dante and His Circle* (London: Ellis and White, 1874) ('Rossetti Dante').
10. Letter of 29 October 1917 to Gregory, *CL InteLex* 3350.
11. Letter of 17 June 1935 to Dorothy Wellesley, *CL InteLex* 6257.
12. Letter of 21 March 1937 to Shri Purohit Swami, *CL InteLex* 6873.
13. Letter of 4 March 1935, *CL InteLex* 6194.
14. Letter of 21 December 1936, *CL InteLex* 6759.
15. Letter of 28 November 1936, *CL InteLex* 6731.
16. Erich Neumann, *The Great Mother* (New York: Pantheon, 1955) ('Great Mother'), Schema III (after p. 82).

17. Curtis Bradford, 'The Order of Yeats's *Last Poems*', *Modern Language Notes*, vol. 76, no. 6 (1961) 515–16.
18. W.B. Yeats, Preface to Margot Ruddock, *The Lemon Tree* (London: Dent, 1937) ('Lemon Tree') xiv.
19. Julia Kristeva, *Tales of Love*, trans. By Leon S. Roudiez (New York: Columbia University Press, 1987) ('Tales of Love') 287.
20. Jahan Ramazani, '"A Little Space": The Psychic Economy of Yeats's Love Poems', *Criticism*, winter 1993 Vol. xxxv, no. 1, 67 ('Psychic Economy') at 70, 83 (emphasis supplied).
21. Letters to and from Yeats are quoted without altering spelling or punctuation.
22. 'A General Introduction for My Work' (*E&I* 509).
23. Elizabeth Butler Cullingford, *Gender and History in Yeats's Love Poetry* (Cambridge: Cambridge University Press, 1993) ('Gender and History') 5.

CHAPTER 1

1. John Harwood, *Olivia Shakspear and W.B. Yeats* (New York: St. Martin's Press, 1989) ('OS') 6.
2. Letter of 31 January 1909 from Ezra Pound to Isabel W. Pound in Omar Pound and A. Walton Litz, eds. *Ezra Pound and Dorothy Shakespear: Their Letters 1909–1914* (London: Faber, 1985) ('EP-DS Letters') xi.
3. Letter of 23 July 1892 to John O'Leary, *CL 1*, 302.
4. C.G. Jung, *The Structure and Dynamics of the Psyche* (London: Routledge & Kegan Paul, 1960) 150–2.
5. Letter to William Sharp, *C.* 25 August 1896, *CL 2*, 47–49.
6. Yeats made use of the archer vision in the 1933 poem 'Parnell's Funeral' (*VP* 541), where the archer is described as an image of 'the Great Mother.'
7. Gustave Flaubert, *The Temptation of Saint Antony*, trans. by D. F. Hanningan (London: H.F. Nichols, 1895) ('Temptation'). See *YL* 97. Yeats discussed *The Temptation of St. Antony* in his 1897 review of Maeterlink's *Aglavine and Selysette* (*UP 2*, 52) and in his 1898 essay, 'The Autumn of the Body' (*E&I* 189).
8. G. R. S. Mead, *Simon Magus an Essay* (London: Theosophical Publishing Society, 1892) ('Simon Magus'). Mead, along with Mrs. Besant, was Secretary of the Esoteric Section of the Theosophical Society during the time of Yeats's membership. George Mills Harper, *Yeats's Golden Dawn* (London: Macmillan, 1974) ('YGD') 8. Although Yeats's Esoteric Section Journal for 20 December 1889 describes Mead's intellect as 'that of a good sized whelk' (*Mem* 282), that did not prevent him from reading Mead's books, two of which were in his library, one of them bearing marginal strokes. *YL* 172.
9. Simon Magus 8–11; 20–1; 30 and Hans Jonas, *The Gnostic Religion*, 2d ed. rev. (Boston: Beacon Press, 1963) ('Gnostic Religion') 107–9.
10. Harold Bloom, *Poetry and Repression* (New Haven: Yale University Press, 1976) 205.
11. W.B. Yeats, ed., *Fairy and Folk Tales of the Irish Peasantry* (London: Walter Scott, 1888) ('FFT') 81.

Endnotes

12. R.E. Witt, *Isis in the Ancient World* (Baltimore: The Johns Hopkins University Press, 1997) ('Witt') 20.
13. Symons' poem as eventually published under the title 'To a Woman Seen in Sleep' is quoted in *CL 2*, 659.
14. The title of the poem in *The Wind Among the Reeds* was 'Aedh Gives his Beloved Certain Rhymes.' Similarly, two other poems discussed in the text had the following titles in *The Wind Among the Reeds*: 'Michael Robartes Remembers Forgotten Beauty' and 'Aedh laments the Loss of Love.'
15. The first is 'He bids His Beloved Be at Peace.'
16. Richard Ellmann, 'Discovering Symbolism' in *Golden Codgers* (New York: Oxford University Press, 1973) ('Discovering Symbolism') 101, 111.
17. Letter of 25 August 1934, *CL InteLex* 6087.
18. Yeats was specifically referring to 'He bids his Beloved be at Peace,' 'He gives His Beloved certain Rhymes' and 'A Poet to his Beloved.' (*Id.*)
19. Helen Vendler, *Our Secret Discipline: Yeats and Lyric Form* (Cambridge: Harvard University Press, 2007) ('Secret Discipline') 107.
20. Although 'The Song of Wandering Aengus' is sometimes said to refer to Maud Gonne because its reference to 'apple blossom' echoes Yeats's account of his first meeting Gonne (e.g. *NC* 53–4), Deirdre Toomey has shown that the apple blossom references have an ancestry in both Irish and Greek sources for the poem. Deirdre Toomey, 'Bards of the Gael and Gall: An Uncollected Review by Yeats in the *Illustrated London News*,' *YA* 5 (1987) 203–7. Nothing in the poem compels its association with any particular woman.
21. James Joyce, *Ulysses* (New York: Random House, 1934), 12.
22. James Joyce, *A Portrait of the Artist as a Young Man* (London: Penguin, 2000), 273.
23. Luke 7:44–47.
24. Holly E. Hearon, *The Mary Magdalene Tradition* (Collegeville: Liturgical Press, 2004) 4 n. 9.
25. Francesco Petrarca, *Rerum senilium, libri* xv, 15, trans. by Aldo S. Bernardo, Saul Levin and Reta Bernardo, *Letters of Old Age* (Baltimore: The Johns Hopkins University Press, 1992) 597.
26. Allen R. Grossman, *Poetic Knowledge in the Early Yeats* (Charlottesville: University Press of Virginia, 1969) ('Poetic Knowledge') 157, 159.
27. Jean Paul Richter, ed., *The Literary Works of Leonardo DaVinci* (London: Sampson, Low, Marston, Searle and Rivington, 1883) II, 291. Yeats's truncated misquotation appears in 'The Tables of the Law' (M 2005 197).
28. Ezra Pound and Maureen Spann, eds., *Confucius to Cummings: An Anthology of Poetry* (New York: New Directions, 1964) 327.
29. 'He tells of a Valley full of Lovers' (*VP* 163), published in January 1897, is a more sincere, and thus somewhat bewildered, expression of the emotions engendered by Gonne's displacement of Shakespear.
30. *Id.*, quoting Warwick Gould's transcription of the Vision Notebook.

31. Deirdre Toomey, '"Worst Part of Life": Yeats's Horoscopes for Olivia Shakespear' in *YA* 6 (1988) 222, 224.
32. Graham Hough, *The Last Romantics* (London: Duckworth, 1949) ('Last Romantics') 233.
33. Moshe Lazar, *Fin 'Amor* in F. R. P. Akehurst & Judith M. Davis, *A Handbook of the Troubadours* (Berkeley: University of California Press, 1955) 81–3; Dante Alighieri, *La Vita Nuova*, trans. by Dante Gabriel Rossetti in *Dante and His Circle* (London: Ellis and White, 1874) ('Rossetti Dante') 227.
34. Thomas Taylor, trans., *The Six Books of Proclus on the Theology of Plato* (London: Law & Co., 1816) II, 294.
35. *Ibid.*
36. Rossetti Dante 59.
37. Deirdre Toomey, 'The Worst Part of Life', YA 6 at 225.
38. See *Life 1*, 169. (Yeats and Gregory met in August 1896).
39. Foster (*Life 2*, 609–10 n. 17) reads the fifteen years as invoking Shakespear, based on their love affair beginning in 1895 and the poem being written at the end of 1910.
40. Letter of 8 October 1938 to Dorothy Wellesley, *CL InteLex* 7311. Similarly, Yeats's draft insists that the shared '[d]elight of mind in mind' persisted even though 'we could part in tears.' (*ISW MM* 225)
41. Arlene Croce. 'Is the Muse Dead?', *The New Yorker*, February 26, 1996, 164 ('Croce') 168.
42. Letter of 5 May 1896, *CL 2*, 28.
43. Psychic Economy 70. Elsewhere, Ramazani associates the 'pearl-pale' and 'white woman' descriptions with the 'consumptive sublime' of the Decadent poets and Pre-Raphaelite painters. Jahan Ramazani, *Yeats and the Poetry of Death* (New Haven: Yale University Press, 1990) ('Poetry of Death') 18.
44. Francesco Petrarca, Sonnet 216 in Thomas Campbell, ed., *The Sonnets, Triumphs, and other Poems of Petrarch* (London: George Bell and Sons, 1907).
45. David R. Clark, *Yeats at Songs and Choruses* (Gerrards Cross: Colin Smythe, 1983) 65–89.

CHAPTER 2

1. Josephine Johnson, *Florence Farr: Bernard Shaw's 'New Woman'* (Gerrards Cross: Colin Smythe, 1975) ('FF') 38–9.
2. Mark Bostridge, *Florence Nightingale: The Making of a Legend* (New York: Farrar Strauss Giroux, 2008) 262n.
3. John Todhunter, *A Sicilian Idyll: A Pastoral Play in Two Scenes* (London: Elkin Mathews, 1890) ('Idyll') 30.
4. See YGD 8 and n. 40. (date of Yeats's initiation) and FF 72 (date of Farr's entry).
5. Florence Farr, 'An Introduction to Alchemy and Notes by S.S.D.D.', in *A Short Inquiry Concerning the Hermetic Art by a Lover of Philalethes*, London, 1714 in

Collectanea Hermetica, Vol. 3, ed., Wynn Westcott (London: Theosophical Publishing Society, 1894).
6. Herodotus states that Demeter is Isis in Egyptian. *Histories* 2.59; 165.5; D. Flusser, 'The Great Goddess of Samaria', *Israel Exploration Journal* 25 (1975) 16–19, identifies Isis with Selene. See also Witt 67, 138–9, 149.
7. Letter of 28 March 1896, in George Mills Harper, *W.B. Yeats and W. T. Horton: The Record of an Occult Friendship* (Atlantic Highlands, N.J.: Humanities Press, 1980) 93.
8. Letter of 10 April 1896, C*L 2*, 19.
9. See n. 214. The final version was probably written in 1902, *SB* xvi, but Isis appears in drafts dating from 1896, *id.*, 83.
10. T. S. Eliot, *The Use of Poetry and the Use of Criticism: Studies in the Relation of Criticism to Poetry in England* (London: Faber, 1933) 118–19.
11. CW VII, 39.
12. Mabel Dolmetsch, *Personal Recollections of Arnold Dolmetsch* (London: Routledge & Kegan Paul, 1957) 31.
13. The photograph is in the Special Collections of the University of Reading Library. See Ian Fletcher, ' Bedford Park: Aesthete's Elysium?' in Ian Fletcher, ed., *Romantic Mythologies* (New York: Barnes & Noble, 1967) ('Fletcher') 197 and photograph facing 195. See also A. M. Gibbs, *Bernard Shaw: A Life* (Gainesville: University of Florida Press, 2005) ('Shaw') 160. Tony Gibbs drew my attention to the echo of the play in the inscription.
14. George Bernard Shaw, 'An Explanatory Word From Shaw' in Clifford Bax, ed., *Florence Farr, Bernard Shaw, and W.B. Yeats* (Dublin: Cuala Press, 1941) ('FSY').
15. Letter of 20 August 1891 to Farr, FSY 7.
16. Shaw letter 1891 to Farr, FSY 4.
17. 'An Explanatory Word From Shaw', *above* n. 14.
18. Shaw letter to Farr, 1 May 1891, FSY 1.
19. As discussed below, Horniman, Farr, and Yeats were fellow members of the Hermetic Order of the Golden Dawn.
20. Shaw letter of 29 March 1894, Burgunder Collection, Cornell University Library, quoted in Margot Peters, *Bernard Shaw and the Actresses* (New York: Doubleday, 1980) 126.
21. Jane Harrison, *Prolegomena to the Study of Greek Religion* (Cambridge: Cambridge University Press, 1903) ('Harrison') 187–8.
22. An Introduction to Alchemy and Notes by S.S.D.D., n. 5 above.
23. Florence Farr, *The Dancing Faun* (London: Elkin Mathews and John Lane, 1894).
24. Letter of 14 October 1896 to Farr, FSY 15.
25. Farr's publications included 'The Magic of a Symbol', *Occult Review* 7, no. 2 (1908) 82–93; 'On the Kabalah', *Occult Review* 7, no. 4 (1908) 213–18; 'On the Play of the Image Maker', *Occult Review* 8, no. 2 (1908) 87–91; 'Egyptian Magic by S.S.D.D. in *Collectanea Hermetica* (Vol. 8, ed. Wynn Wescott (London: Theosophical Publishing Society, 1896); 'The Philosophy Called Vedanta', *Occult Review* 7,

no. 6 (1908) 333–8; 'The Roiscrucians and Alchemists', *Occult Review* 7, no. 5 (1908) 259–64; 'The Tetrad, or the Structure of the Mind', *Occult Review* 8, no. 1 (1908) 34–40. Yeats's library contained a copy of Farr's 'Egyptian Magic' that bears marks indicating a close reading. *YL* 94.
26. Quoted in YGD 10–11.
27. Quoted in *CL 3*, 725.
28. Plato, *Ion*.
29. Richard Ellmann, *James Joyce* (New York: Oxford University Press, 1982) 67.
30. Horniman notes quoted in YGD 43.
31. Florence Farr, *The Music of Speech* (London: Elkin Mathews, 1909) ('Music') 16.
32. W.B. Yeats, 'Literature and the Living Voice', *Ex* 202, 220.
33. The handbill is reproduced as Plate 3 in Ronald Schuchard, *The Last Minstrels: Yeats and the Renewal of the Bardic Arts* (Oxford: Oxford University Press, 2008) ('Minstrels').
34. Robert Bridges, *Poems* (London: Bumpus, 1879) 14–15.
35. Steve L. Adams and George Mills Harper, 'The Manuscript of Leo Africanus', *YA* 1 (1982) 22.
36. Witt 85, 124.
37. See also Minstrels 54–5. Yeats contributed by writing the essay 'Speaking to the Psaltery' and donating his earnings. See Letter of 21 November 1901 to Gregory, *CL 3*, 121. The plays were published by Gordon Craig in 1901. They are reprinted in Florence Farr and Olivia Shakespear, *The Serpent's Path: The Magical Plays of Florence Farr* (Sequim: Holmes, 2005).
38. Farr's and Shakespear's *The Shrine of the Golden Hawk* was on the same bill. Minstrels 181.
39. George Yeats, 'A Forward to the Letters of W.B. Yeats' ('A Forward') in FSY 43; Ellmann, MBM xxiv.
40. Ellmann notes of interviews with George Yeats 8 December 1947, McFarlin Library, University of Tulsa. Ellmann's notes are transcribed in Warwick Gould, '"Gasping on the Strand": Richard Ellmann's W.B. Yeats Notebooks', *YA* 16 (2005) 279.
41. Letter of 3 November 1910, *CL InteLex* 1455.
42. Florence Farr, *Modern Woman: Her Intentions* (London: Frank Palmer, 1910) 44.
43. Letter of 7 July 1914 from Florence Farr to John Quinn, John Quinn Papers, Manuscript and Archives Division, The New York Public Library, Astor, Lenox and Tilden Foundation ('Quinn Papers').
44. These lines, slightly revised, were added to *On Baile's Strand*. See *VPl* 495–96.
45. Letter of 13 July 1906, quoted in *CL 4*, 237, n. 2.
46. Letter of 18 February 1907, *CL 4*, 630.
47. See *CL* 4 630 n. 14; Letter of April 1907, *CL 4*, 651.
48. Letter of 11 April 1908, *CL InteLex* 853.
49. Letter of 21 April 1908, *CL InteLex* 873.

Endnotes 219

50. '"Electra"/Mrs. Patrick Campbell's Triumph', *Liverpool Courier*, October 22 1908, 8 (Quoted in Minstrels 249).
51. Letter of 2 August 1909 from Ezra Pound to Homer Pound. Beinecke Rare Book and Manuscript Library, Yale University ('Beinecke').
52. Letter of 10 December 1910, *CL InteLex* 1473.
53. Letter of 21 January 21 1911, *CL InteLex* 1506.
54. Letter of 28 January 1911, *CL InteLex* 1522.
55. Letters of 31 January and 3, 5, and 8 February 1911, *CL InteLex* 1526, 1534, 1535, 1536.
56. Yeats sent a draft to Gregory on 1 January 1911. *CL IntLex* 1485.
57. Letter of 26 August 1907 to A.A. Bullen, *CL 4*, 712–13.
58. Florence Farr, *The Solemnization of Jacklin* (London: A.C. Fifield, 1912) ('Jacklin').
59. T. Sturge Moore, 'Yeats', *English* 2 (Summer 1939) 277.
60. Letter of 18 June 1912. Quinn Papers.
61. H. W. Nevinson Journal, The Bodleian Library, University of Oxford, MSS. Eng. misc. e. 610–28 quoted in Ronald Schuchard, 'An Attendant Lord: H.W. Nevinson's Friendship with W.B. Yeats' in *YA* 7 (1990) 90 ('An Attendant Lord') 116.
62. Kelly Chronology 156; WBY Letter of 27 June 1912 to Farr, *CL InteLex* 1931 and WBY Letter of late July 1912 to William Rothenstein, *CL InteLex* 1954.
63. Poetry Review, I (September 1912) 424.
64. *CL InteLex* 6204.
65. Ezra Pound 'Portrait d'une Femme', *Ripostes* (London: Swift, 1912), rept. in M.J. King, ed., *Collected Early Poems of Ezra Pound* (New York: New Directions, 1976) 184–5.
66. Letter of 5 July 1912 from Dorothy Shakespear to Ezra Pound, EP-DS Letters 132. The letter also refers to Dorus as a young man 'who lay among lillies all night & is Oscar, without the bitter-sweetness.'
67. Rachel Blau Du Plessis, 'Propounding Modernist Maleness: How Pound Managed a Muse' in *Modernism/Modernity*, Vol. 9, no. 3 (Sept. 2002) 389–405 at 392–3.
68. Letter of 5 July 1912 from Ezra Pound to Dorothy Shakespear, EP-DS Letters 130.
69. Letter of 11 June 1908, *CL InteLex* 915.
70. George Bernard Shaw, 'The Quintessence of Ibsenism' rpt. in *Bernard Shaw: Major Critical Essays* (Harmondsworth: Penguin, 1986) 135.
71. Florence Farr, 'Ibsen's Women, No. 1. Hedda Gabler,' *The New Age*, I, 25, Oct. 17, 1907, 389.
72. Letter of 18 February 1913, *CL InteLex* 2092.
73. Letter of 3 September 1912 from Ezra Pound to Homer Pound, Beinecke.
74. Letter of 12 June 1913, *CL InteLex* 2179.
75. Letter of 4 October 1914, *CL InteLex* 2519.
76. Letter of 19 August 1916, *CL InteLex* 3021.
77. Letter of 7 December 1916, British Library, Add. MS 50533, fol. 11–12, quoted in Josephine Johnson, 'Florence Farr: Letters to W.B. Yeats 1912–1917' in *YA* 9 (1992) 216–54 ('F-YL') at 251.

78. Letter of 18 January 1917, *YA* 9 at 249.
79. *CL InteLex* 3177.
80. *YA* 9 at 250.
81. *CL InteLex* 2620.
82. *YL* 95 George Yeats's automatic writing of June 1918 instructed Yeats to 'Read Fechner.' *YVP 1*, 508.
83. See Walter Kelly Hood, '"Read Fechner", The Spirit Said: W.B. Yeats and Gustav Theodor Fechner' *YAACTS* 7 (1989) 91, 96.
84. Theodor Fechner, *On Life After Death*, trans. by Hugo Wernekke, 3rd ed. (Chicago and London: Open Court Publishing, 1914).
85. Paul Muldoon, *The End of the Poem* (London: Faber & Faber, 2007) 10.
86. Letter of 24 November 1921, *CL InteLex* 4026.
87. Letter of 23 September 1916, *YA* 9 at 247–8.
88. Letter of 18 February 1913, *CL InteLex* 2092. Beardsley's heroism is the subject of 'Upon a Dying Lady' (*VP* 362). In equating the soul's forgetting its broken toys with becoming 'both Chance and Choice', 'All Souls' Night' uses the language of 'Solomon and the Witch', where eternal bliss is a state of 'Chance being at one with Choice at last....' (VP 388).
89. Letter of 7 October 1920, *CL InteLex* 3791.
90. Information from Dorothy Paget Rhodes to Josephine Johnson, quoted in FF at 180.

CHAPTER 3

1. C. S. Lewis famously observed that 'everyone knows' that courtly love appeared 'quite suddenly' in Languedoc at the end of the eleventh century. *The Allegory of Love* (Oxford: Oxford University Press, 1936) 2. Denis de Rougemont suggests a twelfth-century origin in *Love in the Western World*, trans. by Montgomery Belgion, rev. ed. (New York: Pantheon, 1956) ('Western World') (originally published as *Amour et l'Occident* (Paris: Plon, 1939)) 107.
2. In the 'final' version of the *Speckled Bird* (composed in 1902), the Yeats-like character, Michael Hearne, has read *The Mabinogian* and *Morte d'Arthur*. *SB* 23, 27. Yeats owned a copy of *Morte d' Arthur*. *YL* 164.
3. Bernard O'Donoghue, *The Courtly Love Tradition* (Manchester: Manchester University Press, 1982) 5.
4. Frederick Goldin, *The Mirror of Narcissus in the Courtly Love Lyric* (Ithaca: Cornell University Press, 1967) ('Mirror') 2.
5. See Maurice Valency, *In Praise of Love* (New York: Shocken Books, 1982) ('In Praise of Love') 151, 219–20.
6. Although Yeats's letters to Lady Gregory of 17 and 19 January 1911 show that Florence Farr was reading him Chrétien de Troyes, the context suggests she was reading the story of Sir Lancelot rather than lyric poetry. *CL InteLex* 1497 and 1503.

Yeats's intense interest in Rossetti and his knowledge of Rossetti's translation of *La Vita Nuova* make it likely that he knew Rossetti's *Dante and His Circle* (London: Ellis and White, 1874) ('Rossetti Dante'), which contained Guido Guinicelli, 'He perceives his Rashness in Love, but has no choice', at 295, and Guido Calvacanti, 'Of the Eyes of a certain Mandetta, of Thoulouse, which resemble those of his Lady Joan, of Florence', at 139.
7. 'The Arrow' is discussed below.
8. Thomas Malory, *Le Morte d'Arthur*, (London: Dent, 1893) Book III, Ch 20.
9. Dante Alighieri, *Purgatorio*, trans. by Charles Shadwell in *The Purgatory of Dante Alighieri* (London: Macmillan 1892–99) Book xxiv. Blake's aphorism is contained in his letter to Thomas Butts of 6 July 1803, which appears in Geoffrey Keynes, ed. *Blake Complete Writings* (Oxford: Oxford University Press, 1972) 825.
10. Nancy Cardozo, *Lucky Eyes and a High Heart* (New York: Bobbs-Merrill, 1978) ('Lucky Eyes') 25; *Life 1*, 91.
11. See, e.g. Letter of July 1905 to WBY, *G-YL* 208.
12. Gloria Kline's conclusion that Gonne was simply the projection of 'those traits that were femininity as [Yeats] dreamed of it' does not do justice to the very real qualities Yeats found in Gonne. Gloria C. Kline, *The Last Courtly Lover* (Ann Arbor: UMI Research Press, 1983) 10.
13. *E&I* 173; see Matthew Arnold, *On the Study of Celtic Literature* (London: Smith, Elder & Co. 1867) 100–9.
14. Seamus Heaney, 'William Butler Yeats', in Seamus Deane, gen. ed., *The Field Day Anthology of Irish Writing* (Derry: Field Day Publications, 1991) II, 784.
15. Neil Mann, 'W.B. Yeats and the Vegetable Phoenix', *YA* 17 (2007) 20–1.
16. Mary Colum, *Life and the Dream* (London: Macmillan, 1947) 112.
17. Marie Nic Shiubhlaigh, *The Splendid Years: Recollections of Marie Nic Shiubhlaigh as Told to Edward Kenny* (Dublin: James Duffy & Co. 1955) 19.
18. Adrienne Rich, *On Lies, Secrets, and Silence* (New York: Norton, 1979) ('On Lies') 39.
19. Unless otherwise stated, dates of composition are based on A. Norman Jeffares' *New Commentary*.
20. She left the Order in December 1894, finding its members 'the very essence of British middle-class dullness' and suspecting a connection with Masonry, which she regarded as unacceptably British. *SQ* 211–12.
21. Michael Sidnell discusses Yeats as memorialist in 'The Presence of the Poet: or What Sat Down at the Breakfast Table' in A. Norman Jeffares, ed., *Yeats the European* (Gerrards Cross: Colin Smythe, 1989) 131.
22. See *Au* 76 and Letter of 21 March [1889] to Catherine Tynan, C*L 1,154*.
23. Letter of 6 September 1897, *G-YL* 77.
24. An analogous idea had been presented in more palatable form in 'The White Birds' (1891) (*VP* 121), in which Yeats expressed the wish that he and his beloved 'were changed to white birds on the wandering foam ... Where time would surely forget us, and Sorrow come near us no more....'

25. Letter from Maud Gonne to WBY, postmarked Jy 3, 97, *G-YL* 72–3; see *Mem* 113.
26. See *Life 1*, 216.
27. Joseph Hone, *W.B. Yeats* (London: Macmillan, 1942) ('Hone') 321.
28. P.I.A.L. Notebook, NLI MS 36, 276, also quoted in Virginia Moore, *The Unicorn* (New York: Macmillan, 1954) ('Unicorn') 197.
29. Deirdre Toomey, 'Labryinths: Yeats and Maud Gonne', *YA* 9 (1992) 95, 100–2.
30. See White Goddess 68, 169.
31. The draft is transcribed in WRMM 129–32. The quotation in the text follows Foster in reading 'wood' instead of 'crowd' in the penultimate line. See *Life 1*, 239 and n. 55.
32. E.g. Croce 165.
33. Conrad A. Balliet, 'The Lives – and Lies – of Maud Gonne', *Eire-Ireland* 14:3 (1979) at 31.
34. See Mirror 66–7.
35. Letter of 11 January 1905 to Gregory, *CL InteLex* 93.
36. Letter of 9 January 1905 to Gregory, *CL InteLex* 92.
37. Letter of 11 March 1905 to John Quinn, *CL InteLex* 123.
38. See n. 28 above.
39. Letter of 26 July 1908, *G-YL* 257.
40. Letter of 26 June 1908, *G-YL* 256.
41. See Chapter 3.
42. Catullus, Poem 85 in Kenneth Quinn, ed., *Catullus: The Poems* (New York: St. Martin's Press, 1970) 78.
43. Anthony Storr, *The Dynamics of Creation* (New York: Atheneum, 1972) 196.
44. Preface to the first edition of John M. Synge's *Poems and Translations* (*E&I* 306, 308).
45. Mario Praz, *The Romantic Agony*, trans. Angus Davidson (New York: Meridian Books, 1956) 28–45.
46. Richard Ellmann, Notes, 17 June 1946, McFarlin Library, University of Tulsa.
47. Letter of 20 June 1908, *CL InteLex* 919.
48. Letter of 17 Aug. 1910, *CL InteLex* 1411.
49. A.E. Waite, *Lives of Alchemystical Philosophers* (London: G.P. Redway, 1888) 117–18. Yeats owned this work (*YL* 210), which was also available in the Golden Dawn library. See M 2005, 370.
50. Robert Graves, *The Greek Myths* (Harmondsworth: Penguin, 1955) I, 207.
51. See Chapter 1.
52. Letter of 27 November 1910, quoted in A. Walton Litz, 'Pound and Yeats: The Road to Stone Cottage' in George Bornstein ed., *Ezra Pound Among the Poets* (Chicago: University of Chicago Press, 1985) 132–3.
53. See Chapter 1.
54. *Id.*
55. Letter to Harriet Monroe, 15 December 1915, quoted in James Longenbach, *Stone Cottage: Pound, Yeats & Modernism* (Oxford: Oxford University Press, 1988) 183.

Endnotes

56. William Wordsworth, 'Expostulation and Reply' in Wordsworth at 130.
57. Seamus Heaney, 'Sixth sense, seventh heaven' in Brendan Barrington, ed. *The Dublin Review Reader* (Dublin: Dublin Review Books, 2007) 201. The inspirational force behind 'The Cold Heaven' was so potent that it has had a distinguished afterlife. Heaney's essay reveals that his experience of reading 'The Cold Heaven' was the 'lived experience' that inspired his poem 'Shiftings.'
58. Heaney relates these stages to the systematic account of the creative process in Jacques Maritain, *Creative Intuition in Art and Poetry* (New York: Meridian Books, 1955).
59. Diary entry, dated Christmas 1912, quoted in M&M 214.
60. *G-YL* 31, 175–8.
61. Letter of 10 February 1903, *G-YL* 166 (emphasis in original). Foster points out that the penultimate stanza directly transposes a letter Gonne had sent Yeats in 1907 with respect to nationalist criticism upon the collapse of her marriage to MacBride. (*Life 2*, 10).
62. Letter of 20 March 1915, *G-YL* 356–7.
63. See Croce 166.
64. See Gender and History 4.
65. 'The Folly of Being Comforted' (*VP* 199) and 'Broken Dreams' (*VP* 355).
66. See Gender and History 4.
67. Propertius, *Elegies*, II, 2.
68. Quoted in *Life 1*, 507.
69. Ovid, *Metamorphoses*, ed. Brookes More (Boston: Cornhill Publishing Co., 1922) I, 681 *et seq*.

CHAPTER 4

1. Harold Bloom, *Yeats* (New York: Oxford University Press, 1972) ('Bloom') 198. It goes without saying that today's scholarship stands on the shoulders of John Kelly, General Editor of the *Collected Letters*, Roy Foster, Yeats's biographer, and Warwick Gould and Deirdre Toomey, Editor and Research Editor of the *Yeats Annual*. The late A. Norman Jeffares' pioneering work respecting Iseult Gonne, cited below, is particularly pertinent. Other scholarship focusing on Iseult Gonne includes Amanda French ' "A Strangely Useless Thing": Iseult Gonne and Yeats', *Yeats Eliot Review* 19 (2002) 13–24, and Virginia D. Pruitt, 'W.B. Yeats, Iseult Gonne and the Mask,' *Yeats Eliot Review* 10 (1989) 52–6.
2. Vladimir Nabokov, *Lolita* (1955; ann. ed., New York: Vintage, 1991) 16–17.
3. Lionel Trilling, 'The Last Lover: Vladimir Nabokov's "Lolita" ' *Encounter* 11, No. 4 (Oct. 1958) 9 at 12.
4. Jenefer Shute, ' "So Nakedly Dressed": The Text of the Female Body in Nabokov's Novels,' in Ellen Pifer, ed., *Vladimir Nabokov's Lolita: A Casebook* (Oxford: Oxford University Press, 2003) 112.

Endnotes

5. A. Norman Jeffares, 'Iseult Gonne,' *YA* 16 (2005) 197 ('IG') 204. Even in Maud Gonne's autobiography, published in 1938, she refers to her daughter as 'a charming child I had adopted called Iseult.' (SQ 288).
6. Letter of 19 September 1917, *CL InteLex* 3325.
7. Letter of January 1918, quoted in A. Norman Jeffares, Anna MacBride White and Christina Bridgewater, eds., *Letters to W.B. Yeats and Ezra Pound from Iseult Gonne* (Basingstoke: Palgrave, 2004) ('IGL') 95.
8. Letter of 21 June 1908, *CL InteLex* 921.
9. Ella Young, *Flowering Dusk: Things Remembered Accurately and Inaccurately* (New York: Longmans Green & Co., 1945) 102.
10. A. Norman Jeffares, *W.B. Yeats: Man and Poet* (London: Routledge & Kegan Paul, 1978) ('Man and Poet') 190.
11. Letter of 4 May 1910, *CL InteLex* 1346.
12. Quoted in IG, *YA* 16 at 227.
13. Letter of 12 September 1914, *CL InteLex* 2513.
14. Letter of 13 October 1917, *CL InteLex* 3340.
15. Sigmund Freud, 'The Uncanny,' in *The Standard Edition of the Complete Psychological Works of Sigmund Freud* (London: Hogarth Press, 1953–74) ('SE') XVII, 237.
16. Indeed, it was one of the moments of crisis Yeats would later explore in automatic writing sessions with his wife. (*YVP 3*, 225)
17. Michael Holroyd, *Augustus John* (New York: Holt, Rinehart and Winston, 1974) 226, 231–3.
18. Harold Bloom, *The Anxiety of Influence*, 2d ed. (Oxford: Oxford University Press, 1997) 61–3.
19. See Chapter 1.
20. *M 2005*, 202; 425–28.
21. Letter of 8 September 1917, *CL InteLex* 3320.
22. Letter of 21 March 1916 from Maud Gonne to WBY, *G-YL* 369–70.
23. Letter of 25 August [?] 1915 to WBY, IGL 60.
24. *CL InteLex* 2958.
25. *CL InteLex* 2964.
26. Letter of 8 November 1916, *G-YL* 384.
27. Letter of 3 July 1916, *CL InteLex* 2996.
28. Letter of 5 March 1917, *CL InteLex* 3177.
29. *CL InteLex* 3005.
30. Letter of 14 August 1916, *CL InteLex* 3017.
31. *CL InteLex* 3019.
32. *CL InteLex* 3030.
33. Letter of 12 August 1916 to Gregory, *CL InteLex* 3016.
34. Letter of 10 August 1916 to T. Sturge Moore, *CL InteLex* 3014.
35. The Jammes poem was 'Le Poète et L'Oiseau,' 1899, rpt in Francis Jammes, *Oeuvre Poétique Complète* (Biarritz: Atlantica, 2006) 296–306.
36. Letter of 6 June 1917, IGL 84.

37. Iseult may have been referring to the text, rather than the illustrations, which Yeats, in his 1897 essay 'William Blake and His Illustrations to the Divine Comedy,' thought, 'a noisy and demagogic art.' (*E&I* 140) In a 26 June 1926 letter to T. Sturge Moore, Yeats thought Shadwell's opinion that Doré's illustrations were 'magnificent works' an example 'English provincialism.' *TSMC* 104 (*CL IntelLex* 4887).
38. Letter of 9 November 1916, IGL 67–8.
39. In his biography, *Ezra Pound: Poet* (Oxford: Oxford University Press, 2007) 339, A. David Moody says 'there is no deposit of definite evidence in the record' of such a relationship. Given Jeffares' extended conversations with Iseult, his testimony, buttressed by the intimate tone of Iseult's letters to Pound, suffices. Moreover, Iseult told her husband, Francis Stuart, that she and Pound had been lovers. Kevin Kiley, *Francis Stuart Artist and Outcast* (Dublin: The Liffey Press, 2007) 39.
40. Pound to Eva Hesse, 5 November 1954. Collection of Dr. Eva Hesse (quoted in IGL 138).
41. IGL 79.
42. Letter of [?] July 1917, IGL 85.
43. E.g., Letter of 2 October 1918, IGL 62.
44. Letters of 7 September and 2 October 1916 and 30 January 1917, IGL 61, 62 and 76.
45. Letter of 15 October 1916, IGL 64.
46. Letter of 9 November 1916, IGL 68.
47. The quotation is taken from the English edition, *By Way of Sainte-Beuve*, trans. Sylvia Townsend Warner (London: Chatto & Windus, 1958) 18–19.
48. Letter of 1 August 1916, *CL IntelLex* 3012.
49. IGL 68.
50. IGL 62.
51. Quoted in *Life 1*, 518–19.
52. Steve L. Adams and George Mills Harper, eds., 'The Manuscript of Leo Africanus,' *YA* 1 (1982) 13.
53. Tony Tanner, *Venice Desired* (Cambridge: Harvard University Press, 1992) 243.
54. Jacques Derrida, 'Différance' in *Margins of Philosophy*, trans. by Alan Bass (Chicago: University of Chicago Press, 1982) 1–27.
55. Sigmund Freud, 'Creative Writers and Day-Dreaming,' IX SE 143–53.
56. The published essay refers to '[t]he doctors of medicine,' rather than Freud, but as Foster points out, the draft (NLI MS 30,368) refers to 'Dr Freud and his pupils' and Jung's observations on group hysteria. *Life 2*, 76.
57. NLI MS 30, 368.
58. Letter of 2 February 1916, J.B. Yeats, *Letters To His Son W.B. Yeats and Others 1869–1922* (London: Faber & Faber, 1944) 216.
59. *English Review* 26 (1918) 515.
60. George Yeats told Ellmann that the opening lyric referred to Iseult Gonne. (Ellmann notes of 17 January 1947 Interview. McFarlin Library, University of Tulsa).

61. The shell as symbolic of Iseult's beauty can be traced to the automatic writing experiments Yeats undertook with his wife, during the course of which, on 7 January 1918, the symbol of 'bird & shell' was associated with the character Eithne Inguba who is Iseult's surrogate in *The Only Jealousy of Emer*. (*YVP 1*, 217–18)
62. Iseult, along with Wordsworth, Keats, and Tennyson, is listed as an example of phase 14 on a sheet in George Yeats's hand with some changes by Yeats that is filed with the automatic script for 2 June 1918. (*YVP 1*, 549 n. 5)
63. William Butler Yeats, *Four Plays for Dancers* (London: Macmillan, 1923), *VPI* 566.
64. *CL InteLex* 3300 and 3305.
65. *CL InteLex* 3320.
66. *CL InteLex* 3322.
67. See Chapter 2.
68. *CL InteLex* 3325.
69. A. Norman Jeffares, Introduction to *G-YL* 40.
70. Letter of 13 October 1917, *CL InteLex* 3340.
71. Letter of 8 September 1917, *CL InteLex* 3320.
72. Letter of 13 October 1917 to Gregory, *CL InteLex* 3340.
73. *CL InteLex* 3328.
74. Letter of 29 October 1917, *CL InteLex* 3350.
75. Letter of 13 October 1917, *CL InteLex* 3340.
76. Letter of 22 September 1917, *CL InteLex* 3328. Elizabeth Heine, in a theory given prominence in Brenda Maddox's *George's Ghosts* (Basingstoke: Picador, 1999), speculates that because a horoscope prepared for Yeats in 1907 'indicated some major romantic event' for 1917, Yeats, in that year, 'sought a marriage partner until he found one.' Elizabeth Heine, 'W.B. Yeats' map in his own hand', *Biography*, 1:3 (1978) 37–50, at 44 and 48. Although Yeats was greatly influenced by astrological factors – and worried in a letter to George just prior to their wedding about the possible interference of 'that old intreaguer Neptune' (*CL InteLex* 3332) – the contemporaneous evidence of Yeats's thinking does not suggest that he believed he labored under a 31 December 1917 deadline for 'some major romantic event.' In any event he seemed to approach his marriage as an escape *from* romance to routine and order. (Heine does not discuss Yeats's reference to Neptune, but elsewhere associates Neptune with illusion. Heine, 'Yeats and Maud Gonne: Marriage and the Astrological Record, 1908–09', *YA* 13 (1998) 3 at 33.)

CHAPTER 5

1. Letter of 29 October 1917 to Gregory, *CL InteLex* 3350.
2. IG, *YA* 16 at 235. Iseult's reply refers to her having burned Yeats's letter. Letter of 26 October 1917, IGL 91.
3. Margaret Mills Harper, *Wisdom of Two: The Spiritual and Literary Collaboration of George and W.B. Yeats* (Oxford: Oxford University Press, 2006) ('Wisdom of Two') 8–11; *YVP* 3, 1–7, 119.

Endnotes 227

4. George Mills Harper and John S. Kelly, 'Preliminary Examination of the Script of E[lizabeth] R[adcliff]', in *Yeats and the Occult*, ed. George Mills Harper (Toronto: Macmillan, 1975) ('Occult') 130.
5. Letter of 30 September 1917 from Nelly Tucker to Lady Gregory. Berg Collection, New York Public Library. (quoted in BG 93).
6. Letter of 28 November 1917, *CL InteLex* 5428.
7. Yeats's materials relating to the Radcliffe automatic writing include a paper signed by 'G. Hyde-Lees' containing information about one of the people referred to in Radcliffe's automatic writing. (Occult at 141 and 152)
8. This dating is based on notations that George Yeats made on a copy of *Collected Poems* indicating numerous dates and 'noting on the fly leaf that "The poems that have been dated in pencil on this book are dated by authority of MSS".' *YL* 313. George's notes indicate that these poems were written in Glendalough in 1918. *Id.* at 316, 317. The Yeatses stayed in Glendalough in March of that year. John S. Kelly, *A W.B. Yeats Chronology* (Basingstoke: Palgrave Macmillan, 2003) ("Kelly Chronology") 199.
9. *CL InteLex* 3354. Yeats wrote Gregory that he had finished the play on 14 January 1918 (*CL Intelex* 3390), but wrote Pound on 6 June that 'the "Only Jealousy"... will be the better of two more lyrics.' *CL InteLex*, 3447.
10. R.F. Foster, 'Yeats and the Death of Lady Gregory', *Irish University Review*, 34.1 (2004) 109, 120.
11. As further evidence of Fand's status as Muse, Helen Vendler notes that she sheds her light at the fifteenth phase of the moon, at which, according to *A Vision*, ' "all thought becomes an image" and aesthetic activity occurs.' Helen Vendler, *Yeats's Vision and the Later Plays* (Cambridge: Harvard University Press, 1963) ('Vision and Later Plays') 219.
12. *YVP 1*, 164–8; 204; 217–20; 223–5; 253–6. See also George Mills Haprer's illuminating table at *MYV 1*, 150.
13. There is a draft of the poem dated April 1918, *WSC MM* 391, and Yeats's letter to Pound of 6 June 1918 recites that he has completed 'two philosophic poems', likely 'The Phases of the Moon' and 'The Double Vision of Michael Robartes.' *CL InteLex* 3447.
14. Ellmann suggests that the girl of the vision 'is primarily an image of art.' Richard Ellmann, *The Identity of Yeats* (New York: Oxford University Press, 1964) ('Identity') 255.
15. See Chapter 3.
16. See Chapter 3.
17. See Chapter 3.
18. *YL* 317. Jeffares suggests the poem was written in 1919. *NC* 184.
19. That Iseult is the 'fellow artist' addressed in 'To a Young Beauty' is apparent from its context and was confirmed by George Yeats (*YL* 316) and by Iseult's letter of February 1918 thanking Yeats 'for the little poem; it might almost be used as an exorcism.' (IGL 97)

20. Joyce Carol Oates, ' "At Least I Have Made a Woman of Her": Images of Women in Twentieth-Century Literature,' *Georgia Review* 37 (Spring 1983) 7, 17. Marjorie Perloff advances a similar critique in 'Between Hatred and Desire: Sexuality and Subterfuge in "A Prayer for My Daughter" ', *YA* 7 (1990) 29–50.
21. Letter of 8 June 1917 from John Butler Yeats to W.B. Yeats in Lennox Robinson, ed., *Further Letters of John Butler Yeats* (Dundrum: Cuala Press, 1920) 39.
22. Although Yeats elsewhere suggests that women hold to their opinions more firmly than men, this Yeatsian opinion is more socially constructed than essentialist because it is based on the view that 'because the main event of their lives has been a giving themselves and giving birth, they give all to an opinion as if it were some terrible stone doll.' (*Au* 504) Moreover, Yeats concedes in his journal that he himself is 'too full of belief in whatever thought lays hold on me', whereas Lady Gregory, like Synge, isolates herself 'from all contagious opinions of poorer minds....' (*Mem* 154).
23. Edna Longley, 'Helicon and ni Houlihan: Michael Robartes and the Dancer', in Jonathan Allison ed., *Yeats's Political Identities: Selected Essays* (Ann Arbor: University of Michigan Press, 1996) ('Political Identities') 203, 208–9.
24. Letter of 21 September 1927 to T. Sturge Moore, *CL InteLex* 5030.
25. Stephen MacKenna, trans., *Plotinus, The Enneads* (London: Warner, 1917–35) I, 35 (translation of Preller-Ritter Conspectus). See T.R. Henn, *The Lonely Tower*, 2d ed. (London: Methuen, 1965) ('Lonely Tower') 88.
26. Warwick Gould, ' "A Lesson for the Circumspect": W.B. Yeats's Two Versions of *A Vision* and the *Arabian Nights*', in Peter L. Caracciolo, ed., *The Arabian Nights in English Literature* (London: Macmillan, 1988) 244–80 at 246.
27. See Samuel Johnson, *Lives of the English Poets* (London: John Murray, 1854) 156.
28. W.B. Yeats, Note to *The Resurrection* (*VPl* 932).
29. Lonely Tower 15.
30. G.P.E. Lessing, *Laocoön, Nathan the Wise & Minna Von Barnhelm*, trans., William Steel (London: Dent, 1930) 14.
31. Helen Vendler deftly shows how these two poems are variants of the sonnet form. Secret Discipline 170–7.
32. Yeats's note to *The Resurrection* wonders whether he had begun *On Baile's Strand* when he began to imagine the image. He describes evoking such an image with MacGregor Mathers' symbols in his autobiographical account of 'Four Years: 1887–1891.' (*Au* 185–6) The writing of *On Baile's Strand* began in August 1901. (Kelly Chronology 76)
33. E.W. Emerson, ed., *The Complete Works of Ralph Waldo Emerson* (Boston, New York: Houghton, Mifflin, 1903–4), II 7–8. The pertinence of the Emerson and Blake quotations was noted in Thomas R. Whittaker, *Swan and Shadow: Yeats's Dialogue with History* (Chapel Hill: University of North Carolina Press, 1964).
34. Eight poems in addition to those discussed in this chapter have been identified (see *BG* 343 and n. 86) as bearing a 'direct relationship to the philosophical system' developed in conjunction with George's mediumship – 'The Wheel', 'The Fool by the Roadside', 'Shepherd and Goatherd', 'Under the Round Tower', 'The Four Ages

Endnotes   229

of Man', 'The Saint and the Hunchback', 'The Spirit Medium', and 'The Gyres' – but it is not clear that the automatic writing contributed anything of great significance to the achievement of these verses as poetry.
35. Letter of 15 July 1918, *CL InteLex* 3461.
36. Both date the poem as having been written in 1919. See *NC* 181 and Identity 255.
37. See n. 13 above.
38. Letter of 23 April 1924 to Edmund Dulac, *CL InteLex* 4525.
39. Letter of 27 December 1930 to Olivia Shakespear, *CL InteLex* 5428.
40. Michael Wood, *The Road to Delphi* (New York: Farrar, Straus and Giroux, 2003) ('Road') 20, 104.
41. Indeed, the communicators insisted on so proceeding. (*AVB* 10–11)
42. Lisa Maurizio, 'The Voice at the Center of the World: The Pythias' Ambiguity and Authority', in André Lardinois and Laura McClure, eds., *Making Silence Speak: Women's Voices in Greek Literature and Society* (Princeton: Princeton University Press, 2001) 38–54 at 44.
43. See Chapter 4.
44. *CL InteLex* 3332.
45. *CL InteLex* 3337.
46. John Butler Yeats letter to Oliver Elton, 9 April 1911. Quoted in William M. Murphy, *Prodigal Father* (Ithaca: Cornell University Press, 1978) 384.
47. *CL InteLex* 3337.

CHAPTER 6

1. Foster also cites a November 1927 letter expressing George's view that her role in her family could easily be filled by 'a nurse a governess a secretary & a housekeeper...' (*id.* at 351), and notes that, by 1931, George's frustration with her life was apparent in letters to her friends (*id.* at 420).
2. Letter of 2 July 1926, *CL InteLex* 4891.
3. See Chapter 3.
4. *Among School Children* was written in June 1926.
5. See Chapter 1.
6. Marjorie Perloff suggests that the mermaid is Maud Gonne, but does not explain the basis for her attribution. Marjorie Perloff, '"Heart Mysteries", The Later Love Lyrics of W.B. Yeats,' *Contemporary Literature* 10.2 (1969) 266, 270.
7. E.g. Letter of 18 April 1937 to George Yeats, *CL InteLex* 6908.
8. BG 119.
9. Nicholas Grene, *Yeats's Poetic Codes* (Oxford: Oxford University Press, 2008) 121.
10. Letter of 23 September 1935 to Maurice Wollman, *CL InteLex* 6358.
11. Letter of 9 August 1921, *CL InteLex* 3960.
12. *CL InteLex* 4920.
13. Letter of 25 April 1928, *CL InteLex* 5104.

14. Although Wade (*L* 716) relied on Mrs. Yeats's identification of the enclosed poem as 'The Friends of His Youth,' Patrick Keane has pointed out that the poem had already been published at the time of Yeats's letter and 'A Last Confession' is the only poem of the series of women's voices that fits Yeats's question whether the poem would be 'less shocking' if he put 'a capital to "he" in the last stanza. Patrick J. Keane, *Yeats's Interaction with Tradition* (Columbia: University of Missouri Press, 1987) 128 n. 28.
15. Samuel Hynes, 'All the Wild Witches: The Women in Yeats's Poems', *Sewanee Review* lxxxv Vol. no. 4 (1977) 565, 579.
16. Letter of 17 August 1933, *CL InteLex* 5925.
17. Baron Frederick von Hügel, *The Mystical Element of Religion as Studied in St. Catherine of Genoa and her Friends* (London: Dent, 1927) ('Mystical').
18. Crazy Jane on God (*VP* 512) and Crazy Jane on the Day of Judgment (*VP 510*).
19. Yeats's letter at n. 10 above approves this interpretation in Maurice Wollman's *Modern Poetry 1922–1934* (London: Heinemann, 1935).
20. Preface to *The King of the Great Clock Tower* (*VP* 855).
21. Letter of 27 January 1934, *CL InteLex* 5998.
22. Vision and Later Plays 139–53.

CHAPTER 7

1. Richard Ellmann, *W.B. Yeats's Second Puberty* (Washington: Library of Congress, 1985) ('Second Puberty') 7.
2. Virginia D. Pruitt and Raymond D. Pruitt, 'Yeats and the Steinach Operation: A Further Analysis', *YAACTS* 1 104 (1983) (no physical effect). But see *Life 2*, 498–9.
3. Letter of 17 June 1935 to Dorothy Wellesley, *CL InteLex* 6257.
4. Letter of 21 March 1937 to Shri Purohit Swami, *CL InteLex* 6873.
5. 'Ribh at the Tomb of Baile and Aillinn ' (*VP* 554–5).
6. Letter of 25 August 1934, *CL InteLex* 6087.
7. BG 538 (citing letter from Ellmann).
8. See Chapter 3.
9. Roger McHugh, Introduction to Roger McHugh, ed., *Ah Sweet Dancer: W.B. Yeats and Margot Ruddock* (New York: Macmillan, 1970) ('LMR') 9.
10. McHugh recounts that Lovell later 'had many important parts in films, appearing in *The Man in Grey, Alibi, 49th Parallel, Caesar and Cleopatra, Pickwick Papers* and others.' He died in 1953. (*Id.*)
11. Letter of 24 September 1934, *CL InteLex* 6100.
12. Lemon Tree, ix-x.
13. Letters of 24 September and 11 October 1934, *CL InteLex* 6100 and 6110.
14. Letter of 13 November, *CL InteLex* 6124.
15. Homer, *The Odyssey*, XII, 50–3, trans. Robert Fagles (New York: Viking, 1996).
16. See, e.g. White Goddess at 409 and Jed Rasula, 'Gendering the Muse' in *Sulfur* 35:159 at 164.

Endnotes 231

17. Jean-Pierre Vernant, 'Feminine Figures of Death in Greece' in Froma I. Zeitlin, ed., *Mortals and Immortals* (Princeton: Princeton University Press, 1991) 95 at 104.
18. Plutarch, *Symposiacs*, Book IX, question XIV in W. Lloyd Bevan, ed., *Plutarch's Complete Works*, vol. III, *Essays and Miscellanies* (New York: Thomas Y. Crowell, 1909) 352.
19. W.B. Yeats, *A Full Moon in March* (London: Macmillan 1935) v-vi.
20. Letter of 17 November 1934, *CL InteLex* 6126.
21. Letter of 22 May 1936 from WBY to Dorothy Wellesley, *CL InteLex* 6560.
22. Letter of April 1936, *CL InteLex* 6532.
23. Ruddock's account ('Ecstasy') is reprinted in *LMR* 91 ss.
24. Letter of 22 May 1936 to Dorothy Wellesley, *CL InteLex* 6561.
25. Frank Kermode, *Romantic Image* (London: Routledge & Kegan Paul, 1957) 48.
26. Ethel Mannin, TS Diary in Boston University, cited in *Life 2*, 510. See Mannin *Privileged Spectator* (London: Jarrolds, 1939) 80–1.
27. Ethel Mannin, *Confessions and Impressions* (London: Jarrolds, 1931) 183.
28. Mannin's self-assessment is contained in Privileged Spectator, 28.
29. *Saturday Review* (London), 9 January 1926.
30. Letter of 27 December 1934, *CL InteLex* 6158.
31. *Life 2*, 511.
32. *CL InteLex* 6162.
33. See Chapter 1.
34. Letter of 8 January 1935, *CL InteLex* 6170.
35. Warwick Gould unravels the drafts of this poem and, differing from Ellmann who believed it to be a part of the poem to 'Margot,' suggests that the lines were intended for Mannin. Warwick Gould, '"Portrayed before his Eyes": an abandoned late poem,' *YA* 6 (1988) 214.
36. *CL InteLex* 6716.
37. *CL InteLex* 6194.
38. Gary Snyder, 'Forward' to Edward Schafer, *The Divine Woman: Dragon Ladies and Rain Maidens in T'ang Literature* (San Francisco: North Point, 1980) xi.

CHAPTER 8

1. Letter to Wellesley of 11 August 1935, *CL InteLex* 6317.
2. Dorothy Wellesley, *Far Have I Travelled* (London: James Barrie, 1952) ('FT') 34.
3. Victoria Glendinning, *Vita, The Life of Vita Sackville-West* (New York: Knopf, 1983) 129.
4. Letters of 2 September 1927 to Vita Sackville-West and 22 August 1936 to Ethel Smyth, in Nigel Nicolson and Joanna Trautman, eds., *The Letters of Virginia Woolf* (New York: Harcourt Brace Jovanovich, 1977–80) 3:415, 6:66.
5. Yeats's comment appears in the draft of his introduction to Wellesley's *Poetry of Ten Years*, which he sent to her by letter of 8 September 1935, *CL InteLex* 6335.
6. Letter of 25 August 1934, *CL InteLex* 6087.

7. Letter of 14 June 1935, *CL InteLex* 6252. Wellesley's selection from the Yeats correspondence omits the comparison to Sackville-West. *LDW* 3–4.
8. Letter of 9 July 1936, *CL InteLex* 6609.
9. Yeats forwarded a draft of his introduction to Wellesley by letter of 8 September 1935. See n. 5 above; W.B. Yeats, ed., *The Oxford Book of Modern Verse* (New York: Oxford University Press, 1936) ('*OBMV*') xxxii.
10. Letter of 15 November 1935, *CL InteLex* 6446.
11. Letter of 29 October 1936, *CL InteLex* 6688.
12. Letter of 28 November 1936, *CL InteLex* 6731.
13. Letter of 21 December 1936, *CL InteLex* 6759.
14. Letter of 4 May 1937, *CL InteLex* 6922.
15. The *Times Literary Supplement* of 23 April 1949 lamented 'if only the attempts at philosophy could have been left out; though Yeats would not have agreed with this.' A similar note, more pungently expressed, is found in Vita Sackville-West's observation in the DNB that 'Fancying herself as something of a philosopher, ... she often imposed upon her verse a weight it should never have been asked to carry.' E.T. Williams, H.N. Palner, eds., *Dictionary of National Biography* 1951–1960 (Oxford: Oxford University Press, 1971) ('*DNB*') 1041.
16. OBMV xxxii.
17. Dorothy Wellesley, *Early Light: The Collected Poems of Dorothy Wellesley* (London: Rupert Hart-Davis, 1955) ('Early Light') 221.
18. Letter of 6 April 1936, *CL InteLex* 6531.
19. Letter of 25 September 1935, *CL InteLex* 6363.
20. Letter of 30 June 1936 to Wellesley from WBY, *CL InteLex* 6596. The exchange respecting these ballads, and the entire scope of the Yeats-Wellesley relationship, is carefully discussed in Deborah Ferrelli, 'W.B. Yeats and Dorothy Wellesley', *YA* 17 (2007) 227–305.
21. 'The Lady's First Song' (*VP* 572).
22. See 'The Chambermaid's First Song' (VP 574) and 'The Chambermaid's Second Song' (*VP* 575).
23. Letter of 25 November 1936, *LDW* 106.
24. Letters of 8 November 1936 and 9 November 1936, *CL InteLex* 6701, 6705.
25. Letter of 21 July 1936, *CL InteLex* 6619.
26. Letter of 21 December 1936, *CL InteLex* 6759.
27. Hélène Cixous, 'The Laugh of the Medusa' in E. Marks and I. de Courtivron, eds., *New French Feminisms* (New York: Schocken, 1981) 245–6, 254.
28. Harrison 213 ss.
29. See Introduction, n. 16.
30. Dorothy Wellesley, *Beyond the Grave: Letters on Poetry to W.B. Yeats from Dorothy Wellesley* (Tunbridge Wells: Baldwin, 1952) 7.
31. Letter of 5 August 1936, *CL InteLex* 6630.
32. Letter of 21 January 1937 to Wellesley, *CL InteLex* 6785.

33. Letter of 28 November 1936, *CL InteLex* 6731. Rage and hatred as sources of Yeats's inspiration are discussed in Joseph M. Hassett, *Yeats and the Poetics of Hate* (Dublin: Gill and Macmillan; New York: St. Martin's Press, 1986).
34. Letter of 9 December 1936, *CL InteLex* 6746.
35. Letter of 23 December 1936 to Dorothy Wellesley, *CL InteLex* 6762.
36. Theodor W. Adorno, 'Late Style in Beethoven' in Adorno, *Essays on Music*, Richard Leppert, ed., Susan H. Gillespie, trans. (Berkeley: University of California Press, 2002) ('EM').
37. Edward W. Said, *On Late Style* (New York: Random House, 2006) 16–17.
38. Letter of 11 March 1937, in Richard J. Finneran, George Mills Harper and William M. Murphy, eds., *Letters to W.B. Yeats* (New York: Columbia University Press, 1977) II, 587–9.
39. Letter of 22 May 1936 to Dorothy Wellesley, *CL InteLex* 6560.
40. Letter of 22 May 1936 to Wellesley from WBY, *CL InteLex* 6560.
41. Kathleen Raine, Introduction to *LDW*.
42. Letter of 15 November 1936 to Ethel Mannin, *CL InteLex* 6716.

CHAPTER 9

1. Letter of 16 June 1938 to Maud Gonne, *CL InteLex* 7273.
2. Quoted in Heald's obituary, *Times* of London, 10 November 1976, 18.
3. *Id.*
4. Diana Souhami, *Gluck 1895–1978: Her Biography* (London: Pandora, 1988) ('Gluck').
5. *The Sunday Express*, July 5, 1925 at 7.
6. *The Sunday Express*, July 19, 1925 at 7.
7. *The Sunday Express*, October 17, 1926 at 11.
8. Letter of 18 May 1937, *CL InteLex* 6934.
9. Letter of 16 June 1937, *CL InteLex* 6966.
10. Letter of 16 June 1937, *CL InteLex* 6967.
11. Letter of 22 June 1937, *CL InteLex* 6978.
12. Letters of 4 and 12 September 1937, *CL InteLex* 7054 and 7066.
13. Letter of 2 March 1938, *CL InteLex* 7193.
14. Letter of 15 March 1938, *CL InteLex* 7201.
15. Letter of 16–20 March 1938, *CL InteLex* 7202.
16. Letter of 5 September 1937, *CL InteLex* 7055.
17. *Life 2*, 587.
18. Letter of 11 August 1935, *CL InteLex* 6316.
19. Quoted in Jeremy Silver, 'George Barnes's "W.B. Yeats and Broadcasting" 1940', *YA* 5 (1987) 194.
20. Last Poems MM 253.

21. Henry More, *The Immortality of the Soul* (London, 1659), Book III, Ch. 9. F.A.C. Wilson pointed out the pertinence of this passage in *W.B. Yeats and Tradition* (New York: Macmillan, 1958) 214.
22. Daniel Albright, *The Myth Against Myth* (London: Oxford University Press, 1972) 118.
23. Last Poems MM 299–301.
24. See Letter of 27 October 1937 to George Yeats, *CL InteLex* 7103.
25. Chapter 7, text at notes 17 and 18.
26. Letter of 24 October 1938, *CL InteLex* 7317.
27. Letter of 20 November 1937, *CL InteLex* 7122.
28. Warwick Gould, '"What is the explanation of it all?": Yeats's "little poem about nothing"', *YA* 5 (1987) 212–13.
29. Introduction, n. 17.
30. *Id.*
31. Letter of 12 August 1937, *CL InteLex* 7039.
32. Letter of 24 May 1938, *CL InteLex* 7243.

CHAPTER 10

1. Letters of 6 and 12 May 1938 from George Yeats to Edith Shackleton Heald, quoted in Glucks 217.
2. Letter of 18 September 1937 to Dorothy Rhodes, *CL InteLex* 7068.
3. Letter of 5 November 1937, *CL InteLex* 7108.
4. What Foster deftly calls the 'eugenicist hectoring' of the concluding lines (*Life 2*, 641) ought not mar this concluding affirmation of Gonne's central role as Muse.
5. *CL InteLex* 7273.
6. Maud Gonne MacBride, 'Yeats and Ireland' in Steven Gwynn, ed., *Scattering Branches: Tributes to the Memory of W.B. Yeats* (London: Macmillan, 1940) 25.
7. Letter of 8 October 1938, *CL InteLex* 7311.
8. Letter of 1 January 1939 to Edith Shackleton Heald, *CL InteLex* 7360.
9. *The Irish Times*, 28 January 1989, *rept'd* in Political Identities 257.
10. Last Poems MM 142–7.
11. Quoted in *Life 2*, 650.

Bibliography

I. BY YEATS

A Full Moon in March (London: Macmillan, 1935).
Autobiographies (London: Macmillan, 1955).
A Vision: An Explanation of Life Founded upon the Writings of Giraldus and upon certain Doctrines attributed to Kusta Ben Luka (London: privately printed for subscribers only by T. Werner Laurie, Ltd., 1925).
A Vision (London: Macmillan, 1937).
The Collected Letters of W.B. Yeats: Volume I, 1865–1895, ed. John Kelly and Eric Domville; *Volume II, 1896–1900*, ed. Warwick Gould, John Kelly, Deirdre Toomey; *Volume III, 1901–1904*, and *Volume IV, 1905–1907*, eds. John Kelly and Ronald Schuchard (Oxford: Clarendon Press, 1986, 1997, 1994, 2005).
The Collected Letters of W.B. Yeats, gen. ed. John Kelly, Oxford University Press (InteLex Electronic Edition) 2002.
Essays and Introductions (London and New York: Macmillan, 1961).
Fairy and Folk Tales of the Irish Peasantry (London: Walter Scott, 1888)
The Gonne-Yeats Letters 1893–1938: Always Your Friend, ed. Anna MacBride White and A. Norman Jeffares (London: Hutchinson, 1992).
The Letters of W. B. Yeats, ed. Allan Wade (London: Rupert Hart-Davis, 1954; New York: Macmillan, 1955).
Letters on Poetry from W.B. Yeats to Dorothy Wellesley, intro. Kathleen Raine (London and New York: Oxford University Press, 1964).
Memoirs: Autobiography – First Draft: Journal, transcribed and edited by Denis Donoghue (London: Macmillan, 1972; New York: Macmillan, 1973).
Mythologies (London and New York: Macmillan, 1959).
Mythologies, ed. by Warwick Gould and Deirdre Toomey (Basingstoke: Palgrave Macmillan, 2005).
The Oxford Book of Modern Verse (New York: Oxford University Press, 1936).
The Secret Rose, Stories by W.B. Yeats: A Variorum Edition, eds. Warwick Gould, Phillip L. Marcus, and Michael J. Sidnell (London: Macmillan, 1992). Second edition, rev. and enl.
The Speckled Bird by William Butler Yeats: An Autobiographical Novel With Variant Versions: New Edition, incorporating recently discovered manuscripts, edited and annotated by William H. O'Donnell (Basingstoke: Palgrave Macmillan, 2003).

W. B. Yeats and T. Sturge Moore: Their Correspondence, 1901–1937, ed. Ursula Bridge (London: Routledge and Kegan Paul; New York: Oxford University Press, 1953).

The Variorum Edition of the Poems of W. B. Yeats, ed. Peter Allt and Russell K. Alspach (New York: Macmillan, 1957).

The Variorum Edition of the Plays of W. B. Yeats, ed. Russell K. Alspach, assisted by Catherine C. Alspach (New York: Macmillan, 1969).

Yeats's Vision Papers (London: Macmillan, 1992; Palgrave, 2001), gen. ed. George Mills Harper, assisted by Mary Jane Harper, Vol. 1: *The Automatic Script: 5 November 1917–18 June 1918*, eds. Steve L. Adams, Barbara J. Frieling and Sandra L. Sprayberry; Vol. 2: *The Automatic Script: 25 June 1918–29 March 1920*, eds. Steve L. Adams, Barbara J. Frieling, and Sandra Sprayberry; Volume 3: *Sleep and Dream Notebooks, Vision Notebooks 1 and 2, Card File*, eds. Robert Anthony Martinich and Margaret Mills Harper; *Vol. 4: 'The Discoveries of Michael Robartes' Version B ['The Great Wheel' and 'The Twenty-Eight Embodiments']*, eds. George Mills Harper and Margaret Mills Harper, assisted by Richard W. Stoops, Jr.

II. ABOUT YEATS

Adams, Steve L. and Harper, George Mills, 'The Manuscript of Leo Africanus', *YA 1* (1982) 3–47.

Albright, Daniel, *The Myth Against Myth* (London: Oxford University Press, 1972).

Bloom, Harold, *Yeats* (Oxford: Oxford University Press, 1970).

Bradford, Curtis, 'The Order of Yeats's *Last Poems*', *Modern Language Notes*, vol. 76, no. 6 (1961).

Clark, David R., *Yeats at Songs and Choruses* (Gerrards Cross: Colin Smythe, 1983).

Cullingford, Elizabeth Butler, *Gender and History in Yeats's Love Poetry* (Cambridge: Cambridge University Press, 1993).

Ellmann, Richard, *The Identity of Yeats* (New York: Oxford University Press, 1964).

—— *Golden Codgers* (New York: Oxford University Press, 1973).

—— *W.B. Yeats: The Man and the Masks* (New York: Norton, 1978).

—— *W.B. Yeats's Second Puberty* (Washington: Library of Congress, 1985).

Finneran, Richard J., Harper, George Mills and Murphy, William M., eds., *Letters to W.B. Yeats* (New York: Columbia University Press, 1977).

Foster, R. F., *W.B. Yeats: A Life, I: The Apprentice Mage* (Oxford and New York: Oxford University Press, 1997).

—— *W.B. Yeats: A Life II: The Arch-Poet* (Oxford and New York: Oxford University Press, 2003).

—— 'Yeats and the Death of Lady Gregory', *Irish University Review*, 34.1 (2004) 109–21.

French, Amanda, '"A Strangely Useless Thing": Iseult Gonne and Yeats', *Yeats Eliot Review* 19 (2002) 13–24.

Gould, Warwick, '"A Lesson for the Circumspect": W.B. Yeats's Two Versions of *A Vision* and the *Arabian Nights*', in Peter L. Caracciolo, ed., *The Arabian Nights in English Literature* (London: Macmillan, 1988).

Grene, Nicholas, *Yeats's Poetic Codes* (Oxford: Oxford University Press, 2008).

Grossman, Allen R., *Poetic Knowledge in the Early Yeats* (Charlottesville: University Press of Virginia, 1969).

Harper, George Mills, *Yeats's Golden Dawn* (London: Macmillan, 1974).

—— *W.B. Yeats and W. T. Horton: The Record of an Occult Friendship* (Atlantic Highlands: Humanities Press, 1980).

—— *The Making of Yeats's "A Vision": A study of the Automatic Script* (London: Macmillan; Carbondale and Edwardsville, Ill.: Southern Illinois University Press, 1987). 2 vols.

—— and Kelly, John S., 'Preliminary Examination of the Script of E[lizabeth] R[adcliff]', in *Yeats and the Occult*, ed. George Mills Harper (Toronto: Macmillan, 1975).

Harper, Margaret Mills, *Wisdom of Two: The Spiritual and Literary Collaboration of George and W.B. Yeats* (Oxford: Oxford University Press, 2007).

Harwood, John, *Olivia Shakspear and W.B. Yeats* (New York: St. Martin's Press, 1989).

Hassett, Joseph M., *Yeats and the Poetics of Hate* (Dublin: Gill and Macmillan; New York: St. Martin's Press, 1986).

Heaney, Seamus, 'William Butler Yeats' in Seamus Deane, gen. ed., *The Field Day Anthology of Irish Writing* (Derry: Field Day Publications, 1991) 91–8.

Heine, Elizabeth, 'W.B. Yeats' map in his own hand', *Biography* 1:3 (1978) 37–50.

—— 'Yeats and Maud Gonne: Marriage and the Astrological Record, 1908–09', *YA* 13 (1998) 3–33.

Henn, T. R., *The Lonely Tower*, 2d ed. (London: Methuen, 1965).

Hone, Joseph, *W.B. Yeats* (London: Macmillan, 1942).

Hood, Walter Kelly, '"Read Fechner", The Spirit Said: W.B. Yeats and Theodor Fechner', *YAACTS* 7 (1989) 91–8.

Hynes, Samuel, 'All the Wild Witches: The Women in Yeats's Poems', *Sewanee Review* lxxxv Vol. no. 4 (1927) 565–82.

Jeffares, A. Norman, *A New Commentary on the Poems of W.B. Yeats* (London: Macmillan; Stanford: Stanford University Press, 1984).

Jeffares, A. Norman, 'Iseult Gonne', *YA* 16 (2005) 197–278.

Jeffares, A. Norman, White, Anna MacBride and Bridgewater, Christina, eds., *Letters to W.B. Yeats and Ezra Pound from Iseult Gonne* (Basingstoke: Palgrave, 2004).

Keane, Patrick J., *Yeats's Interaction with Tradition* (Columbia: University of Missouri Press, 1987).

Kelly, John S., *A W.B. Yeats Chronology* (Basingstoke: Palgrave Macmillan, 2003).

Kline, Gloria C., *The Last Courtly Lover* (Ann Arbor: UMI Research Press, 1983).

Litz, A. Walton, 'Pound and Yeats: The Road to Stone Cottage', in Bornstein, George, ed., *Ezra Pound Among the Poets* (Chicago: University of Chicago Press, 1985).

Longenbach, James, *Stone Cottage: Pound, Yeats & Modernism* (Oxford: Oxford University Press, 1988).

Longley, Edna, 'Helicon and ni Houlihan: Michael Robartes and the Dancer' in Jonathan Allison, ed., *Yeats's Political Identities: Selected Essays* (Ann Arbor: University of Michigan Press, 1996).

MacBride, Maud Gonne, 'Yeats and Ireland' in Steven Gwynn, ed., *Scattering Branches: Tributes to the Memory of W.B. Yeats* (London: Macmillan, 1940) 16–33.

Mann, Neil, 'W. B. Yeats and the Vegetable Phoenix', *YA* 17 (2007) 3–35.

McHugh, Roger, ed., *Ah, Sweet Dancer: W.B. Yeats and Margot Ruddock* (New York: Macmillan, 1970).

Moore, T. Sturge, ' Yeats ', English 2 (Summer 1939) 273–8.

Moore, Virginia, *The Unicorn* (New York: Macmillan, 1954).

Oates, Joyce Carol, '"At Least I Have Made a Woman of Her": Images of Women in Twentieth-Century Literature', *Georgia Review* 37 (Spring 1983) 7–30.

Perloff, Marjorie, '"Heart Mysteries", The Later Love Lyrics of W.B. Yeats', *Contemporary Literature* 10.2 (1969) 266–83.

—— 'Between Hatred and Desire: Sexuality and Subterfuge in "A Prayer for My Daughter"', *YA* 7 (1990) 29–50.

Pruitt, Virginia D., 'W.B. Yeats, Iseult Gonne and the Mask', *Yeats Eliot Review* 10 (1989) 52–6.

—— and Pruitt, Raymond D., 'Yeats and the Steinach Operation: A further Analysis', *YAACTS* 1(1983) 104–24.

Ramazani, Jahan, *Yeats and the Poetry of Death* (New Haven: Yale University Press, 1990).

—— '"A Little Space": The Psychic Economy of Yeats's Love Poems', *Criticism*, Vol. xxxv, no. 1 (1993) 67–89.

Schuchard, Ronald, *The Last Minstrels: Yeats and the Renewal of the Bardic Arts* (Oxford: Oxford University Press, 2008).

Sidnell, Michael, 'The Presence of the Poet: or What Sat Down at the Breakfast Table', in A. Norman Jeffares, ed., *Yeats the European* (Gerrards Cross: Colin Smythe, 1989).

Silver, Jeremy, 'George Barnes's "W.B. Yeats and Broadcasting" 1940', *YA* 5 1987.

Toomey, Deirdre, '"Worst Part of Life": Yeats's Horoscopes for Olivia Shakespear', *YA* 6 (1988) 222–6.

—— 'Labryinths: Yeats and Maud Gonne', *YA* 9 (1992) 95–131.

Bibliography

Vendler, Helen, *Yeats's Vision and the Later Plays* (Cambridge: Harvard University Press, 1963).
—— *Our Secret Discipline: Yeats and Lyric Form* (Cambridge: Harvard University Press, 2007).
Wellesley, Dorothy, *Beyond the Grave: Letters on Poetry to W.B. Yeats from Dorothy Wellesley* (Tunbridge Wells: Baldwin, 1952).
Whittaker, Thomas R., *Swan and Shadow: Yeats's Dialogue with History* (Chapel Hill: University of North Carolina Press, 1964).

III. OTHER WORKS

Alighieri, Dante, *Purgatorio*, trans. by Charles Shadwell (London: Macmillan, 1892–99).
Adorno, Theodor W., 'Late Style in Beethoven' in Adorno, *Essays on Music*, Richard Leppert, ed., Susan H. Gillespie, trans. (Berkeley: University of California Press, 2002).
Balliet, Conrad A., 'The Lives – and Lies – of Maud Gonne', *Eire-Ireland* 14:3 (1979) 17–44.
Bax, Clifford, ed., *Florence Farr, Bernard Shaw, and W.B. Yeats* (Dublin: Cuala Press, 1941).
Bergin, Thomas G., ed. *Petrarch: Selected Sonnets, Odes and Letters* (Amilingher Heights: Harlan Davidson, 1966).
Bevan, W. Lloyd, ed., *Plutarch's Complete Works*, vol. III, *Essays and Miscellanies* (New York: Thomas Y. Crowell, 1909).
Bloom, Harold, *Poetry and Repression* (New Haven: Yale University Press, 1976).
—— *The Anxiety of Influence* 2d ed. (Oxford: Oxford University Press, 1997).
Bostridge, Mark, *Florence Nightingale: The Making of a Legend* (New York: Farrar Strauss Giroux, 2008).
Bridges, Robert, *Poems* (London: Bumpus, 1879).
Cardozo, Nancy, *Lucky Eyes and a High Heart* (New York: Bobbs-Merrill, 1978).
Cixous, Hélène, 'The Laugh of the Medusa' in E. Marks and I. de Courtivron, eds., *New French Feminisms* (New York: Schocken, 1981), 245–64.
Colum, Mary, *Life and the Dream*, (London: Macmillan, 1947).
Croce, Arlene, 'Is the Muse Dead?', *The New Yorker*, February 26, 1996, 164–9.
de Rougemont, Denis, *Love in the Western World*, trans. by Montgomery Belgion, rev. ed. (New York, Pantheon, 1956) (originally published as *Amour et l'Occident* (Paris: Plon, 1939)).
Derrida, Jacques, 'Différance' in *Margins of Philosophy*, trans. by Alan Bass (Chicago: University of Chicago Press, 1982).
Dolmetsch, Mabel, 'Personal Recollections of Arnold Dolmetsch' (London: Routledge & Kegan Paul, 1957).

Bibliography

Du Plessis, Rachel Blau, 'Propounding Modernist Maleness: How Pound Managed a Muse' in *Modernism/Modernity*, Vol. 9, no. 3 (Sept. 2002) 389–405.

Eliot, T. S., *The Use of Poetry and the Use of Criticism: Studies in the Relation of Criticism to Poetry in England* (London: Faber, 1933).

Ellmann, Richard, *James Joyce* (New York: Oxford University Press, 1982).

Emerson, E.W., ed., *The Complete Works of Ralph Waldo Emerson* (Boston, New York: Houghton, Mifflin, 1903–4).

Farr, Florence, 'An Introduction to Alchemy and Notes by S.S.D.D.', in *A Short Inquiry Concerning the Hermetic Art by a Lover of Philalethes*, London, 1714 in *Collectanea Hermetica*, Vol. 3, ed. Wynn Westcott (London: Theosophical Publishing Society, 1894).

—— 'Ibsen's Women', No. 1, Hedda Gabler, *The New Age*, I, 25, Oct. 7, 1907, 389.

—— *Modern Woman: Her Intentions* (London: Frank Palmer, 1910).

—— *The Solemnization of Jacklin* (London: A.C. Fifield, 1912).

—— *The Dancing Faun* (London: Elkin Mathews and John Lane, 1894).

—— *The Music of Speech* (London: Elkin Mathews, 1909).

Fechner, Theodor, *On Life After Death*, trans. by Hugo Wernekke, 3rd ed. (Chicago and London: Open Court Publishing, 1914).

Flaubert, Gustave, *The Temptation of Saint Antony*, trans. by D. F. Hanningan (London: H.F. Nichols, 1895).

Fletcher, Ian, ed., *Romantic Mythologies* (New York: Barnes & Noble, 1967).

Freud, Sigmund, *The Standard Edition of the Complete Psychological Works of Sigmund Freud* (London: Hogarth Press, 1953–74).

Gibbs, A.M., *Bernard Shaw: A Life* (Gainesville: University of Florida Press, 2005).

Gill, Stephen, ed., *William Wordsworth: The Major Works* (Oxford: Oxford University Press, 1984).

Glendinning, Victoria, *Vita, The Life of Vita Sackville-West* (New York: Knopf, 1983).

Goldin, Frederick, *The Mirror of Narcissus in the Courtly Love Lyric* (Ithaca: Cornell University Press, 1967).

Graves, Robert, *The Greek Myths* (Harmondsworth: Penguin, 1955).

—— *The White Goddess*, 4th ed. (London: Faber & Faber, 1999).

Harrison, Jane, *Prolegomena to the Study of Greek Religion* (Cambridge: Cambridge University Press, 1903).

Heaney, Seamus, 'Sixth sense, seventh heaven' in Brendan Barrington, ed. *The Dublin Review* Reader (Dublin: Dublin Review Books, 2007).

Hearon, Holly E., *The Mary Magdalene Tradition* (Collegeville: Liturgical Press, 2004).

Hesiod, *Theogony*, tr. Hugh G. Evelyn-White, in *Hesiod: The Homeric Hymns and Homerica* (London: Heineman, 1982).

Homer, *The Odyssey*, trans. by Robert Fagles (New York: Viking, 1996).

Bibliography 241

Hough, Graham, *The Last Romantics* (London: Duckworth, 1949).
Johnson, Josephine, *Florence Farr: Bernard Shaw's 'New Woman'* (Gerrards Cross: Colin Smythe, 1975).
Johnson, Samuel, *Lives of the English Poets* (London: John Murray, 1854).
Jonas, Hans, *The Gnostic Religion*, 2d ed. rev. (Boston: Beacon Press, 1963).
Joyce, James, *Ulysses* (New York: Random House, 1934).
—— *A Portrait of the Artist as a Young Man* (London: Penguin, 2000).
Jung, C.G., *The Structure and Dynamics of the Psyche* (London: Routledge & Kegan Paul, 1960).
Keynes, Geoffrey, ed., *Blake Complete Writings* (Oxford: Oxford University Press, 1972).
Kermode, Frank, *Romantic Image* (London: Routledge & Kegan Paul, 1957).
Kiley, Kevin, *Francis Stuart Artist and Outcast* (Dublin: The Liffey Press, 2007).
Kristeva, Julia, *Tales of Love*, trans. Leon S. Roudiez (New York: Columbia University Press, 1987).
Lazar, Moshe, '*Fin Amor*' in F.R.P. Akehurst and Judith M. Davis, *A Handbook of the Troubadours* (Berkeley: University of California Press, 1955).
Lessing, G.P.E., *Laocoön, Nathan the Wise & Minna Von Barnhelm*, trans., William Steel (London: Dent, 1930).
Lewis, C. S., *The Allegory of Love* (Oxford: Oxford University Press, 1936).
Litz, A. Walton, 'Florence Farr: A "Transitional Woman"', in Maria di Battista and Lucy McDiarmid, eds., *High and Low Moderns: Literature and Culture, 1889–1939* (New York: Oxford University Press, 1996).
MacBride, Maud Gonne, *A Servant of the Queen*, 1938; rpt. (Gerrards Cross: Colin Smythe, 1994).
MacKenna, Stephen, trans., *Plotinus, The Enneads* (London: Warner, 1917–35) vol. I.
Maddox, Brenda, *George's Ghosts* (Basingstoke: Picador, 1999).
Malory, Thomas, *Le Morte d'Arthur*, (London: Dent, 1893).
Mannin, Ethel, *Confessions and Impressions* (London: Jarrolds, 1931).
—— *Privileged Spectator* (London: Jarrolds, 1939).
Maritain, Jacques, *Creative Intuition in Art and Poetry* (New York: Meridian Books, 1955).
Maurizio, Lisa, 'The Voice at the Center of the World: The Pythias' Ambiguity and Authority', in André Lardinois and Laura McClure, eds., *Making Silence Speak: Women's Voices in Greek Literature and Society* (Princeton: Princeton University Press, 2001).
Mead, G.R.S., *Simon Magus an Essay* (London: Theosophical Publishing Society, 1892).
Moody, A. David, *Ezra Pound: Poet* (Oxford: Oxford University Press, 2007).
More, Henry, *The Immortality of the Soul* (London, 1659).
Muldoon, Paul, *The End of the Poem* (London: Faber & Faber, 2007).
Murphy, William M., *Prodigal Father* (Ithaca: Cornell University Press, 1978).

Bibliography

Nabokov, Vladimir, *Lolita*, 1955; ann. ed. (New York: Vintage, 1991).
Neumann, Erich, *The Great Mother* (New York: Pantheon, 1955).
Nic Shiubhlaigh, Marie, *The Splendid Years: Recollections of Marie Nic Shiubhlaigh as Told to Edward Kenny* (Dublin: James Duffy & Co. 1955).
Nicolson, Nigel and Trautman, Joanna eds, *The Letters of Virginia Woolf* (New York: Harcourt Brace Jovanovich, 1977–80).
O'Donoghue, Bernard, *The Courtly Love Tradition* (Manchester: Manchester University Press, 1982).
Ovid, *Metamorphoses*, ed. Brookes More (Boston: Cornhill Publishing Co. 1922).
Petrarca, Francesco, *Rerum senilium libri*, trans. by Aldo S. Bernardo, Saul Levin and Reta A. Bernardo, *Letters of Old Age* (Baltimore: Johns Hopkins University Press, 1992).
Pound, Ezra, 'Portrait d'une Femme' in *Ripostes* (London: Swift, 1912), rep't in M. J. King, ed., *Collected Early Poems of Ezra Pound* (New York: New Directions, 1976).
Pound, Ezra, and Spann, Maureen, eds., *Confucius to Cummings: An Anthology of Poetry* (New York: New Directions, 1964).
Pound, Omar, and Litz, A. Walton, *Ezra Pound and Dorothy Shakespear: Their Letters 1909–1914* (London: Faber, 1985).
Praz, Mario, *The Romantic Agony*, trans. Angus Davidson (New York: Meridian Books, 1956).
Preminger, Alex, and Brogan, T.V.F., eds., *The New Princeton Encyclopedia of Poetry and Poetics* (Princeton: Princeton University Press, 1993).
Quinn, Kenneth, ed., *Catullus: The Poems* (New York: St. Martin's Press, 1970).
Rich, Adrienne, *On Lies, Secrets, and Silence* (New York: Norton, 1979).
Richter, John Paul, ed., *The Literary Works of Leonardo DaVinci* (London: Sampson, Low, Marston, Searle and Rivington, 1883).
Ruddock, Margot, *The Lemon Tree* (London: Dent, 1937).
Rossetti, Dante Gabriel, *Dante and His Circle* (London: Ellis and White, 1874).
Said, Edward W., *On Late Style* (New York: Random House, 2006).
Shaw, George Bernard, 'The Quintessence of Ibsenism' rpt. in *Bernard Shaw: Major Critical Essays* (Harmondsworth: Penguin, 1986).
Shute, Jenefer, '"So Nakedly Dressed": The Text of the Female Body in Nabokov's Novels' in Ellen Pifer, ed., *Vladimir Nabokov's Lolita: A Casebook* (Oxford: Oxford University Press, 2003).
Snyder, Gary, 'Forward' to Edward Schafer, *The Divine Woman: Dragon Ladies and Rain Maidens in T'ang Literature* (San Francisco: North Point, 1980).
Souhami, Diana, *Gluck 1895–1978: Her Biography* (London: Pandora, 1988).
Storr, Anthony, *The Dynamics of Creation* (New York: Atheneum, 1972).
Synge, J. M. *Poems and Translations* (Dundrum: Cuala Press, 1909).
Tanner, Tony, *Venice Desired* (Cambridge: Harvard University Press, 1992).

Bibliography

Taylor, Thomas, trans., *The Six Books of Proclus on the Theology of Plato* (London: Law & Co., 1816).

Todhunter, John, *A Sicilian Idyll: A Pastoral Play in Two Scenes* (London: Elkin Mathews, 1890).

Trilling, Lionel, 'The Last Lover: Vladimir Nabokov's "Lolita"' *Encounter* 11, No. 4 (Oct. 1958).

Valency, Maurice, *In Praise of Love* (New York: Shocken Books, 1982).

Vernant, Jean-Pierre, 'Feminine Figures of Death in Greece' in Froma I. Zeitlin, ed., *Mortals and Immortals* (Princeton: Princeton University Press, 1991).

von Hügel, Baron Frederich, *The Mystical Element of Religion as Studied in St. Catherine of Genoa and her Friends* (London: Dent, 1927).

Waite, A.E., *Lives of Alchemystical Philosophers* (London: G.P. Redway, 1888).

Wellesley, Dorothy, *Early Light: The Collected Poems of Dorothy Wellesley* (London: Rupert Hart-Davis, 1955).

Witt, R.E., *Isis in the Ancient World* (Baltimore: The Johns Hopkins University Press, 1997).

Wollman, Maurice, *Modern Poetry 1922–1934* (London: Heinemann, 1935).

Wood, Michael, *The Road to Delphi* (New York: Farrar, Straus and Giroux, 2003).

Yeats, John Butler, *Letters to His Son W.B. Yeats and Others 1869–1922* (London: Faber & Faber, 1944).

—— *Further Letters of John Butler Yeats*, ed. Lennox Robinson (Dundrum: Cuala Press, 1920).

Young, Ella, *Flowering Dusk: Things Remembered Accurately and Inaccurately* (New York: Longmans Green & Co., 1945).

Index

Note: Illustrations are indicated by bold entries

Adorno, Theodor 194–5
Aeschylus 192
Africanus, Leo (spirit) 119, 133
Albright, Daniel 204
Allgood, Molly 50
Armstrong, Laura 73
Ashton, Frederick 172

Barnes, George 179
Beardsley, Aubrey 42
Beardsley, Mabel 27, 59
 and joy in face of death 61
Beauclerc, Helen 197
Bennett, Arnold 199
Bergson, Henri 14
Bloom, Harold 15, 103, 109, 110–11, 120
Bridges, Robert 47

Campbell, Lawrence 210
Campbell, Mrs Patrick 57
Cixous, Hélène 190
Clark, David 33
Collis, Jack 172
Colum, Mary 71
courtly love tradition 65–8
 and core of 66
  Yeats on monstrosity of 109
 and Gonne as Muse of 3–4, 65–8, 99–100
 and unattainability of beloved 2, 66
 and Yeats' abandonment of 103, 128–9
 and Yeats' concept of the Muse 1
Croce, Arlene 32, 68
Cullingford, Elizabeth Butler 9, 75, 94–5

Daniel, Arnaut 66
Dante Alighieri 2, 17
 and courtly love tradition 67–8
 and 'Ego Dominus Tuus' 119–20
 and joy 27
 and poetry of praise 80, 89
 and sweetness 28, 95
da Vinci, Leonardo 23
de Rougemont, Denis 66, 67, 68

Dickinson, Mabel 57, 89–90, 110
Dolmetsch, Arnold 40, 46, 47, 55
Dolmetsch, Mabel 40
Dulac, Edmund 151, 197, 203
Du Plessis, Rachel Blau 56, 57

Eliot, T S 39
Ellis, Edwin 150
Ellman, Richard 18, 19, 26, 50, 86, 131, 150, 156, 169, 171, 205
Emerson, Ralph Waldo 149–50
Emery, Edward 37
Ennoia 15, 16, 111

Farr, Florence **36**
 as actress:
  in *Arms and the Man* 43
  in *A Comedy of Sighs* 42
  in *The Countess Cathleen* 44–5
  in *Deirdre* 53
  in *Electra* 53
  in *Rosmersholm* 41
  in Shaw's plays 41–2
  in *A Sicilian Idyll* 37, 40
 and beautiful voice 38, 39
 and cancer 58–9
 and death of 59
 on Ibsen's Hedda Gabler 57
 and independence of 50, 57
 and leaves for Ceylon 55, 62
 and magic 38, 44
 and marriage and divorce 37
 and Pound's 'Portrait D'une Femme' 55–7
 and Shakespear, co-authorship with 48
 and Shaw 40–1
  acts in plays of 41–2, 43
  influence on novel 43
  loved by 41
 and solo performances 52
  final psaltery performance 55
 and tour of America 52
 and vision of Isis 38–9
 and the Wisdom Goddess 38

Farr, Florence (*continued*)
   mask of Medusa 42–3
   and works of:
     The Beloved of Hathor 48
     The Dancing Faun 43
     'The Earth and We' 59–60
     Modern Woman: Her Intentions 50
     The Shrine of the Golden Hawk 48, 49, 175
     The Solemnization of Jacklin 54, 59
   and Yeats:
     asks for payment for reading to 53
     associated with White Goddess by 37–8, 48
     conflict within Order of the Golden Dawn 45–6
     consider joint USA tour 52
     construction of a spoken poetry 39
     continuing friendship with 58
     creation of a poet's theatre 44–5
     demands pay increase from 53
     as enchantress of 39
     end of affair with 50–1
     exasperation of 54–5
     Fechner's ideas 59
     his memories of in old age 209–10
     influence on 3
     Irish Literary Theatre 44–5
     joint performances 47
     last letter to 59
     lists her gifts 37–8
     as Muse to 40, 51, 52, 57
     praised by 54
     reaction to her performance in *Rosmersholm* 41
     refusal to be cast as Muse by 57–8
     rhythmic chanting of poetry 40, 45, 46–9
     romantic relationship 49
     soul's journey after death 61, 62
     too close to be a Muse 49–50
     use of psaltery in recitations 46
   and Yeats's writings:
     'Against Witchcraft' 51–2
     'All Souls' Night' 3, 59, 60–1, 62–3
     excluded from 'Friends' 53–5
     'The Players ask for a Blessing on the Psalteries and on Themselves' 47–8
Farr, William 37
Fechner, Theodor 59
Flamel, Nicholas and Pernella 90–1
Flaubert, Gustave 1, 15, 16, 111

Foster, Roy 11, 68, 110, 157, 161, 182, 199
Freud, Sigmund 109, 110–11, 122, 123, 128, 169
Furies 190, 192–5

Glendinning, Victoria 185
Gluckstein, Hannah 199
Golden Dawn, Order of the, *see* Order of the Golden Dawn
Goldin, Frederick 66, 84
Gonne, Iseult **102**
   and conception of 72, 104, 126
   and jobs 113
   as nymphet 105
   and uselessness of being a Muse 124–5
   and writings of 113
   'The Shadow of Noon' 124–5
   and Yeats:
     anti-self, or daimon 118–19
     breaks from 127–8
     celebrates her beauty 125–6
     constructed as Muse by 107–9, 124
     constructed as object of desire by 106–7
     deepening of relationship 113, 114
     his attraction to 106–7
     his memories of in old age 210
     illusions 118
     influence on 4
     intellectual collaboration 116–17
     lyric borrowed by 125
     memory of her singing 105
     rejects marriage proposal by 4, 114–15
     role of absence 117–18
     semi-paternal relationship 105–6, 113, 115
     she suggests marriage 106
     as teacher 106
     unease over role of 109
   and Yeats's writings:
     'The Death of the Hare' 159–60
     'Lines written in Dejection' 115–16
     'Men Improve with the Years' 115, 124
     'Michael Robartes and the Dancer' 124, 140–1
     The Only Jealousy of Emer 125–6
     'On Woman' 107–8, 124
     'Owen Aherne and his Dancers' 132, 160
     Per Amica Silentia Lunae 116, 119–23
     'Presences' 109–13

Index

'To a Child Dancing in the Wind' 104, 105
'To a Young Beauty' 141
'To a Young Girl' 108–9
'Two Songs of a Fool' 160
'Two Years Later' 106, 107
'Why Should Not Old Men be Mad?' 117
Gonne, Kathleen 81, 106
Gonne, Maud **64**
  as actress 71
  and beauty of 68, 69, 71
  and conversion to Catholicism 83, 84
  and identity 68
  and Irish nationalism 65, 69
  violence 93
  and joins Order of the Golden Dawn 72
  and MacBride 78, 81
  end of marriage 84–5
  marriage to 83, 84
  and Millevoye 68, 76
  and mystery 68
  and political activity 73, 74, 75
  and slanderous gossip about 75–6
  and unattainability of 4, 84
  and Yeats:
    analogizes to Helen 92–3
    associated with White Goddess by 25–6, 93
    brother and sister relationship 70–1
    consigned to past by 103
    creation of new Irish consciousness 69–70
    denies her entry to house 142
    difficulty in eradicating her image of Muse 139–40
    disputes between 97
    dreams of marriage to 76
    effects of relationship on poetry 87–8
    end of marriage to MacBride 84–5
    enmity between 88–9
    as father of poems of 83
    final meeting with 210–11
    first meeting 40, 65, 68–9
    on her career as Muse to 99
    on her conversion to Catholicism 84
    on her loss of solitariness 83–4
    impact of marriage on 84
    influence on 3–4
    justifies her violence 92–3
    marriage to MacBride 83–4, 91–2
    memorialist poetry 98
    as Muse of courtly love tradition 65–8, 99–100
    as Muse to 95–6, 97
    necessity of unattainability 87
    physical relationship 86
    poetry of praise 80–1, 90
    prevents her joining demonstration 75, 92
    primacy as Muse to 95
    reasons for his attraction to 69
    rejected as Muse by 142
    rejects marriage proposal by 4, 71, 77, 82–3, 114, 127, 128
    reveals vulnerability to 76–8
    shared belief in power of dreams 70
    shared vision 77
    spiritual marriage 76–7, 90
    spiritual relationship 86, 87
    summary of relationship with 103–4
    vision of 85–6
    waning influence on 89
  and Yeats's writings:
    'Adam's Curse' 66, 68, 81–3
    'Against Unworthy Praise' 94
    'Among School Children' 153, 158–9
    'The Arrow' 80–1
    'Broken Dreams' 100
    'A Bronze Head' 92, 210
    Cathleen ni Houlihan 71
    'The Cold Heaven' 95–7
    The Countess Cathleen 69, 71
    'The Death of the Hare' 159–60
    'A Deep-sworn Vow' 95
    'A Dialogue of Self and Soul' 140
    'The Double Vision of Michael Robartes' 139–40
    'A Dream of Death' 73
    'Easter 1916' 113–14
    'Fallen Majesty' 103
    'First Love' 158
    'The Fish' 76
    'The Folly of Being Comforted' 81
    'Friends' 29, 94–5
    'The Friends of His Youth' 158
    'Her Praise' 98
    'He thinks of those who have Spoken Evil of his Beloved' 75–6
    'He wishes for the Cloths of Heaven' 76
    'He wishes his Beloved were Dead' 74–5, 92
    'His Memories' 158

Gonne, Maud (*continued*)
    'His Phoenix' 98
    'Human Dignity' 158
    'King and No King' 91
    'Leda and the Swan' 93
    'The Lover pleads With His Friend
        for Old Friends' 73–4
    'A Man Young and Old' 86
    'A Memory of Youth' 103–4
    Nicholas and Pernella Flamel
        poems 90–4
    'No Second Troy' 92–4
    'The Old Age of Queen Maeve' 84
    'The People' 98–9
    'A Prayer for my Daughter' 88
    'Quarrel in Old Age' 164–5
    'Reconciliation' 91–2
    'Subject for lyric' 78–80, 140
    'Summer and Spring' 158, 159
    'A Thought From Propertius' 100
    'The Tower' 77
    'When Helen Lived' 98
    'When You are Old' 72
    'A Woman Homer Sung' 92, 140
    'Words' 87–8
Gore-Booth, Eva 11, 81
Gould, Warwick 111, 145
Graves, Robert:
    and definition of the Muse 33
    and the Muse poet 2
    and poetic practice 20
    and White Goddess 1–2
Gregory, Lady Augusta 26, 27
    and death of 165
    in 'Friends' 26, 29–31, 32
Gregory, Robert 27
Grene, Nicolas 160
Grossman, Ellen 22–3, 32

Haire, Norman 169, 181
Harrison, Jane 42
Hartley, L T 181
Harwood, John 29, 30
Heald, Edith Shackleton 7–8, 171, 186,
    198
    and ambiguous sexuality of 199
    and journalism of 199–201
    and myth of the 'adored one' 200
    and societal ideas of beauty 199–200
    and suits by wives for loss of husbands'
        affection 200–1
    and Yeats:
        desire expressed by 202–3
        intimate letters from 201–2

    introduced to 197
    as Siren to 202
    visits by 201
Heald, Ivan 199
Heald, Nora 199
Heaney, Seamus 70, 96–7, 211
Helena 15, 16, 111
Henn, T R 148, 189–90
Hermetic Order of the Golden Dawn, *see*
    Order of the Golden Dawn
Hesiod 1
Hoffmann, E T A 109
Hofmannsthal, Hugo von 53
Holroyd, Michael 110
Homer 1
Hone, Joseph 133
Horniman, Annie 42, 45
Horton, W T 15, 32, 38, 60, 115
Hough, Graham 26
Hügel, Baron Frederich von 163
Hyde-Lees, George, *see* Yeats, George (née
    Hyde-Lees)
Hynes, Samuel 163

Ibsen, Henrik 41, 57
Irish Literary Theatre 44
Irish Republican Brotherhood 93

Jeffares, A Norman 29, 106, 108, 110,
    150
John, Augustus 110
Johnson, Lionel 12, 192
Joyce, James 21
Jung, Carl Gustav 13

Kermode, Frank 178
Kristeva, Julia 8, 99

late style 194–5
Leanhaun Shee 15–16, 138
Lessing, G P E 148
Longley, Edna 143
Lovell, Raymond 172

MacBride, Major John 78, 81, 83, 84,
    93, 113
McHugh, Roger 172
Malory, SIr Thomas 65–6
Mann, Thomas 206
Mannin, Ethel 6, **180**
    and achievements of 181
    and Yeats 182–3, 197
    first meeting 181
    'Love's levelling bed' 182

as moon goddess to 182–3
as Muse to 182–3
Markieweicz, Constance 81, 164
Martyn, Edward 14
Mathers, MacGregor 14, 38, 44, 60
Mathers, Moina 14, 33
Matheson, Hilda 185, 211, 212
Mead, G R S 1, 15, 22, 111
Millevoye, Lucien 68, 76, 78
Mnemosyne 1
Monro, Harold 55
Monroe, Harriet 94
moon:
  and Mannin associated with 182–3
  and Shakespear associated with 16–17
  as symbol of feminine Wisdom principle 1–2
  and the White Goddess 16, 18
  and Yeats's archer vision 14–15
Moore, George 44, 100
Moore, Sturge 54
More, Henry 203
Muckerjee, Divabrata 106
Muldoon, Paul 60
Muse(s):
  and courtly love tradition 65–8
  and feminist critique of 32
  and Greek idea of 1
  as harlots 110–12
  and incarnation as living woman 15–16
  and Yeats:
    changes in idea of 8
    changes in idea of after marriage 141
    child/harlot categorization 111–12
    concept of 1–2, 212
    conflicting attraction of attainable and unattainable 24
    crisis in career as Muse poet 128–9
    daimon, or anti-self 135
    Farr as Muse 40, 49–50, 51, 52, 57–8
    Furies 190, 192–5
    Gonne (Iseult) as Muse 107–9, 124
    Gonne (Maud) as Muse 65–8, 89, 95–6, 97, 99–100, 139–40, 142
    harlots 110–12
    Mannin as Muse 182–3
    mediation between material and spiritual 21–2
    redefinition of 141, 144
    relationship to 120–2
    restoration of youthful Muses 164–5
    Ruddock as Muse 179
    Shakespear as Muse 32–4
    source of poetic inspiration 1, 8
    timeless Muse 162–5
    Wisdom figure 1–2
    Yeats (George) as Muse 144, 154–6

Nabokov, Vladimir 105
Neo-Platonism, and delight 28
Neumann, Erich 7, 192
Nevinson, H W 55, 85
Nic Shiubhlaigh, Marie 71
Nightingale, Florence 37

Oates, Joyce Carol 142–3
O'Connor, Frank 169
O'Donoghue, Bernard 66
O'Leary, John 65
Order of the Golden Dawn:
  and Farr 38, 44
  and Farr-Yeats conflict 45–6
  and Gonne (Maud) joins 72
  and Hyde-Lees joins 133–4
  and women in 44
  and Yeats joins 14

Paget, Dorothy 42, 48, 62, 209
Patterson, Jenny 42
Pelham, Lady Elizabeth 195–7
Petrarch 1
Pilcher, Thora 115
Plato 1, 28, 45, 81, 124, 138, 158
Plutarch 174, 204
Pound, Ezra 12, 23–4, 53, 61, 133
  'Portrait D'une Femme' 55–7
  and Yeats's development as poet 93–4
  and Yeats's relationship with Iseult Gonne 107, 117
Praz, Mario 89
Proust, Marcel 118
psaltery 40, 46
Purohit Swami, Shri 176

Quinn, John 51, 52, 55, 118, 134

Radcliffe, Elizabeth 90, 133, 134
Raine, Kathleen 197
Ramanathan, Sir Ponnambalan 55
Ramazani, Jahan 8, 32, 62
Rhodes, Dorothy Paget, see Paget, Dorothy
Rhymers Club 2
Rich, Adrienne 72, 73, 81, 90
Riding, Laura 196
Robins, Elizabeth 42

Rossetti, Dante Gabriel:
  and influence on Yeats 1, 65
  and translations of Italian poets 66
Ruddock, Margot 6, **166**
  and death of 178–9
  and early life 172
  and mental breakdown 177–8
  and poetry of:
    'The Apple' 179
    'Autumn, crystal Eye' 176
    'I take thee, Life' 175–6
  and Yeats:
    estimation of her verse 175–6
    failed sexual relations with 173
    first contact with 171–2
    first meeting 172
    on her potential as actress 172
    meeting in Majorca 176–7
    as Muse to 179
    as Siren to 173–4, 179
  and Yeats's writings:
    'A Crazed Girl' 178
    A Full Moon in March 174–5, 179
    'The Man and the Echo' 179–81
    'Margot' 172–3, 174
    'Sweet Dancer' 177–8
Russell, George 44, 72, 104

Sackville-West, Vita 185, 186
Saddlemyer, Ann 108, 134, 147, 150–1, 154
Said, Edward 195
Schepeler, Alick 110
Scott, Dixon 53
Shakespear, Dorothy 12, 107, 133
Shakespear, Henry Hope 12, 17
Shakespear, Olivia **10**
  and appearance 11
  and death of 211
  and education 11
  and Farr, co-authorship with 48
  and Yeats:
    advice to under semi trance 14
    associated with White Goddess by 14–15, 16–17, 18, 22
    distracted by Maud Gonne 23
    first meeting 11, 12
    his memories of in old age 211
    his regrets over leaving 25
    impact of introduction to sexual love 12–13
    influence on 2–3

    intensity of passionate relationship 21–2
    as life-long stimulus to creativity of 26
    as Muse to 32–4
    parting from 23–4
    resumption of affair 26
    resumption of friendship 24
    sexual relationship 11, 12
    symbol of forgotten beauty 18–19
    Wisdom figure 22
  and Yeats's writings:
    'After Long Silence' 33–4
    'The Empty Cup' 25, 159
    'Friends' 26, 29–30, 32, 33
    'He gives His Beloved certain Rhymes' 16–17
    'He remembers Forgotten Beauty' 18–19, 21, 32
    'The Lover mourns for the Loss of Love' 23–4
    'The Mermaid' 159
    'A Poet to his Beloved' 17
    'The Secrets of the Old' 159
    'The Travail of Passion' 21–3, 32
Sharp, William 14
Shaw, George Bernard:
  and *Arms and the Man*, opening night 43
  and Farr 40–2, 43
Shelley, Percy Bysshe, and Yeats' symbolism theories 13–14
Shute, Jenefer 105
Simon Magus 15, 111
Sirens 173–4, 179, 202, 204
Snyder, Gary 183
Steinach, Eugen 169
Steinach operation 6, 169–70
Storr, Anthony 89
Stuart, Francis 160
Symons, Arthur 15, 53
Synge, John 122, 143, 209

Tagore, Rabindranath 55, 58, 106
Tanner, Tony 122
Todhunter, John 37, 40, 42
Toomey, Deirdre 26, 29, 30, 77, 111
Trilling, Lionel 105
Troyes, Chrétien de 66
Turner, W J 188, 212

uncanny 109, 128

Index

Valency, Maurice 66
Vendler, Helen 20–1, 108, 166
Vernant, Jean-Pierre 173
Villiers de l'Isle-Adam, Auguste, and
  Yeats's review of *Axël* 74–5

Wellesley, Dorothy **184**
  and background of 185
  and Sackville-West 185
  and writings of:
    'Matrix' 185, 187–8
    'Matrix' rewritten by Yeats 189–90
    and Yeats 197
  creative potential of androgeny 190
  influence on 6–7
  joint project with 188–9
  masculinity of verse praised by 186, 187
  poetry praised by 185, 187
  regular visits by 186
  rewrites poem of 189–90
  shared inspiration in anger 190–1
  and Yeats's writings:
    'Hound Voice' 204
    'The Lover's Song' 189–90
    'The Three Bushes' 189
    'To Dorothy Wellesley' 109, 190, 191–3
Wellesley, Lord Gerald 185
White Goddess:
  and Graves' theory 1–2
  and Yeats 14
    archer vision 14–15
    Farr's association with 37–8, 48
    Gonne's (Maud) association
      with 25–6, 93
    moon's association with 18
    Shakespear's association with 14–15, 16–17, 18, 22
Whittal, Mary Elizabeth 37
Wisdom figure:
  and concept of the Muses 1–2
  and Farr 38
  mask of Medusa 42–3
  and Mary Magdalene 22
  and the moon 16
  and Shakespear 22
  and Yeats 15
Woolf, Virginia 185
Wordsworth, William 2, 18, 96

Yeats, George (née Hyde-Lees) 49, 50, **130**
  and automatic writing:
    Anima Mundi 134
    fakes receipt of spiritual message 131–2
    The Only Jealousy of Emer 138–9
    as product of Yeats's poetry 150–1
    role of sexual satisfaction and
      inspiration 135–7
    significance of 151–4
    validation of Radcliffe's automatic
      writing 133, 134
    variety of subjects 134
    Yeats encourages 132–3
  and joins Order of the Golden
    Dawn 133–4
  as medium 5
  and occult interests 133
  and Yeats:
    attitude towards extra-marital
      relationships of 171
    changes in his idea of Muse after
      marriage 141
    daughter born 141
    decides to marry her 127
    displaces Gonnes as Muse 144
    erotic relationship 154–5, 157
    first meeting 133
    influence on 5
    marriage 4
    marriage as threat to poetry of 131
    as Muse to 154–6
    as oracle to 154
    organizing his last years 209
    prophetic poetry 150
    reassurances from 144–5
    role as medium praised by 145–7
    role of sexual satisfaction and
      inspiration 135–7
    rootedness after marriage 141, 143
    as Sibyl to 154
    significance of automatic writing
      for 151–4
    as source of wisdom for 144–5, 147
  and Yeats's writings:
    'Among School Children' 152
    'Byzantium' 152, 153
    'The Double Vision of Michael
      Robartes' 150
    'The Gift of Harun Al-Rashid'
      145–7, 156
    'Gratitude to the Unknown
      Instructors' 154
    'An Image from a Past Life' 144

Yeats, George (*continued*)
 'Leda and the Swan' 147, 148–9
 The Only Jealousy of Emer 137–9
 'The Phases of the Moon' 147
 'A Prayer for my Daughter' 141–4
 'The Second Coming' 147, 148, 149
 'Solomon and the Witch' 136–7
 'Solomon to Sheba' 136
 'The Tower' 152–3, 157
 'Two Songs of a Fool' 141
 'Under Saturn' 144–5
 'Words for Music Perhaps' 147
Yeats, John Butler 123, 143, 155
Yeats, W B 44, **130**, **184**, **198**
 and chooses role as lover 2, 9
 and clarity of vision 148
 and communication with spiritual world 133
 and courtesy 144
 and courtly love tradition 65–8, 82
  abandonment of 103, 128–9
  Gonne as Muse of 3–4, 65–8, 99–100
  monstrosity of core concept 109
 and creation of an Irish national literature 69, 70
 and creative process 96–7
  anger and rage 190–5
  bitterness 161–2, 193
  desire 121–2, 202–3
  disappointment 123
  dreams 122–3
  'Ego Dominus Tuus' 119–20
  feminine part of psyche 183, 186
  'First Principles' 97, 171
  impact of Steinach operation 169–70
  inspiration 149
  late style 194–5
  masculine/feminine tensions 187
  Per Amica Silentia Lunae 119–23
  relationship to Muse 120–2
  rootedness 143
  sublimation 122
 and creative states 26–7
  delight 28, 61
  ecstasy 28, 31–2
  joy 27–8, 95
  sweetness 28, 95
 and cyclical theory of history 147–8
 and daimon, or anti-self 118–19, 120, 121, 134–5
 role as Muse 135
 and death 204–5
 and death of 212
 and Dickinson 110
 affair with 89–90
 and drama, importance of poetical culture 39–40
 and escape from romantic agony 89–90
 and Farr 3
  'Against Witchcraft' 51–2
  'All Souls' Night' 3, 59, 60–1, 62–3
  asks for payment for reading 53
  associates with White Goddess 37–8, 48
  beautiful voice 38, 39
  conflict within Order of the Golden Dawn 45–6
  consider joint USA tour 52
  construction of a spoken poetry 39
  continuing friendship with 58
  creation of a poet's theatre 44–5
  demands pay increase 53
  as enchantress 39
  end of affair 50–1
  exasperation with 54–5
  excluded from 'Friends' 53–5
  Fechner's ideas 59
  Irish Literary Theatre 44–5
  joint performances 47
  last letter from 59
  memories of in old age 209–10
  as Muse 40, 51, 52, 57
  'The Players ask for a Blessing on the Psalteries and on Themselves' 47–8
  praise of 54
  qualities of 37–8
  reaction to performance in *Rosmersholm* 41
  refusal to be cast as Muse 57–8
  rhythmic chanting of poetry 40, 45, 46–9
  romantic relationship 49
  soul's journey after death 61, 62
  too close to function as Muse 49–50
  use of psaltery in recitations 46
 and Furies and Muses 190, 192–5
 and Gonne (Iseult) 4
  anti-self, or daimon 118–19
  attraction to 106–7
  beauty of 125–6
  borrows lyric from 125

breaks from 127–8
child/harlot categorization 111–12
constructed as Muse 107–9, 124
construction as object of desire 106–7
'The Death of the Hare' 159–60
deepening of relationship 113, 114
illusions 118
intellectual collaboration 116–17
'Lines written in Dejection' 115–16
marriage proposal rejected 4, 114–15, 127, 128
memories of in old age 210
memory of her singing 105
'Men Improve with the Years' 115, 124
'Michael Robartes and the Dancer' 124, 140–1
The Only Jealousy of Emer 125–6
'On Woman' 107–8, 124
'Owen Ahern and his Dancers' 132, 160
Per Amica Silentia Lunae 116, 119–23
'Presences' 109–13
on role of absence 117–18
semi-paternal relationship 105–6, 113, 115
she suggests marriage 106
as teacher to 106
'To a Child Dancing in the Wind' 104, 105
'To a Young Beauty' 141
'To a Young Girl' 108–9
'Two Songs of a Fool' 160
'Two Years Later' 106, 107
unease over role of 109
on uselessness of being a Muse 124–5
'Why Should Not Old Men be Mad?' 117
and Gonne (Maud):
'Adam's Curse' 66, 68, 81–3
'Against Unworthy Praise' 94
'Among School Children' 153, 158–9
analogizes to Helen 92–3
'The Arrow' 80–1
associates with White Goddess 25–6, 93
'Broken Dreams' 100
'A Bronze Head' 92, 210
brother and sister relationship 70–1
Cathleen ni Houlihan 71
'The Cold Heaven' 95–7
consigns to past 103
conversion to Catholicism 84
The Countess Cathleen 69, 71
creation of new Irish consciousness 69–70
'The Death of the Hare' 159–60
'A Deep-sworn Vow' 95
denies entry to house 142
'A Dialogue of Self and Soul' 140
difficulty in eradicating as image of Muse 139–40
disputes between 97
'The Double Vision of Michael Robartes' 139–40
'A Dream of Death' 73
dreams of marriage 76
'Easter 1916' 113–14
effects of relationship on poetry 87–8
end of marriage to MacBride 84–5
enmity between 88–9
'Fallen Majesty' 103
as father of poems 83
final meeting with 210–11
'First Love' 158
first meeting 40, 65, 68–9
'The Fish' 76
'The Folly of Being Comforted' 81
'Friends' 29, 94–5
'The Friends of His Youth' 158
on her career as Muse 99
'Her Praise' 98
'He thinks of those who have Spoken Evil of his Beloved' 75–6
'He wishes for the Cloths of Heaven' 76
'He wishes his Beloved were Dead' 74–5, 92
'His Memories' 158
'His Phoenix' 98
'Human Dignity' 158
impact of marriage of 84
influence of 3–4
justifies her violence 92–3
'King and No King' 91
'Leda and the Swan' 93
loss of solitariness 83–4
'The Lover pleads With His Friend for Old Friends' 73–4
'A Man Young and Old' 86
marriage proposal rejected 4, 71, 77, 82–3, 114
marriage to MacBride 83–4, 91–2

Yeats, W B (*continued*)
  memorialist poetry 98
  'A Memory of Youth' 103–4
  as Muse 65–8, 95–6, 97, 99–100
  necessity of unattainability 87
  Nicholas and Pernella Flamel
    poems 90–4
  'No Second Troy' 92–4
  'The Old Age of Queen Maeve' 84
  'The People' 98–9
  physical relationship 86
  poetry of praise 80–1, 90
  'A Prayer for my Daughter' 88
  prevents from joining demonstration 75, 92
  primacy as Muse 95
  'Quarrel in Old Age' 164–5
  reasons for attraction to 69
  'Reconciliation' 91–2
  rejection as Muse 142
  reveals vulnerability 76–8
  shared belief in power of dreams 70
  shared vision 77
  spiritual marriage 76–7, 90
  spiritual relationship 86, 87
  'Subject for lyric' 78–80, 140
  summary of relationship with 103–4
  'Summer and Spring' 158
  'A Thought From Propertius' 100
  'The Tower' 77
  vision of Yeats 85–6
  waning influence as Muse 89
  'When Helen Lived' 98
  'When You are Old' 72
  'A Woman Homer Sung' 92, 140
  'Words' 87–8
  writes play for 69
  and Gregory (Lady Augusta) 26, 27
  'Friends' 26, 29–31, 32
  and Heald 7–8, 186
    desire 202–3
    intimate letters to 201–2
    introduced to 197
    as Siren 202
    visits to 201
  and impotence 169, 186
  and language:
    magical use of 20–1
    need for mastery of 20
  and longing for ordinariness 129
  and loss of inspiration 169
  and love and desire 179, 202
  and lust 194, 202, 203
  on lyric poetry 2
  and magic 44
    central role of 13
    Egyptian magic 38
    joins Order of the Golden Dawn 14
    temporal world as mirror of eternal world 19
    use of language 20–1
  and Mannin 6, 197
    first meeting 181
    'Love's levelling bed' 182
    as moon goddess 182–3
    as Muse 182–3
    and memories of past loves as inspiration 157–62
    bitterness 161–2
    restoration of youthful Muses 164–5
    timeless Muse 162–5
  and the moon:
    archer vision 14–15
    association with White Goddess 18
    Mannin's association with 182–3
    as powerful symbol 18
    Shakespear's association with 16–17
  and Moore's satire of 100
  and Muse(s):
    changes in idea of 8
    changes in idea of after marriage 141
    child/harlot categorization 111–12
    concept of 1–2, 212
    conflicting attraction of attainable and unattainable 24
    crisis in career as Muse poet 128–9
    daimon, or anti-self 135
    Farr as Muse 40, 49–50, 51, 52, 57–8
    Furies 190, 192–5
    Gonne (Iseult) as Muse 107–9, 124
    Gonne (Maud) as Muse 65–8, 89, 95–6, 97, 99–100, 139–40, 142
    harlots 110–12
    incarnation as living woman 15–16
    Mannin as Muse to 182–3
    mediation between material and spiritual 21–2
    redefinition of 141, 144
    relationship to 120–2
    restoration of youthful Muses 164–5
    Ruddock as Muse 179
    Shakespear as Muse 32–4
    source of poetic inspiration 1, 8
    timeless Muse 162–5
    Wisdom figure 1–2
    Yeats (George) as Muse 144, 154–6

and opinions/convictions
  distinction 143
 and Pelham 195–7
 and review of de l'Isle-Adam's
  Axël 74–5
 and rhythmic chanting of poetry 39,
  44, 45, 46–7
 use of psaltery 46
 and Ruddock 6
 'A Crazed Girl' 178
  death of 178–9
  estimation of verse of 175–6
  failed sexual relations with 173
  first contact with 171–2
  first meeting 172
  A Full Moon in March 174–5, 179
  'The Man and the Echo' 179–81
  'Margot' 172–3, 174
  meeting in Majorca 176–7
  mental breakdown 177–8
  as Muse 179
  on potential as actress 172
  as Siren 173–4, 179
  'Sweet Dancer' 177–8
 and seances 119, 133
 and Shakespear:
  advice under semi trance 14
  'After Long Silence' 33–4
  associates with White Goddess
   14–15, 16–17, 18, 22
  death of 211
  description of 11
  'The Empty Cup' 25, 159
  first meeting 11, 12
  'Friends' 26, 29–30, 32, 33
  'He gives His Beloved certain
   Rhymes' 16–17
  'He remembers Forgotten Beauty'
   18–19, 21, 32
  impact of introduction to sexual
   love 12–13
  influence of 2–3
  intensity of passionate relation-
   ship 21–2
  as life-long stimulus to creativity 26
  'The Lover mourns for the Loss of
   Love' 23–4
  memories of in old age 211
  'The Mermaid' 159
  as Muse 32–4
  parting from 23–4
  'A Poet to his Beloved' 17
  regret at leaving 25
  resumption of affair 26
  resumption of friendship 24
  'The Secrets of the Old' 159
  sexual relationship 11, 12
  as symbol off forgotten beauty 18–19
  'The Travail of Passion' 21–3, 32
  Wisdom figure 22
 and Shaw, opening night of *Arms and
  the Man* 43
 and Steinach rejuvenation operation 6,
  169–70
 and symbolism theories 13–14, 17–18
  access to the great Memory 13
  importance of language 20
  love poetry 19–20
  mediation between material and
   spiritual 19
  symbols as greatest power 39
  use of moon as symbol 18
  use of natural elements 18
 and Wellesley 197
  creative potential of androgeny 190
  'Hound Voice' 204
  influence of 6–7
  joint project with 188–9
  'The Lover's Song' 189
  praises masculinity of verse 186,
   187
  praises poetry of 185, 187
  regular visits to 186
  rewrites poem by 189–90
  shared inspiration in anger 190–1
  'The Three Bushes' 189
  'To Dorothy Wellesley' 109, 190,
   191–3
  unsatisfied desire 186–7
 and the White Goddess 14
  archer vision 14–15
  Farr's association with 37–8, 48
  Gonne's (Maud) association
   with 25–6, 93
  moon's association with 18
  Shakespear's association
   with 14–15, 16–17, 18–22
 and Wisdom figure 1–2, 15, 16
  Farr 38, 42–3
  Shakespear 22
 and Yeats (George) 5
  'Among School Children' 152
  Anima Mundi 134
  attitude towards extra-marital
   relationships 171
  automatic writing 132–3
  automatic writing as product of
   poetry 150–1

Yeats, W B (*continued*)
  'Byzantium' 152, 153
  changes in idea of Muse after marriage 141
  daughter born 141
  decides to marry 127
  'The Double Vision of Michael Robartes' 150
  erotic relationship 154–5, 157
  fakes receipt of spiritual message 131–2
  first meeting 133
  'The Gift of Harun Al-Rashid' 145–7, 156
  'Gratitude to the Unknown Instructors' 154
  'An Image from a Past Life' 144
  'Leda and the Swan' 147, 148–9
  marriage as threat to poetry 131
  marriage to 4
  as medium 5
  as Muse 144, 154–6
  The Only Jealousy of Emer 137–9
  as oracle 154
  organizing his last years 209
  'The Phases of the Moon' 147
  praises role as medium 145–7
  'A Prayer for my Daughter' 141–4
  prophetic poetry 150
  reassurances to 144–5
  role of sexual satisfaction and inspiration 135–7
  rootedness after marriage 141, 143
  'The Second Coming' 147, 148, 149
  shared interest in occult 133–4
  as Sibyl 154
  significance of automatic writing 151–4
  'Solomon and the Witch' 136–7
  'Solomon to Sheba' 136
  as source of wisdom 144–5, 147
  'The Tower' 152–3, 157
  'Two Songs of a Fool' 141
  'Under Saturn' 144–5
  validation of Radcliffe's automatic writing 133, 134
  'Words for Music Perhaps' 147
Yeats, W B, writings of:
  'An Acre of Grass' 191
  'Adam's Curse' 3, 31, 66, 68, 81–3
  The Adoration of The Magi (story) 111, 148
  'After Long Silence' 33–4, 63
  'Against Unworthy Praise' 94
  'Against Witchcraft' 51–2
  'All Souls' Night' 3, 59, 60–1, 62–3
  'Among School Children' 31, 152, 153, 158–9
  'Ancestral Houses' 28
  'The Arrow' 66, 80–1
  'The Binding of the Hair' 17
  'Broken Dreams' 100
  'A Bronze Head' 92, 210
  'Byzantium' 152, 153
  Cathleen ni Houlihan 71
  'The Circus Animals' Desertion' 7, 205
  'The Cold Heaven' 95–7
  Collected Poems 8
  'Come Gather Round me, Parnellites' 193
  'Coole Park' 29
  The Countess Cathleen 44–5, 69, 71
  'The Countess Cathleen in Paradise' 163
  'A Crazed Girl' 6, 178
  Crazy Jane poems 163
  'Cuchulain Comforted' 211
  'The Curse of Cromwell' 193
  The Death of Cuchulain, 111, 211
  'The Death of the Hare' 159–60
  'A Deep-sworn Vow' 95
  Deirdre 52, 53
  'A Dialogue of Self and Soul' 95, 140
  'The Double Vision of Michael Robartes' 139–40, 150
  'A Dream of Death' 73
  'Easter 1916' 113–14
  'Ego Dominus Tuus' 4, 119–20
  'The Empty Cup' 25, 159
  'Fallen Majesty' 103
  'First Love' 25–6, 158
  'First Principles' 171
  'The Fish' 76
  'The Fisherman' 96
  'The Folly of Being Comforted' 81
  Four Plays for Dancers 126
  'Friends' 26–7, 29–32, 33, 53–5, 94–5
  'The Friends of His Youth' 158
  A Full Moon in March 174–5, 179
  'The Ghost of Roger Casement' 193
  'The Gift of Harun Al-Rashid' 145–7, 156
  'Gratitude to the Unknown Instructors' 154
  The Green Helmet and Other Poems 90–1

Index

'He and She' 19, 170–1
'He gives His Beloved certain Rhymes' 16–17
'He hears the Cry of the Sedge' 32
'He remembers Forgotten Beauty' 2–3, 18–19, 21
'Her Praise' 98
'He thinks of his Past Greatness when a Part of the Constellations of Heaven' 32
'He thinks of those who have Spoken Evil of his Beloved' 75–6
'He wishes for the Cloths of Heaven' 76
'He wishes his Beloved were Dead' 74–5, 92
'His Memories' 158
'His Phoenix' 98
'His Wildness' 160–1
'Hound Voice' 204
'Human Dignity' 158
'An Image from a Past Life' 144
'An Introduction for My Plays' 112
The Island of Statues 73
'J.M. Synge and the Ireland of His Time' 113
'King and No King' 91
The King of the Great Clock Tower 48–9, 166, 171, 203–4
  rewriting of 174–5
The King's Threshold 46
The Land of Heart's Desire 12, 42, 54
'Lapis Lazuli' 28
'A Last Confession' 162
'Leda and the Swan' 93, 147, 148–9
'Letter to Ezra Pound' 191
'Lines written in Dejection' 115–16
'Literature and the Living Voice' 46
'The Living Beauty' 128–9
'Long-legged Fly' 112
'The Lover mourns for the Loss of Love' 23–4
'The Lover pleads With His Friend for Old Friends' 73–4
'The Lover's Song' 189–90
'Magic' 13
'The Man and the Echo' 179–81
'A Man Young and Old' 86, 157
'Margot' 172–3, 174
'The Mask' 90
'Meditations in Time of Civil War' 143
'A Memory of Youth' 103–4
'Men Improve with the Years' 115, 124

'The Mermaid' 159
'Michael Robartes and the Dancer' 124, 140–1
'The Municipal Gallery Revisited' 143
'News for the Delphic Oracle' 203–4
'No Second Troy' 92–4
'The Old Age of Queen Maeve' 84
The Only Jealousy of Emer 125–6, 137–9
'On Woman' 107–8, 124
'Owen Aherne and his Dancers' 132, 160
Oxford Book of Modern Verse 185, 187, 192
'The People' 98–9
Per Amica Silentia Lunae 4, 28, 116, 119–20, 134, 183
'The Phases of the Moon' 147
'The Philosophy of Shelley's Poetry' 13–14, 18
'The Players ask for a Blessing on the Psalteries and on Themselves' 47–8
Poems (1895) 71–2
'Poetry and Tradition' 27, 99, 144, 194
'Politics' 7, 205, 206–7
'Portrayed Before His Eyes' 6, 182
'A Prayer for my Daughter' 28, 61–2, 88, 141–4
'A Prayer for Old Age' 171
'Presences' 109–13
'Quarrel in Old Age' 164–5
'Reconciliation' 91–2
'Red Hanrahan' 24
Responsibilities 100, 101
'The Results of Thought' 164
'Ribh considers Christian Love insufficient' 171
'Ribh Denounces Patrick' 19
Rosa Alchemica (story) 148
'Sailing to Byzantium' 6, 161, 162
'The Second Coming' 147, 148, 149
'The Secrets of the Old' 159
In the Seven Woods 54
The Shadowy Waters 49
'Solomon and the Witch' 136–7
'Solomon to Sheba' 136
'A Song' 129
'The Song of Wandering Aengus' 20–1
'Speaking to the Psaltery' 46
The Speckled Bird (unpublished novel) 38, 91
'The Spur' 7, 194

Yeats, W B, writings of: (*continued*)
Stories of Red Hanrahan 16
'Stream and Sun at Glendalough' 165–6
'Subject for lyric' 78–80, 140
'Summer and Spring' 158, 159
'Supernatural Songs' 170–1
'Swedenborg, Mediums and Desolate Places' 58
'Sweet Dancer' 177–8
'The Symbolism of Poetry' 17–18, 19–20
'Those Images' 112, 205–6
'A Thought From Propertius' 100
'The Three Bushes' 7–8, 189, 207
'To a Child Dancing in the Wind' 104, 105
'To a Young Beauty' 141
'To a Young Girl' 108–9
'To Dorothy Wellesley' 7, 109, 190, 191–3
'The Tower' 77, 152–3, 157
'The Tragic Generation' 192
'The Travail of Passion' 21–3
The Trembling of the Veil 9, 39, 54–5, 135
'Two Songs of a Fool' 141, 160
'The Two Trees' 210
'Two Years Later' 106, 107
'Under Ben Bulben' 212
'Under Saturn' 144–5
'Upon a House Shaken by The Land Agitation' 31
'Vacillation' 27
A Vision 6, 14, 62, 105, 111, 145, 147, 151, 152, 183, 202
The Wanderings of Oisin 65
'When Helen Lived' 98
'When You are Old' 72
'Why Should Not Old Men be Mad?' 117
'The Wild Old Wicked Man' 195–7
The Wind Among the Reeds 2–3, 18, 22
'A Woman Homer Sung' 92, 140
'A Woman Young and Old' 157, 163
'Words' 4, 87–8
'Words for Music Perhaps' 147
Young, Ella 106

Zeus 1

Printed and bound by CPI Group (UK) Ltd, Croydon, CR0 4YY